The
Illuminati
Facts & Fiction

The
Illuminati
Facts & Fiction

Mark Dice

The Resistance
San Diego, CA

Table of Contents

Preface

The Illuminati: Facts & Fiction is a book that separates and analyzes the various claims and evidence about the Illuminati, their history, beliefs, members, organizations, and activities. This is a supplement for my first book on the subject, *The Resistance Manifesto*, which focuses more on the New World Order, the 9/11 attacks, Big Brother, and how the political agendas of elite secret societies are fulfilling Bible prophecy.

The Illuminati: Facts & Fiction focuses more on the Illuminati secret society and historical evidence pointing to its existence and actions. The trail of information discussing the Illuminati is traced back to the original sources, as each one is analyzed with regards to its authorship and the information found in each source. This book is also about debunking various frauds, exaggerations, and disinformation involving the organization and also highlights the rare instances that the Illuminati or subsidiary organizations are mentioned in mainstream media or incorporated into fictional films, books, and TV shows. The motives for the writers incorporating such ideas in their fictional works are also analyzed. Their intentions are not always to educate people about the Illuminati or tell a captivating story, but instead is sometimes an attempt to spread disinformation and make the audience believe that certain actual conspiracies are the creation of Hollywood or a novelist, when in fact they actually happened.

The deeper one goes down the rabbit hole, the more bizarre the information becomes. When one is new to this path, what appears to be a misunderstanding, an exaggeration, or a lie, often is found to be factual and thoroughly documented by reliable sources. In this book I have taken an objective and skeptical view of the topic and have sifted through the volumes of information to get to the truth and the sources which lead to its discovery so we can leave the fiction, distortions, and lies by the wayside and not be fooled or distracted by them. While some of the allegations and stories about the Illuminati sound far fetched, you will find, as the cliché goes, the truth *is* stranger than fiction.

About the Author

For most of his life growing up Mark Dice had a burning desire for understaning the spiritual and mystical principles at work in the world and in his own life. His quest for truth, knowledge, and wisdom lead him on a path to find answers to the difficult questions one can ponder when seeking a comprehensive understanding of their existence.

He searched for answers to the struggles of humanity, of war and poverty, of love and hate, of wealth and power. His hunger for knowledge lead him to discover a powerful secret society and their pivotal, yet hidden role in the world. He found that the mysteries of life and world events were not so mysterious once he began to understand the workings of the Illuminati.

Mark meticulously researched and documented his findings to share with anyone who had the same burning desire to understand the world and their place in it. In 2005 he published *The Resistance Manifesto*, his magnum opus exposing the hidden Illuminati's plans for a New World Order and the organizations and philosophies that accompany it. He immediately became active in exposing the lies coming from the elite Illuminati who maintain political power around the world. While being only twenty-eight years old when *The Resistance Manifesto* was first published, Mark immediately gained the respect and endorsement of best selling authors twice his age. Veteran researchers Jim Marrs, Texe Marrs, Anthony J. Hilder, and other younger film makers such as Alex Jones gave their endorsement to Mark and his Manifesto.

Mark has a gift for explaining esoteric and complex issues in a way that can be easily understood by almost anyone and meticulously cites the sources of his evidence.

While having respect for all authentic religions and belief systems, Mark Dice is a Christian and holds a bachelors degree in communication. He lives in San Diego, California.

Introduction

The infamous Illuminati secret society has remained the focus of so-called "conspiracy theorists" for hundreds of years. They have been called the puppet masters who secretly pull the strings of the world's events from elections to revolutions, and from business monopolies to stock market crashes. A significant number of researchers and ordinary citizens have varying degrees of suspicion that somehow, somewhere, a secret agenda is continuously lurking behind the scenes.

When unexpected events occur in the world, these people don't see them as a random occurrence, but as the work of an unseen hand which has orchestrated or encouraged these events to happen for the personal, professional, or financial gain of certain individuals. Often such speculation is given the label of a "conspiracy theory" and dismissed as imaginative thinking. Yet many of the world's events don't make complete sense, even to the so-called experts who study them. Something is missing from a solid explanation. There is more to the story than meets the eye, but these supposed experts are often afraid to speculate on what that missing piece of the puzzle is.

People look at catastrophic events like the attacks on the World Trade Center on 9/11 and wonder how such a thing could happen without law enforcement and intelligence agencies knowing about it. People look at the mortgage collapse of 2008 and the following economic repercussions of bank failures and government bailouts and wonder how such a thing could happen. People see their standard of living going down and a two income household barely able to get by and wonder how can this be? People hear on the news that child molesters and rapists get out of prison after only a few years, yet others are locked up for decades after getting busted with some marijuana.

So people turn to the television to keep their mind off such things. With the push of a button their mind is relaxed with the soothing images of watching beautiful contestants compete to be this season's American Idol, or they get an adrenaline rush as their favorite football team scores a winning touchdown with just seconds left on the clock. These things make sense to them, and it's what others will talk about the next day at work and if they want to feel connected with others then they had better participate in these pointless activities.

The fact of the matter is that when you step back and take a closer look at the world that we are living in and at what really matters, at the sources of information we habitually rely on, and assemble various pieces of this mysterious puzzle called life, a different picture begins to emerge. What should be the top story on the evening news is mitigated to a small and unsuspecting article in the back half of the paper and is completely omitted from broadcast news. What should be contained in celebrity gossip magazines is found as the top story on the major TV networks. Why does this happen?

When one discovers the very concrete reality of secret societies and their influence and power, one begins to see things much differently. When one discovers, as in recent years, the growing credible information about these secret societies, their membership, goals and accomplishments, one sees a gaping hole in the legitimacy and accuracy of mainstream media and general knowledge.

Any talk about a "conspiracy" or secret agenda being carried out by an organization of rich and powerful men is almost always countered with laughter by the average Joe who mindlessly follows the herd.

Is it that hard to believe an organization of powerful men has made a pact with each other to secretly further their agendas? Is it that hard to design a self perpetuating structure that would allow such an organization to continuously function regardless of who specifically occupies any one position at any given time? Is it far fetched to think that these individuals would purchase and control the mainstream media and use this powerful tool to further their goals?

One of the first reality shows ever created was called *Survivor*, which began airing in May of 2000. The show featured sixteen people who were put on a secluded island and competed for one million dollars as each week a contestant was voted off the show by their fellow castaways. As the show went on, several people on the island would secretly make an agreement to help each other out at the expense of others who were not part of their agreement. The outsiders had no idea such an agreement was made, and if and when ill will fell upon them, they didn't suspect anything other than bad luck. But unknown to them, they were a victim of a conspiracy. A victim of the workings of a secret society within the group of contestants.

As future seasons of *Survivor* were aired, the secret alliances would become a common theme of the show to viewers who had an eagle eye of the workings of all who were on the island. Devious contestants always found such an idea a practical and effective way to get ahead.

If the formation of a secret alliance among members on *Survivor* became a common method to gain advantage over others and to "survive," is it that far fetched to believe that similar secret alliances occur in business or politics? It seems that the idea to form a secret alliance exclusively for the benefit of those involved is a perfectly logical idea, and the best way to protect such an alliance and ensure its success is to prevent others who are not a part of it from becoming aware that such a thing even exists.

We know for a fact that secret societies exist in politics, business, and religion. Many of these associations have existed for hundreds of years. The existence of such societies spawns speculation from outsiders, and sometimes paranoia. With little information to work from to formulate a reliable theory as to what these people are doing and what the consequences of their actions may be, it is often difficult to accurately understand the workings of a secret society or alliance. But just like the most careful criminal, secret societies often leave clues behind. No matter how many precautions one takes to prevent any knowledge of their actions, it is nearly impossible to execute a plot flawlessly and without leaving evidence behind. As with some murder cases, the evidence may not be understood immediately after the crime, or it may not even be noticed as evidence at all. As time passes, other clues from similar crimes may emerge and shed new light on things that were once overlooked.

In regards to the Illuminati, clues have been discovered over the last several hundred years. Something is definitely being kept secret by some very rich and powerful individuals. A network, an agenda, a source of wealth and power, a reason for the secrecy, and more. In more modern times starting in about the late 1970s, various people have come forward and claimed to be actual members of this illusive group and said they had defected and turned to Christianity. These men have told stories claiming to expose some of the history, beliefs, and goals of the Illuminati secret society. Some of their claims seem reasonable, others stretches of the imagination, and others obvious lies. Their testimony along with any inconsistencies will be addressed in this book.

Also covered are compilations of countless pieces of evidence about the Illuminati, including original writings that were seized in 1786 from the home of one of the members. These writings are indeed authentic, and there is no scholar or historian who will refute that. The only refutations are as to whether or not the organization was able to carry on its work in the years following its original exposure to the public, over two hundred years ago. When one reads the words of founder Adam Weishaupt, it seems impossible that the organization didn't continue to exist, and later thrive. It seems foolish to believe that their goals would simply be abandoned because its leadership was discovered.

Had Adam Weishaupt not formulated and documented the plans for such an organization, surely it seems that another power hungry diabolical man would have done the same. After all, if Thomas Edison had not invented the light bulb, surely you would not be reading these words by candle light. Another man would have harnessed the power of electricity just as effectively. Such an invention was inevitable, and other men who had no connection with Edison were working towards the same goal. Cultures around the world throughout history that have had no contact with each other have made similar and often identical discoveries and innovations. Mankind's curiosities are similar around the world, just as our moral shortcomings are.

The very concept of a secret alliance among men to further each other's goals at the expense of others and under a shroud of secrecy surly isn't a novel idea. Mafias and organized criminal enterprises have sprung up around the world and have similar structures and methods, yet few have been influenced by another.

The idea of a secret group which has pledged allegiance to each other over all others should be as fundamental to our lives as falling in love. And just as this human condition of interpersonal relationships has become a classic theme in Hollywood movies, we should suspect that a similar basic theme would be found as well. And it is. A secretive group of bad guys who plot greed, harm, or destruction.

While an array of classic Hollywood narratives continue to be produced, with many of them involving secret criminal alliances, it is interesting that a rare number of them will actually incorporate plots very similar to events in reality that are attributed to the workings of the Illuminati. Even more rare, the name "Illuminati" is actually used to describe the group that is behind the events in these films. After analyzing Illuminati themes, symbolism, and references in popular Hollywood movies, one can come to no other conclusion than the writers and producers of those very films have detailed knowledge of the Illuminati itself.

While they are not producing a documentary film trying to expose the organization like the various ones that will be discussed in this book, one can't help but think that they are trying to get the point across to the audience in a similar way. After all, one can learn a lesson from reading the facts, or by hearing a story about such events in the form of a fable or allegory much like Aesop's fables contain underlying moral messages that are conveyed through fictional stories. Some of the themes in these Hollywood movies include plotlines surrounding terrorism, mind control, Big Brother, secret societies, and occult mysticism and magic.

While some uninformed skeptics believe that when someone talks about the Illuminati they got the idea from a Hollywood movie, the reverse is actually true, and many writers and producers have actually gotten their ideas from the historical and factual Illuminati.

In October of 1963 a man named Joe Valachi testified before the McClellan Congressional Committee on organized crime where he proceeded to tell the authorities about the inner workings of the Italian Mafia and how far-reaching their organization was. He explained how they controlled an array of industries and had police and judges in their pockets from either threats or payoffs. When Valachi was first taken into custody and began telling police about the Mafia, the story was too unbelievable for the authorities. They couldn't understand how a secret criminal enterprise could be so successful and operate without notice in so many sectors of society. Valachi was locked away in a mental hospital and was thought to be insane. Only later did authorities realize he was telling the truth and as La Cosa Nostra was uncovered, the extend of their criminal empire began to be understood.

The subject of "the Mafia" continues to fascinate people and if one didn't know their history, they may believe that well known Hollywood movies such as *Goodfellas* and *Casino* are entirely fictional, but in fact are based on true stories and the gangsters portrayed in these films did live lives of luxury and incredible influence. They were also ruthless killers.

One can't help but notice the strange and deafening silence on certain issues by so-called experts in the mainstream media. How is it that year after year Rush Limbaugh, Sean Hannity, Alan Colmes, Bill O'Reilly and others ignore issues surrounding the Illuminati? Issues with tangible solid evidence that is undeniable. The annual Bilderberg meeting for example, or the Cremation of Care ceremony at the Bohemian Grove, or true workings of the Federal Reserve Bank. Surely these are at least interesting enough stories for an occasional segment, yet for decades these so-called political experts and commentators mysteriously omit any mention of such issues and organizations from their shows.

The answer is that most of these individuals know very well about these issues. Many of them are willing accomplices and participants in such things. These people are paid millions of dollars a year to entertain the public with issues of little significance, and to set the agenda of the public mindset in a way that excludes any real answers to what is at stake and what is happening in Washington. These propagandists parrot talking points that are given to them daily by the people who sign their paychecks and are careful to act as gate-keepers whenever a sensitive issue may be addressed. These talking heads can't plead ignorance because they are often a part of the very inner circle of which they protect. Even during call-in radio talk shows when the format is relaxed and the hosts tell the audience that "any topic is fair game," they don't really mean what they say. Any relevant question that falls outside of the prescribed paradigm they are perpetuating is dropped by the call screener, or if it makes it on the airwaves, the caller gets hung up on immediately and their question either ridiculed or ignored.

Some key players in positions of power and influence may not be a member, or even aware that they are serving the Illuminati, or that the society exists at all. These individuals are carrying out a self-serving agenda for the benefit of those who have promised them rewards in return, or advancements for their participation. While these players know that they are a part of a private or secretive agreement pushing an agenda, many do not realize that they are a pawn in a larger conspiracy. Their only motives are money, power, and prestige. Some of their activities are criminal, and some have been caught and sent to prison. The point is that there are countless willing servants who go along with Illuminati schemes while not seeing the underlying forces that are directing a larger operation.

Information is power, and the Illuminati knows this. Having access to accurate and reliable information is power, and the ability to dispense false and misleading information is also power. As one reads the words of the original writings of the Illuminati, one finds that the founding members understood this in the late 1700s, well before the communication age. By monopolizing the mainstream media in all forms as it developed; print, radio, and television, they have been able to contain information and dispense misleading or useless stories to the public. If people didn't see it on Fox News or CNN, then it must not be happening, they think. It has only been through books published by small independent publishers, and in the later years the advent of the Internet that has allowed those who are hungry for the truth to find something solid to satisfy their desires. Websites like Infowars.com and to a lesser extent, DrudgeReport.com have allowed us to bypass the monopoly control of information dispensed by the mainstream media.

In the following pages this author has compiled both information from the original writings of the Illuminati and some of the first authors to write books exposing them and their goals, as well as the most accurate writers and researchers who have carried on that tradition. You will find the testimony of men and women who either claimed to have been a part of the Illuminati, or a victim of some of its members. You will also find a compilation of the rare instances that Illuminati related topics are mentioned or alluded to in mainstream media sources. Many, if not most of the confirmed or suspected Illuminati created and controlled organizations are also rarely mentioned in the mainstream news, and these unique occurrences have been compiled in this book. Finally, you will find a summary of various references, both direct and indirect to the Illuminati and their activities that are found in popular Hollywood films, TV shows, and novels. Such obscure mentions go unnoticed by viewers who are unaware of the deeper meanings that these plot lines and characters have.

With bits and pieces of reliable information about some fairly prominent secret societies and organizations like the Skull and Bones society, the Bohemian Grove, and the Bilderberg group being released to the public, we have concrete evidence of just who is involved with such organizations. Authentic membership lists have been stolen or otherwise obtained from the Bohemian Grove, and guest lists have been obtained in similar fashion regarding Bilderberg attendees. In some cases, as with President George W. Bush and Senator John Kerry, men have publicly admitted being members of Skull and Bones, but refused any comment beyond that. So we have a clear idea of who is involved in such organizations and we can see by their résumés that they have achieved personal, political, and financial success far beyond other competitors. It would be foolish not to see a clear pattern in all of this.

These secret societies, organizations, and meetings exist. This is often beyond a doubt and with mountains of indisputable evidence to support this conclusion. They exist for a purpose, and have often existed for hundreds of years. Their existence and purpose goes beyond a mere social gathering, as this is what cocktail parties and dinners are for. After looking at all the evidence, one should reasonably conclude that they exist partly to further each others careers by means of secret alliances, and quid pro quos, a Latin phrase meaning "something for something" or a mutual agreement between two parties where each other provides a good or service in return for a good or service. Once this is realized, one has a better idea of how the political landscape is formed. There is also a larger agenda that is being carried out, and is directed by those at higher levels of power within the Illuminati. There is a satanic and occult agenda fueling the construction of the New World Order and the systematic enslavement of the human race.

If this level of understanding is reached by an outsider, it is only the result of their paradigm being challenged after they discover the reality of mysticism and occult philosophies and rituals that are a part of many of these organizations. It is one thing to observe and understand secret alliances among the rich and powerful meant for their own personal and professional enhancement. It is something entirely different to see these alliances in the context of elaborate and bizarre satanic rituals, as in the case of the initiation into the Skull and Bones society, or the annual Cremation of Care ritual in the secluded redwood forest of the Bohemian Grove.

These are grown men we are talking about. The most sophisticated, educated, and wealthy men in the world from prominent families, yet they participate in such things. At first it seems so far fetched that it is understandable how one could easily dismiss such allegations as fanciful rumors, or the ramblings of a mentally deranged person. Yet, the closer one looks into these things, the more irrefutable such claims become.

One who ponders these issues also ultimately arrives at the question of what is the Illuminati's ultimate purpose? Why construct the New World Order global government? What then? What role do the occult rituals and mysticism play in all of this? The answers are found both in Bible prophecy, and within the teachings of occult and New Age organizations. They eerily parallel each other all the way to their conclusions, at which point they dramatically differ.

New Age and occult teachings predict that when the New World Order infrastructure and ideologies are complete, that from within the hierarchy of the Illuminati will arrive the long awaited messiah. They believe that he will unite all the world's religions into one compatible formula, and that he will fulfill all prophecies of the coming world savior. They also say that at this time the secret hierarchy of enlightened masters will then be able to come out from the shadows in what is called the externalization of the hierarchy, and then finally show themselves to the world and reveal the hidden wisdom that they had kept sheltered for countless generations.

The appearance of this New Age Christ will then eliminate all pain and suffering from the world. All poverty and sickness, all prejudice and crime. All shortages and scarcity, all fears and anxiety. It is at this point that the world and all who inhabit it will finally be able to live in perfect peace and harmony with each other thanks the revelations of this Illuminati messiah and the hierarchy. They had to work in secret and deny their existence for thousands of years, in order to protect themselves from their enemies. It is only now that their great work is finished that they may finally reveal themselves without any fear of repercussions. This is all, of course, according to the teachings in New Age enlightenment circles and occult hierarchies. These teachings report that this Illuminati Christ will be some kind of super-human demigod or even a being from another planet or dimension.

In contrast, according to Christianity, and even to some extent Islam and other religions, the New World Order global empire will be taken control of by the Antichrist and his supporters. In this view, a man will also claim to be the messiah of the world, and hold the key to solving humanity's troubles. Only in this view, the core of humanity's problems include those who don't agree that he is the messiah. The freedom from prejudice that he promises is impeded by Christians and others who see him as a counterfeit Christ and the Antichrist. The perversions and immorality that he is preaching is resisted and denounced by faithful Christians who see such behaviors as sinful and socially and spiritually destructive.

Just as Adolf Hitler promised peace and economic prosperity in Germany once the Jews were eliminated, the Antichrist will offer the same solution and single out the resistant Christians and others as the obstacle to peace and prosperity. These old fashioned Christians with their outdated traditions and beliefs are what is holding back the unity of mankind, the Antichrist will tell the world. People who still believe in private property, personal privacy, and the principles laid out in the original Constitution of the United States are the ones who are disrupting the new system. Those who will not accept implantable microchips and tracking devices, or neural interfaces wired directly into their brain and those who speak out against such things are the people who need to be eliminated for there to be peace. This, of course, according the to the Illuminati messiah and his supporters.

At some point during this ordeal, Christians believe that Jesus will return to earth and the Apocalypse will occur, exposing the counterfeit Christ and casting him into Hell. God is said to finally unveil the mysteries of existence and the struggles of life, and destroy or punish those who did not follow his rules. Those faithful to God's principles will then be eternally rewarded for their righteousness and courage.

Pre Illuminati Organizations

Most of the information distributed surrounding the Illuminati stems from the Knights Templar, the Freemasons, and the Bavarian Illuminati founded in Germany in 1776. It's important to note that essentially the same type of an organization had existed earlier, for hundreds, if not thousands of years. The Knights Templar date back to the 1100s and the Freemasons to the late 1500s, but before these organizations had formed, secret societies which possessed supposed secret knowledge had existed much earlier, and would later grow into these newer and more sophisticated groups.

Knowledge has always been a source of power, and dating back to ancient Egypt and Greece, groups of men had kept certain knowledge to themselves and only revealed it to others in incremental levels within what were called the Mysteries, or the Mystery schools. As science, medicine, and art were evolving and new discoveries were being made, the adepts or initiates of these Mystery schools were the ones on the cutting edge. These organizations were frequently made up of the brightest men in society.

The Mystery schools also served as a method for spiritual enlightenment as well. Mystical and spiritual principles were taught and acted out in the form of rituals and ceremonies as a way to convey allegorical meanings to the initiates. While these Mystery schools may not have facilitated any ill motives or plotted any diabolical schemes against non members and society as a whole, one can understand how initiates in the Mysteries could develop a superiority complex and use the cover of the organizations to aid them in carrying out their political and professional agendas. Some believe that the Mystery schools once had the highest standards regarding character and integrity of the members, and they were slowly corrupted and such virtues were replaced with selfishness and evil.

The Luciferian Doctrine

It is clear from the writings of prominent Freemasons and Illuminati authors that the religion and philosophy of the elite members is that of Lucifierianism or Satanism. Whether this is a literal belief or a metaphoric or allegorical belief is of little difference. If it were literal, it would then be metaphoric as well. If it were metaphoric, then it also expands into a literal fashion as the actions of the participants manifest themselves.

To sum up Luciferianism or Satanism one must understand the difference between atheistic Satanism, and theistic Satanism. Atheistic Satanism was popularized in the late 1960s by Anton LaVey, the founder of the Church of Satan and the author of *The Satanic Bible*. While misleading and confusing, he and his followers profess that they are atheists and don't believe in a literal Devil, or even God. They don't believe in an afterlife or a Heaven or Hell, either. These individuals choose to call themselves Satanists and use the symbol of Satan for its rebellious and nonconformist connotations. This topic is expanded in greater detail in the section of this book which covers *The Satanic Bible*.

Theistic Satanism, on the other hand, is the belief in a God and a Devil, and supernatural beings. These Satanists take the opposite side of the Christian view concerning the Garden of Eden and the Fall of Man. In Judaism and Christianity, the book of Genesis describes how God created Adam and Eve and how they lived in the Garden of Eden. God was said to have told them that they were not to eat the forbidden fruit from the tree of knowledge of good and evil, for if they did, they would surely die.

As the story goes, Satan appeared to Eve in the form of a snake and tempted her to eat the fruit. Genesis 3:1-7 reads, "The woman said to the serpent, "we may eat fruit from the trees in the garden, but God did say, 'You must not eat fruit from the tree that is in the middle of the garden, and you must not touch it, or you will die.'"

"You will not surely die," the serpent said to the woman. "For God knows that when you eat of it your eyes will be opened, and you will be like God, knowing good and evil."

"When the woman saw that fruit of the tree was good for food and pleasing to the eye, and also desirable for gaining wisdom, she took some and ate it. She also gave some to her husband, who was with her, and he ate it. Then the eyes of both of them were opened, and they realized they were naked; so they sowed fig leaves together and made coverings for themselves."

Theistic Satanists and Luciferians believe that Satan came to the Garden of Eden to save Adam and Eve and mankind from ignorance, and that God didn't want them to have the knowledge because then they wouldn't be his slaves. In this view, God is seen as the oppressor and the evil one, and Satan is seen as the hero and savior. This is why in such books as *The Secret Doctrine*, author Helena Blavatsky calls Satan the holy spirit.

She wrote, "Thus "SATAN," once he ceases to be viewed in the superstitious, dogmatic, unphilosophical spirit of the Churches, grows into the grandiose image of one who made of terrestrial a divine MAN; who gave him, throughout the long cycle of Maha-kalpa the law of the Spirit of Life, and made him free from the Sin of Ignorance, hence of death."[1]

"The true meaning is far more philosophical, and the legend of the first "Fall" (of the angels) assumes a scientific colouring when correctly understood."[2]

This is one of the reasons the Illuminati has a hierarchical structure, and only dispenses knowledge little by

---

[1] Blavatsky, Helena – *The Secret Doctrine* V I p. 198
[2] Blavatsky, Helena – *The Secret Doctrine* V I p. 418

little as members climb the ranks. Knowledge is power, and they have taken the fruit from the tree of knowledge of good and evil and have hid it away, using it as a carrot to entice lower level initiates to do the organization's bidding so they may be rewarded with not only their financial and social support, but with the forbidden occult knowledge of Man's past and of the nature of reality itself. Such forbidden knowledge, they believe, holds the potential for a man to become god-like.

The term Lucifer, which is synonymous with Satan, is Latin for "light bearer," which is why Luciferians and Satanists believe that the Devil is the source of knowledge and wisdom, thus he is good. While in Christianity, Jesus is said to be the light of the world, the Illuminati designate this attribute to Lucifer or Satan. The name Satan actually means "adversary" or accuser, and is hence the adversary of God. The title of Lucifer is given to Satan because he brings the forbidden wisdom that God did not want humanity to have.

In Christianity, as well as Luciferianism and other religions, the term "light" represents love, knowledge, and wisdom. One main difference between most religions and Luciferianism is that Christianity and most religions openly teach their message and welcome everyone to learn it and understand it, where occultism keeps its message hidden from most people and doesn't share its knowledge with others. The word occult means "hidden." The main difference between Luciferianism and Christianity is that traditional Christianity teaches that salvation comes only by believing in Jesus, where occultists believe that one is saved by learning the secret knowledge. While this idea of salvation by knolwege is not overtly evil and diabolical, it is what the Illuminati has done with this concept that proves they are a cabal of liars, hypocrites, and tryants. The term Illuminati is Latin for Illuminated ones, and is also a reference to light, Lucifer, and brilliance.

Inside the Mindset of the Illuminati

When one fully understands the religion of the Illuminati and its subsidiary branches such as high level Freemasons, Skull and Bones members, and Bohemian Grove attendees, one can wrestle with the reality of this Luciferian doctrine. While many publicly known organizations such as the Freemasons pride themselves on instilling moral character in their members, how is it that these elite members can be evil Satan worshipers? Do they really have the truth? Is Satan really the good god, and the God of the Bible is the evil one who is holding knowledge and blessings back from mankind?

If the Illuminati has the truth regarding the history of our creation and existence and the nature of God, then are they betraying their own god by keeping that truth, knowledge, and wisdom from others? What about not only keeping that supposed truth from people, but lying to them, or ruthlessly taking advantage of others or stealing from them? Whatever they think the truth is, they are keeping it for themselves and dispensing a constant stream of propaganda, disinformation, and out-right lies, in order to prevent others from finding that truth.

While practically every religion on the planet from Christianity, to Islam, to Buddhism and Hinduism, wants everyone to have an understanding of what they consider to be the truth, it is the Illuminati who do not abide by these ideals. Elite members do not follow the golden rule of life, that of treating others the way that you want to be treated, instead they violate nearly every major moral code that is found in religions around the world. Do not lie, do not steal, do not murder, do not covet, these rules mean nothing to the elite members of the Illuminati and its subsidiary organizations.

These revelations often lead to the question of whether

these individuals believe in an afterlife or a judgment from God after they die. Most religions believe that when one dies, they will stand before God and be judged for their sins. Under this belief system, even if someone gets through life without getting caught for their misdeeds, they will one day pay the price in the afterlife in a purgatory for temporary punishment, or burning in Hell for an eternity. Therefore one wonders what the Illuminati believe will happen to them when they die. How will they escape Divine justice for all of their crimes?

There are two explanations for this. One is that they don't believe in an afterlife, and that we are just sophisticated animals who have no souls, and when we are dead, there is no afterlife, nor judgment. This would explain their social Darwinist world view and their unfair parasitic practices which rob others of their money, health, freedom, and sanity. Another explanation is that the Illuminati believe that God doesn't judge us in a personal way, but in an impersonal fashion based on a scale of good deeds vs. bad deeds. In this view, one is believed to be able to balance out their Karma, so to speak, and avoid any unwanted repercussions for their indiscretions.

Both of these explanations lead to other questions. Is the Illuminati correct? Are we just animals with no soul or afterlife? If we are a religious person, are *we* the ones living a lie? Let's just say for argument's sake that they are correct that there is no afterlife and no judgment from God after one dies. I certainly hope this is not true, but even if it is the case, if we all were to live by their philosophy, then society would be a dangerous place, and unfulfilling and meaningless. If every man was out for himself and we all would break the basic moral code of the civilized world, then life would be Hell on earth. If there is no afterlife or judgment from God, no Heaven or Hell, then the brief life that we live on this planet would still be infinitely more enjoyable, fulfilling, and safe if we were to live by Biblical principles than if we were to live by the Illuminati's code of do what thou wilt.

The Illuminati may have the entire truth, or they may have a piece of it and think they have it as a whole, like a blind man who grabs an elephant's tale and thinks that it is an elephant, not knowing he is only holding a small part of an elephant and cannot begin to imagine what an elephant really is, based on the small part that he is holding in his hand.

Despite their supposed superior knowledge and wisdom, the Illuminati have been wrong in the past. They have been blinded by their own pride and drunk from their own power. Adolf Hitler along with his elite inner circle of Nazis believed that they would rule the world and build a new race of enlightened super-men. They believed that mystical powers were on their side, and their destiny was to build a thousand year empire with Adolf Hitler as its high priest. Instead, their plans crumbled and Hitler and his closest allies were forced to commit suicide in a cowardly act of defeat.

Jesus said there are two rules in life. The first one is to love God with all your heart, and the second one is to love your neighbor as yourself. Luke 10:25-28 reads, "On one occasion an expert in the law stood up to test Jesus. "Teacher," he asked, "what must I do to inherit eternal life?"

"What is written in the law" he replied. "How do you read it?"

He answered: "Love the Lord your God with all your heart and with all your soul and with all your strength and with all your mind, and love your neighbor as yourself."

"You have answered correctly." Jesus replied. "Do this and you will live."

In philosophy, a consideration called Pascal's wager proposes that if one were to live as though there was no God or final judgment, and they were wrong, they would have a tremendous loss. But if someone were to live as though there is a God, that God has established rules for us to follow, and that each individual will be repaid or punished for their deeds, then if they were wrong, they would lose nothing and would have had a safer more fulfilling life anyway. Pascal proposed that even though we cannot prove the existence of God through reason or scientific inquiry, that people should wager as though he does exist because one has potentially everything to gain and nothing to lose by doing so.

Regardless of one's religion, there is another story in the Bible which helps to explain the philosophy of the Illuminati. In Matthew 4:8-9, it explains how Satan took Jesus to the top of a mountain and told him he would give him control over all the kingdoms of the world if Jesus would worship Satan. Jesus, of course, didn't accept this offer, but this story conveys a deeper meaning than what appears on the surface. By worshiping Satan and turning one's back on God's rules, it is possible to gain control over vast empires and gather enormous riches. But these gains come with a price which is not always seen at the time. Later, when repercussions come from breaking the rules, the empire and riches one had gained will become their very undoing. So when Satan told Jesus, "All this I will give to you if you will bow down and worship me," he was partially telling the truth. He just wasn't disclosing the consequences that would occur from such actions.

So do not let the Luciferian doctrine and the Illuminati's philosophy poison your mind and lead you to abandon the golden rule of life. While learning the details of occult philosophy can cause one to wrestle with their faith, one must understand there are very real consequences and reactions to the way we chose to live our lives.

Whatever one's faith is, there is a universal code of conduct in the world, and it is clear that the Illuminati habitually breaks that code, while presenting a false face to society that they abide by the same rules everyone else is expected to follow.

Why are the Jews Always Blamed?

One can't discuss the Illuminati or the New World Order at any length without coming across anti-Semitism. For a minority of those who are against the New World Order, the Jews are at the heart of every problem, and at the pinnacles of power. The "Jewish bankers" and the "Jews in Hollywood" control it all, they claim. Some still believe that *The Protocols of the Elders of Zion* are authentic Jewish documents that prove the Zionists' sinister plans, and that the Illuminati is controlled by Jews at the very top.

The Protocols are a series of documents which were written from a Jewish perspective which outline the necessary steps for world domination. They describe the need to control the banking system, the media, and political institutions in order to accomplish these goals. They are essentially the Illuminati plan for control written up from the perspective of Jews.

When the documents were "discovered" in 1905 word was spread that they were created by a governing body of the Jews, and the Protocols have been used ever since to inflame hate against the Jewish people. Hitler believed the Protocols were authentic and today some still believe that is the case. The Protocols are examined in further detail later in this book.

One source of anti-Semitism comes from the idea that some Jews believe they are God's chosen people and God's favorite race of humans. Many see the Jews who hold these views as racist and Jewish supremacists. The fact that many Jews believe that God gave them the land of Israel in the Middle East, and that the Palestinians then have no rightful claim to it continues to be a source of conflict today as the two different cultures argue and kill over whose land it rightfully is.

Some see the central theme of Judaism as being

secretive in nature, and an inner circle of Jews secretly controlling the religion and international banking. Certainly the Jewish Pharisees (the religious teachers in the past) kept the spiritual teachings about Judaism to themselves and purposefully kept the masses ignorant and uninformed about the nature of God and the Torah (the Old Testament). Jesus denounced this control, and his main theme of his teaching was that people didn't need the Pharisees to have a connection with God, and that they could have direct access to God themselves and didn't need a "middle man" so to speak.

Some point to the Talmud and Cabala as a continuation of the monopolization of spiritual information on the part of the Jews and see parts of the Talmud as Jewish supremacist in their teachings and give justification for some Jews to believe that their race is the one divinely ordained by God to rule the world.

A rare and unorthodox interpretation of the Book of Genesis and the Fall of Man also fuels anti-Semitism. Adherents to the serpent seed theory believe that Satan had sex with Eve in the garden of Eden and caused Eve to become pregnant with Cain, making him half human, half Devil. Later, as this theory claims, Adam and Eve conceived a child of their own, being Abel. The theory continues that Cain is the patriarch of the Jewish people, and hence they are all descendents of Satan.

Some white supremacists believe that white people, or Aryans, are actually God's chosen race, and that the Jews are falsely claiming they are the chosen ones. This is the case with the Christian Identity movement, who are racist Christians who see themselves as the true heirs to God's blessings, and see the Jews as enemies and counterfeits.

In the Book of Revelation chapter 2 verse 9, the Bible reads, "I know your afflictions and your poverty— yet you are rich! I know the slander of those who say they are Jews and are not, but are a synagogue of Satan."

Later in chapter 3 verse 9, Jesus says, "I will make those who are of the synagogue of Satan, who claim to be Jews though they are not, but are liars—I will make them come and fall down at your feet and acknowledge that I have loved you."

These are two powerful passages that those who often target the Jews as being the root of the world's problems will use as evidence that even Jesus saw that there were counterfeit Jews attempting to fool the people as to their actual beliefs and motives.

Christian Identity's beliefs are in common with British Israelism, which teaches that white Europeans are the literal descendants of the Israelites through the ten tribes that were taken away into slavery by the armies of Assyria.

These beliefs hold that Jesus was an Israelite from the tribe of Judah, and that white European Israelites are still God's chosen people. They also believe that those which most people call modern Jews are not descendents from the Israelites nor Hebrews but are instead actually Khazars who descended from people with Turco-Mongolian blood.

Adolf Hitler seemingly subscribed to these theories and they were used to justify the actions of the Holocaust. Several Aryan Nation organizations and other white supremacist groups incorporate similar beliefs and are used to support their ideologies and actions.

Some Christians subscribe to what is called replacement theology which teaches that people who follow the teachings of Jesus and become Christians are God's chosen people, and that the body of Christ, or the church, replaced the Jews as the chosen people. This is certainly not mainstream Christianity which continues to teach that the Israelites are God's chosen ones. Supporters of replacement theology aren't necessarily racists or white supremacists and should not be confused with Christian Identity believers.

While the Jews continue to be at the center of controversy and blame regarding their alleged control of the

Illuminati, it should be emphasized that members of all races are found within the hierarchy of power. While it is easy to point out wealthy Jews, or powerful Jews in Hollywood and the media, it is more effective to point out the corrupt nature of someone's soul, rather than their racial heritage. While there are Jews who arrogantly place themselves and their personal value above all others because of their racial identity, there are even more who see themselves as most people do, that of members of the human race and equal to all others regardless of race or religion.

Fixing the Fight

Most people who identify strongly with a particular political party believe that most, or everything that their party does or stands for is right, and that most or everything that the opposing party stands for is wrong. This same "us vs. them" attitude is also directed towards prominent members in each political party, and party leaders. Republican supporters believe that the Democratic party and leadership are stupid, incompetent, and sometimes criminal, while believing that members of the Republican party are saints, and have the people's best interests in mind. The same is true of Democratic supporters, in that they blindly view their party as above reproach, and see the opposing party as incompetent, ideologically incorrect, and at times criminal.

This false, left/right paradigm prevents many people from seeing that the leadership at the top of both political parties is controlled by the same private interests. The Illuminati own both horses in the race, so to speak, as was clearly illustrated in the 2004 presidential election when both John Kerry and George W. Bush were facing off against each other for the presidency, and both are members of the ultra elite Illuminati branch, the Skull and Bones society.

The man credited with founding the Illuminati in 1776, Adam Weishaupt, wrote "By this plan we shall direct all mankind. In this manner, and by the simplest means, we shall set all in motion and in flames. The occupations must be so allotted and contrived, that we may, in secret, influence all political transactions."

"This can be done in no other way but by secret associations, which will by degrees, and in silence, possess themselves of the government of the States, and make use of those means for this purpose..."

"...the Order will, *for its own sake*, and therefore

certainly, place every man in that situation in which he can be most effective. The pupils are convinced that the Order *will* rule the world. Every member therefore becomes a ruler."

"I shall therefore press the cultivation of science, especially such sciences as may have an influence on our reception in the world; and may serve to remove obstacles out of the way...Only those who are assuredly proper subjects shall be picked out from among the inferior classes for the higher mysteries...And in particular, every person shall be made a spy on another and on all around him."

"Nothing can escape our sight; by these means we shall readily discover who are contented, and receive with relish the peculiar state-doctrines and religious opinions that are laid before them; and, at last, the trustworthy alone will be admitted to a participation of the whole maxims and political constitution of the Order."

"In a council composed of such members we shall labor at the contrivance of means to drive by degrees the enemies of reason and of humanity out of the world, and to establish a peculiar morality and religion fitted for the great Society of mankind."

High level Republicans, and Republican presidents are the right foot of the Illuminati, and Democrats are the left foot. One foot takes a step forward, then the other, and the process is repeated as the two feet work together to move the Illuminati forward to accomplish their goals of which both conservative and liberal politicians are secretly aiding. This is why we find politicians and presidents whose actions are completely contradictory to their party or the promises they made on the campaign trail. George W. Bush, a supposed conservative, increased government spending more than all previous administrations combined, and while continuously talking about keeping America safe from terrorists, he refused to increase border security and denounced the Minute Men, who voluntarily patrol the U.S. Mexican border, as "vigilantes."

The owners of the NFL (National Football League) couldn't care less which team wins the Super Bowl each year, because no matter which team it is, the NFL makes money. The Illuminati is the same way when it comes to politics. The president of the United States is like a manager at a fast food restaurant. He seems to be the one in charge and the one who takes the brunt of customer complaints, but he is merely working for someone who the customers will never see, or never hear about. The fast food manager is working for the franchise owner, just as the president of the United States is simply a spokesman who is carrying out the orders and agenda of his boss which remains unseen by the public. This boss, is of course, the Illuminati.

Mainstream Media

The control of information, as well as disinformation, is one of the most powerful tools at the Illuminati's disposal. The best way to do this, as they discovered hundreds of years ago, is to own the sources of mainstream media. Television, newspapers, magazine publishers, radio networks, and film studios are largely owned and controlled by Illuminati branches.

Editorial policies are put in place and producers and editors are positioned to act as gate-keepers to prevent any unwanted information from being presented to the masses. While not 100% effective, they have proven their ability to minimize the amount of news stories from making it into print or on the airwaves that will be unfavorable to Illuminati goals and operations.

Aside from acting as gate-keepers, these individuals also receive information from their handlers as to what stories should be produced, and what angle they should have. If a particular issue or person needs to be presented in a favorable light, then this is what will happen. In 2008, former White House press secretary Scott McClellan reported on CNN that the White House gave regular talking points to several hosts at the Fox News Channel. The 2004 documentary *Outfoxed: Rupert Murdoch's War on Journalism* details how Fox News was used as both a mouth piece and an attack dog for the Bush administration. Leaked memos showed that orders came down from the top Fox executives as to which stories to run and what points to focus on, so that broadcasts would fit a prescribed agenda, and not be "fair and balanced" as Fox News claims.

Operation Mockingbird is a program that the CIA and other branches of government implemented back in the 1950s in order to control the mainstream media in America, as well as media in foreign countries. Through congressional hearings it was revealed that hundreds of millions of dollars had been paid to reporters, and that editors in key media intuitions were also on the payroll who often killed certain stories from being printed or aired.

This should come as no surprise. Looking back at the original writings of the Bavarian Illuminati founder, Adam Weishaupt, one can see that back in the late 1700s he understood the power in controlling information. Weishaupt wrote, "By establishing reading societies, and subscription libraries, and taking these under our direction, and supplying them through our labours, we may turn the public mind which way we will."

"In like manner we must try to obtain an influence in the military academies (this may be of mighty consequence) the printing-houses, booksellers shops, chapters, and in short in all offices which have any effect, either in forming, or in managing, or even in directing the mind of man: painting and engraving are highly worth our care."

Illuminati members also understood how powerful controlling newspapers could be to smear their enemies. One letter found in the original Illuminati writings reads, "We get all the literary journals. We take care, by well-timed pieces [articles], to make the citizens and the Princes a little more noticed for certain little slips."

It's not just print and broadcast news that they control. The entertainment business has been fully infiltrated and is now dominated by Illuminati handlers. When one looks at how over just one generation, television shows went from *I Love Lucy* showing a husband and wife sleeping in two separate twin beds because the network wouldn't allow a couple to be shown in bed together, to *Desperate Housewives* and *Nip/Tuck* bordering on soft-core pornography, it is clear a rapid decay in the moral quality of the programming has occurred. One must not even look back as far as the days of *I Love Lucy* to see the dramatic change in standards. This author remembers growing up in the 1980s with such shows as *Family Ties* and *Growing Pains*, which at the time were both entertaining, and usually had a moral to the story. Such shows are now almost non existent and have been replaced with utter filth that is now commonplace.

While many ignorant people claim that television doesn't affect an individual's behaviors, the social and cultural effects of such changes are clearly noticeable. Sexual immorality, violence, and disrespectful and destructive behaviors are celebrated and encouraged by today's most popular television shows and musicians.

The Illuminati elite knew they could change the moral climate of society by giving the impression that women didn't need to follow the basic patterns of behavior that were expected of them. Weishaupt wrote, "There is no way of influencing men so powerfully as by means of the women. These should therefore be our chief study; we should insinuate ourselves into their good opinion, give them hints of emancipation from the tyranny of public opinion, and of standing up for themselves; it will be an immense relief to their enslaved minds to be freed from any one bond of restraint, and it will fire them the more, and cause them to work for us with zeal, without knowing that they do so; for they will only be indulging their own desire of personal admiration."

With most people knowing more about which celebrity recently got pregnant or had a run in with the law, than they know about what's happening in national politics or their community, the Illuminati easily continues to thrive with little opposition. It is no accident that petty issues and celebrity gossip are the top stories in the media, and the majority of the public is oblivious to reality. They are mesmerized by the mainstream media and unconcerned and often unaware of their own ignorance.

Economic Control

Most people do not have the faintest clue about what money really is, how it is created, and how it functions in a society. The financial system is so complicated, many chose not to learn how it works. The Dow Jones Industrial Average, Stocks, Bonds, Treasury Bills, put options, 401k, IRAs, CDs, interest rates, inflation, the Department of the Treasury, the Federal Reserve, etc. etc. It's a lot to digest.

You will often hear people say "the middle class is shrinking" or "the middle class is going to disappear" and wonder how that could happen. When you understand that the Illuminati's central means of power is by controlling money, and when you learn about the mechanisms they use to do this, a clearer understanding of both personal and global finances will occur.

The Illuminati learned at least as far back as the twelfth century, that they could loan money to individuals and governments, and then charge them interest on the money that they had loaned them, thus making money without working. Most people back then, and even today, have to provide a product or service in order to then sell it to someone else interested in that product or service, and that way earn a profit. People worked to build things, grow food, or offer numerous services including preparing food, cleaning, or feeding and tending to livestock.

When civilization was evolving, if someone grew corn, then they could trade a bushel of corn for a cow to a farmer who raised cows. They could also trade that bushel of corn to a man who assembled clothes in exchange for a new pair of pants and some sandals. This is known as the barter system. But there would be a problem if the man who grew corn wanted to trade the corn for a cow but the farmer with the cow didn't want any corn, but instead wanted some wheat, which the corn grower didn't have. For this reason, people agreed on a medium of exchange. This medium of exchange, we'll use gold coins for example, was something that they could trade their corn for, and then take the gold coins and trade those coins for a cow, or for whatever else they wanted that was for sale at the market. The more valuable the product or service was that they provided, the more gold coins they would get in exchange for that product or service. Throughout history, many different items have been used as money, such as sea shells, stones, and gold coins. This item would have to be rare enough so that people couldn't just create more of it, thus creating free money for themselves. For thousands of years, gold and silver coins have been a standard medium of exchange because of their rarity, and difficulty to counterfeit.

Metal coins were often a burden to carry, so a system was devised where people would turn in their gold or silver to a bank and in return they would get paper money which represented the amount of gold and silver they deposited. At any time people could go back to the bank and trade in their paper money for its equivalent in gold and silver. The paper money was basically a receipt for the actual money that they had deposited at the bank. In the market place, people would accept these receipts as payment for goods and services instead of gold and silver coins. Bankers would also loan out the money (gold and silver coins) people had deposited in their vaults, and collect interest on those loans. These bankers also realized that they could loan out money to people they didn't actually have, and then collect the interest on those loans as well. Loaning out money they don't have doesn't seem possible, but all they needed to do to accomplish this was write up a receipt and loan that out to someone, and the person would be able to use that receipt in the marketplace and nobody would know that it didn't actually represent any gold or silver that someone had deposited in the bank. It seems hard to believe, but when you understand how fiat currencies work, it is actually a genius idea on the part of the bankers. It's the ultimate con, and few people are aware of it.

This same system is in place today and has evolved into a complex global economy, but it still operates in the same way. Hundreds of years ago the Illuminati discovered how powerful of a system this is, and that the ones who control the creation and loaning of money can have an unlimited supply of it without actually working. This is the big banking secret of the Federal Reserve system, and the reason the Illuminati have become known as international bankers.

Their ultimate financial goal is to create a socialist system where the government will control all aspects of industry, society, healthcare, real estate, and finances. By building a New World Order where everyone must rely on the government for jobs, healthcare, education, and basic services, the Illuminati will be able to easily dictate to the people what they can and cannot do. Their aim is to permanently establish a two class society where a small percentage of people (the Illuminati and their supporters) will own and control all infrastructure, wealth, and real estate, and the rest of the world will be reduced to slaves with no real assets or power. This is identical to the caste system in ancient India where the children of a laborer was destined to be a laborer, and so would his children, and so on. At the same time, the upper class caste maintains an elite and elegant lifestyle that their children will enjoy, and so will their children's children and so on.

The New World Order will be a self-sustaining structure and intelligent people looking to avoid social and economic slavery will find it nearly impossible unless they are willing to perpetuate the system. Most of the public will willingly accept their present status and economic enslavement since they are amused with televised entertainment and sedated with any number of prescribed pharmaceuticals which alleviate their anxieties, unhappiness, or desire to improve their situation. Any extra money they have at the end of the month is usually squandered away on alcohol or other items of no real value, which keeps them from accumulating any tangible assets. Interest paid on credit card debt also continues to siphon off money that could be used to improve their living conditions. Most of the items purchased with those credit cards were not necessary, but the user's inability to resist their urge to mindlessly consume and purchase excessively expensive items which have no purpose other than to attempt to convey a social status that the person does not have, caused them to compulsively spend.

The Illuminati's creation and control of money, interest rates and inflation allow them to fuel economic booms which they know will ultimately end as they hemorrhage into bubbles which burst and leave a path of economic devastation behind for the average citizen. Since the Illuminati owns real tangible assets, they are immune from the devastating effects of economic bubbles bursting, or stock markets crashing.

In 2007 and 2008 Peter Schiff, the president of Euro Pacific Capitol, a brokerage firm had been warning that the mortgage bubble was soon to burst and the stock market would crash and throw the country into a recession or worse. He was a fairly frequent guest on cable news shows and his forecast was always 180 degrees from the host and other guests. At times other guests on the segments laughed out loud at Schiff's predictions. Schiff was chosen by Congressman Ron Paul to be his economic adviser when he ran for President in 2008. Schiff also predicted the collapse in his 2007 Book *Crash Proof: How to Profit from the Coming Economic Collapse*.

One of the most respected trend forecasters, Gerald Celente, the CEO of the Trends Research Institute, made news late in 2008 by saying that the American economy would completely collapse and that there would be hyper inflation causing prices for food and other goods to skyrocket, causing shortages, long lines, and government

40

price controls to prevent rising prices on necessities. Despite these warnings nothing changed and the American economy began collapsing and set off a chain reaction around the globe.

Soon after the collapse began, in October 2008 an unprecedented 700 billion dollar bailout for failing and struggling banks was proposed. 700 billion is a seven with eleven zeros after it. $700,000,000,000 represented $2,300 for every man woman and child in America. Henry Paulson the Treasurer Secretary at the time, Ben Bernanke the Chairman of the Federal Reserve, and others were saying that if the bailout didn't pass a vote which allowed it to happen, that within weeks the stock market would crash, and the country would suffer unimaginable consequences.

Some members of Congress were privately told that if the bailout didn't pass a vote, America would completely break down and martial law would have to be imposed to thwart massive crime and civil unrest. Congressman Brad Sherman blew the whistle on such threats and called them unjustified fear mongering.[3] California Senator Diane Feinstein publicly admitted that her office received 91,000 phone calls and emails about the bailout, and that 85,000 of them were opposed to it, but she voted for the bailout anyway because people were "confused" and "didn't understand it" and she did what she said was in the best interest of the country.

Immediately after the bailout was passed by Congress, Ben Bernanke, Henry Paulson, and others decided to allot the money to other areas, instead of buying bad mortgage debt that they had originally proposed. The money was already approved by Congress, and no steps were taken to hold these men to their original promise of where the money

---

[3] The Los Angeles Times *Senate approves bailout after revisions, 74-25* October 2 2008

would go. They simply decided to spend the money differently after the "economic stimulus" was passed, and the money was theirs. Months later, the Fed refused to disclose the recipients of two trillion dollars in loans which came from taxpayer money,[4] and many CEOs of failed financial institutions which received billions of dollars of taxpayers money were still allowed to collect their Christmas bonuses of millions, and in some cases tens of millions of dollars.

In November of 2008, Barack Obama was selected to be the next president of the United States, and after being sworn into office on January 20th 2009, he quickly proposed a second "economic stimulus" package which exceeded the size of the first one, just months earlier. Contrary to common sense, president Obama and his economic advisers insisted to the American people that the only thing that would prevent America from going into a depression was if the government would spend nearly 800 billion more dollars.

On February 13th 2009 the 787 billion dollar "stimulus plan" was passed by Congress without a single member even reading it. Seriously, not a single member of Congress read the bill, but passed it anyway. The bill was over 1100 pages long, and from the time it was published to the time of the vote was less than 12 hours. The Obama administration had used fear mongering to scare Congress into passing it immediately and said if they didn't approve it, the economy and the country would collapse. Even after the bill was passed by Congress and then signed into law a few days later by President Obama, the stock market kept dropping hundreds of points a day and by the end of February, the Dow Jones Industrial Average had dropped more than 50% from its high a year earlier to under 7000.

As a result of these "bailouts" and "stimulus packages,"

---

[4] Bloomberg.com *Fed Refuses to Disclose Recipients of $2 Trillion* December 12th 2008 by Mark Pittman

the United States government has become the largest share holder in numerous financial institutions, thus nationalizing them. These once failed banks used to be completely independently owned and operated, but can now be controlled by the government. The auto industry also received billions of dollars in "bailout" money, and now must answer to the federal government in regards to what kind of cars and trucks to produce. The free market system and Capitalism itself have been replaced with socialism as a result. Most of the ignorant public was relieved that the government was trying to "save the economy" from this unforeseen disaster which occurred as a result of the mortgage bubble bursting, but in reality the entire ordeal was orchestrated by the Illuminati. Many experts warned that the "stimulus" packages would only make the economy worse, but the Obama administration rammed their plans through as quickly as they could with no oversight.

In her 1934 book, *A Treatise on White Magic*, Illuminati author Alice Bailey wrote about the financial control of the Illuminati, not to expose their methodologies, but to educate members of the organization. She explains, "[the] group controls and orders the means whereby he [mankind] exists, controlling all that can be converted into energy, and constituting a dictatorship over all modes of intercourse, commerce and exchange. They control the multiplicity of form-objects which modern man regards as essential to his mode of life. Money, as I have before said, is only crystallized energy or vitality,—what the oriental student calls pranic energy. It is a concretisation of etheric force. It is therefore vital energy externalized, and this form of energy is under the direction of the financial group. They are the latest group in point of data, and their work (it should be borne in mind) is most definitely planned by the Hierarchy. They are bringing about effects upon the earth which are most far reaching."[5]

Dating back to the days of the Knights Templars, the Illuminati had learned how powerful they could be if they were to become the masters of money and banking. War has always been a big business for the Illuminati as well. The weapons manufactures earn a continuous stream of profits by supplying the increased demand, and private contractors such as Halliburton earn enormous amounts of money and are paid by the government to do jobs that can often be completed by the military at a fraction of the cost. A powerful film titled *Iraq for Sale* shows just how much money the private contractors are making with no-bid contracts.

Anton LaVey, the founder of the Church of Satan, had his grandson Stanton Zaharoff LaVey named after Sir Basil Zaharoff, an arms dealer, and in LaVey's authorized biography it talks about how much he admired this arms dealer for his cunningness because he would sell weapons to governments of both sides of a conflict in order to make money.[6]

Such a practice has been used for decades, if not centuries. Private banks have lent money to governments to finance conflictions and wars. Interest is then earned on these loans, making the banks a hefty profit. But their scheme doesn't end there. Throughout history, these private banks have loaned money to both sides of a conflict, thus not only prolonging the conflict, but earning interest from both governments that are fighting each other.

The well known saying "the love of money is the root of all evil" can be understood with a deeper level of understanding when the concepts of money and loans are

[5] Bailey, Alice − *A Treatise on White Magic* p. 412
[6] Barton, Blanch − *The Secret Life of a Satanist: The Authorized Biography of Anton LaVey* pages 24-25

fully comprehended. Since a medium of exchange is necessary for today's society to function, it should come as no surprise that the Illuminati has wrapped its tentacles around institutions needed for money to be created and regulated.

Nonfiction Books

Nonfiction books exposing the Illuminati have been in publication since at least the late 1700s when the Bavarian Illuminati was exposed after some of the group's writings had been seized by authorities. Since then, a variety of authors have published books, both exposing the Illuminati and their subsidiary organizations, as well as writing books targeted for elitists and occultists to spread the satanic and occult teachings along with the political and financial aspirations of the secret brotherhood.

Books range from focusing specifically on the original Illuminati, to exposing Skull and Bones, the Bohemian Grove, the Federal Reserve, the Bilderberg group, and more. Titles and descriptions of several of the most reliable and well known books to do so are to follow, as well as some of the information that the authors have uncovered. Also included are books by occultists who wanted to openly spread the Illuminati's philosophies and plans.

Proofs of a Conspiracy

One of the first and most popular books written about the Illuminati was published in 1798 by John Robison, a professor of natural philosophy at Edinburgh University in Scotland. The full title of the book is *Proofs of a Conspiracy Against all the Religious and Governments of Europe Carried on in the Secret Meetings of Freemasons, Illuminati, and Reading Societies.* It is often referred to by the shortened title *Proofs of a Conspiracy.* A copy of his work was sent to George Washington, where he responded with a letter saying that he was aware that the Illuminati had diabolical plans of separating people from their government.

Robison's book is extremely important because it was written at the time the Illuminati was first exposed to the public. It is basically a first hand account of what the Illuminati were doing and how they became known to the public. Robison saw the importance of documenting what was happening and his writings remain essential for anyone looking to fully understand the Illuminati. He included large portions of original writings of Adam Weishaupt and other members which were made public shortly after their discovery. By reading the words of Weishaupt and the plans outlined in his writings, it becomes clear he had intricate sinister goals, and knew exactly how the Illuminati could seize control of the government, media, and other key institutions of influence.

Robison writes, "The association of which I have been speaking, is the order of Illuminati, founded in 1775, by Dr. Adam Weishaupt, professor of Canon law in the university of Ingolstadt, and abolished in 1786 by the Elector of Bavaria, but revived immediately after, under another name, and in a different form, all over Germany. It was again detected and seemingly broken up; but it had by this time taken so deep root that it still subsists without being detected, and has spread into all the countries of Europe. It took its first rise among the Freemasons, but is totally different from Freemasonry."[7]

Robison explains in detail how information about the Illuminati began to be uncovered, and how their original papers had been found and made public. He wrote, "In the beginning of 1783, four professors of the Marianen Academy, founded by the widow of the late Elector, viz. Utschneider, Cossandey, Renner, and Grunberger, with two others, were summoned before the Court of Enquiry and questioned, on their allegiance, respecting the Order of the Illuminati. They acknowledged that they belonged to it, and when more closely examined, they related several

---

[7] Robison, John – *Proofs of a Conspiracy* page 9

circumstances of its constitution and principles. Their declarations were immediately published, and were very unfavorable. The Order was said to abjure Christianity, and to refuse admission into the higher degrees to all who adhered to any of the three confessions."[8]

"A collection of original papers and correspondence was found by searching the house of one Zwack [Xavier von Zwack] (a member) in 1786. The following year a much larger collection was found at the house of Baron Bassus; and since that time Baron Knigge, the most active member next to Weishaupt, published an account of some of the higher degrees, which had been formed by himself."[9]

In a work titled *Literary Memoirs of Living Authors of Great Britain,* published in London in 1798 for R. Faulder it reads, "In the autumn of the year 1797, Professor Robison published an octavo volume, entitled *Proofs of a Conspiracy.* This volume has been favorably received, and although too hasty a performance for a work of so much consequence, is well entitled, both from its subject and its authenticity, to the serious attention of every reader. It arrives at the same remarkable conclusion as the celebrated Memoirs of the Abbe Barruel, illustrating the history of Jacobinism, though the authors were perfectly unconnected with each other, and pursued their inquiries in very different ways. It has raised (we are sorry for such an appearance) a considerable clamor and enmity against the Professor, though it was written, we are fully convinced from the best motives. We cannot conclude this article without observing that the principles, and honest zeal, which Professor Robison has displayed upon this occasion are highly credible to him, and merit the warmest acknowledgments from society in general."

Reverend Dr. Erskine, who was a neighbor to John

[8] Robison, John – *Proofs of a Conspiracy* page 60-61
[9] Robison, John – *Proofs of a Conspiracy* page 76

Robison, wrote in a letter dated September 25, 1800 in Edinburgh, "I think highly of Professor Robison's book. Some of the most shocking facts it contains, I knew before its publication, from a periodical account of the church history of the times, by Professor Koester at Giessen, of which I lent him all the numbers relating to that subject. For three years, that valuable work has been discontinued, whether from the artifices of Illuminati booksellers, to prevent its sale and spread, or from the author's bad health, I know not."

These testimonials and others show that Robison was not a "conspiracy theorist" but was simply documenting what the Illuminati was and what their goals were, immediately after their discovery.

In *Proofs of a Conspiracy*, Robison also describes the initiation ceremony into the "Regent Degree" of the Illuminati which was the near the highest level in the hierarchy. It bears a striking resemblance to the satanic ritual for entry into Skull and Bones at Yale. Robison describes that during the Illuminati's ceremony, the initiate faced a skeleton, and at its feet were a crown and a sword. He was then asked "whether that is the skeleton of a king, nobleman, or a beggar." Despite his choice, the president declared, "The character of being a man is the only one that is important."

The writing inside Skull and Bones headquarters known as the "Tomb" at Yale reads, "Wer war der Thor, wer Weiser, Bettler oder Kaiser? Ob Arm, ob Reich, im Tode gleich." In English it says, "Who was the fool, who was the wise man, beggar or king? Whether poor or rich, all's the same in death." This is just one of many identical connections found between the Bavarian Illuminati and the Skull and Bones society. One of the founders of Skull and Bones, William Huntington Russell, had just returned from studying abroad in Germany shortly before starting Skull and Bones in 1832. "Bonesmen" who will actually talk about the organization admit that Russell had obtained permission from "a German secret society" when he was studying there, and then returned to America to start Skull and Bones. This German secret society was none other than the Illuminati.

John Robison's *Proofs of a Conspiracy* is still in print today and thankfully has not been lost in history. Aside from giving the history of the Illuminati and the circumstances surrounding their discovery, Robison includes entire letters written by Adam Weishaupt himself, as well as other high level members. From these original writings, one learns that the Illuminati were not simply a group of "freethinkers" who feared persecution from the Catholic Church, but were devious, power hungry immoral men who did not want to free society from the grip of the Catholic Church, but instead wanted to replace that position of power themselves and then they could rule over society as kings.

Memoirs Illustrating the History of Jacobinism

In 1797 a French Jesuit priest named Abbe Barruel published a series of books on the Jacobins and their influence on the French Revolution. The Jacobins were a powerful political club in France which helped organize the revolution in the late 1700s. Today the term Jacobin or Jacobinism is sometimes used to describe left-wing revolutionary ideas.

Barruel wrote four different volumes titled *Memoirs Illustrating the History of Jacobinism* in which he explained that the French Revolution was the result of secret societies, largely the Bavarian Illuminati. Two of the volumes focus extensively on Adam Weishaupt and the Illuminati, and Barruel's writings remain important today because they were written at the time Weishaupt and his cohorts were discovered and had their plans exposed to the world.

Barruel's writings contain some of the same warnings and information that John Robison's *Proofs of a Conspiracy* includes, but the two authors had no contact with each other, and were unaware of each other's work until after its publication.

Barruel wrote, "The third conspiracy, which I am now about to investigate, is that of the atheistical Illuminees, which at my outfit I denominated the conspiracy of the Sophisters of Impiety and anarchy against every religion natural or revealed, not only against kings, but against every government, against all civil society, even against all property whatsoever."[10]

Before expanding on the Illuminati's goals and activities, Barruel explains how Weishaupt's and others writings were discovered and made public. "The first is a collection entitled "Some of the Original Writings of the Sect of Illuminees," which were discovered on the 11th and 12th of October, 1786 at Landshut, on a search made in the House of the Sieur Zwack, heretofor Counselor of the Regency; and printed by the Order of His Highness the Elector [in] Munich, by Ant. Franz, Printer to the Court. The second is a supplement to the Original Writings, chiefly containing those which were found on a search made at the castle of Sandersdorf, a famous haunt of thee Illuminees, by order of His Highness the Elector. Munich, 1787. These two volumes contain irrefragable proofs of the most detestable conspiracy. They disclose the principles, the object, and the means of the Sect; the essential parts of their code, the diligent correspondence of the adepts, particularly that of their chief, and statement of their progress and future hopes."[11]

While Adam Weishaupt is credited with creating the

---

[10] Barruel, Abbe – *Memoirs Illustrating the History of Jacobinism* Volume III page v
[11] Barruel, Abbe – *Memoirs Illustrating the History of Jacobinism* Volume III page vi - vii

Illuminati, it is suspected that he had merely been chosen to modernize the organization and formulate updated goals and methods of operation for an advancing society. Barruel had also raised this issue, saying "It is not known, and it would be difficult to discover, whether Weishaupt ever had a master, or whether he is himself the great original of those monstrous doctrines on which he founded his school."[12]

Regardless of whether Weishaupt was the actual mastermind at the top of the Illuminati, or merely credited with the task of modernizing it, their objectives remain the same. "The destruction of Religion, the destruction of society and the civil laws, the destruction of all property— that was the point at which he always aimed," wrote Barruel.[13]

Weishaupt said, "Yes, princes and nations shall disappear from off the face of the earth; yes, a time shall come when man shall acknowledge no other law but the great book of nature: This revolution shall be the work of the secret societies, and that is one of our grand mysteries."[14]

Proof of the Illuminati

Originally published in 1802, *Proof of the Illuminati* by Seth Payson is still in print and available today. It is one of the three primary books that were published at the time that the Illuminati was organized and started gaining power and influence, the others being the works of Robison and Barruel.

Payson was an American and served in the New

---

[12] Barruel, Abbe – *Memoirs Illustrating the History of Jacobinism* Volume III page 5
[13] Barruel, Abbe – *Memoirs Illustrating the History of Jacobinism* Volume III page 11
[14] Barruel, Abbe – *Memoirs Illustrating the History of Jacobinism* Volume III page 15

Hampshire state senate from 1802-1805. Part of his campaign platform was his alarming message found in his book. Payson draws from the writings of Abbe Barruel and John Robison, and quotes both them, as well as the original writings of the Illuminati that were discovered in 1786. While some writers who supported the Illuminati attempted to discredit the work of John Robison, Payson starts off his book with numerous letters from prominent European publications and other scholars who all praise Robison's character and his book, *Proofs of a Conspiracy.*

One endorsement Payson included in his book came from a man he said was one of the most respectable writers in Scotland who said, "Professor Robison's character is so well established among those who know him best, that it would be ridiculous, at Edinburgh, to call in question his veracity or ability. I had read many of his authorities in German originals before his book was published; and the first notice I received of it was in the preface to Dr. Erskine's sketches of ecclesiastical history, where you will see the honorable testimony that he gives Mr. Robison, and the great expectation that he had from his publication."[15]

Payson understood the sinister nature of the Illuminati and made it his mission to inform others. He wrote, talking about Adam Weishaupt, that, "His scheme appears to be calculated, not so much for uniting persons of similar sentiments in one society, as for seducing those of opposite inclinations, and by a most artful and detestable process, gradually obliterating from their minds every moral and religious sentiment. It is in this view principally that this plan of seduction calls for the attention of mankind, as it develops the secret, insidious policy by which the agendas of faction and infidelity lead on their disciples, still concealing their real designs, until the mind is involved in a maze of

---

[15] Payson, Seth — *Proof of the Illuminati* pages 18-19

error, or entangled in snares from which there is no retreat."[16]

Although there was no such thing as radio or television, Payson saw how the Illuminati controlled the flow of information that was available at the time, saying, "But the principle means, on which they depended for corrupting the public mind, were literary societies, or reading clubs; which they labored to set up in every town. These were modifications of Weishaupt's minerval schools; they became very numerous; and it was the business of the secretaries, and initiated booksellers, to have them furnished with books of the most Anti-Christian character."[17]

Payson also explained how members of the Illuminati are indoctrinated with corruption and taught that it is acceptable to use any means necessary to further their order. "He is placed in situations where he hears the more artful sophistry used to prove that patriotism and private affections are narrow-minded prejudices; that the bonds of marriage and parental authority are encroachments on the natural rights of man; that suicide is lawful; that sensual pleasures correspond with the law of nature, and that it is proper to employ, for a good purpose, those means which wicked men use for evil purposes."[18]

While these old books such as Seth Payson's, Abbe Barruel's, and John Robison's explain that the Illuminati existed and had sinister motives and detailed plans, they only show the tip of the iceberg since the Illuminati was only in its infancy. As the years went by, instead of the organization disbanding, they continued their charted course and grew stronger and more powerful than any of these writers would be able to imagine.

---

[16] Payson, Seth — *Proof of the Illuminati* page 64
[17] Payson, Seth — *Proof of the Illuminati* page 100
[18] Payson, Seth — *Proof of the Illuminati* page 114

Secret Societies and Subversive Movements

In 1924 a woman named Nesta Webster published a book titled *Secret Societies and Subversive Movements* that discussed the Illuminati and how secret societies throughout history have used their covert networks to organize revolutions and monopolize power in society. Webster begins her analysis by stating, "Let it be said once and for all, secret societies have not always been formed for evil purposes. On the contrary, many have arisen from the highest aspirations of the human mind—the desire for a knowledge of eternal verities. The evil arising from such systems has usually consisted in the perversion of principles that once were pure and holy."[19]

She goes on to acknowledge that secret societies have been used to pursue esoteric knowledge as well as being used for political purposes noting the French and Bolshevik revolutions. Regarding the esoteric and mystical aspirations of secret societies, Webster explains "For whilst religious leaders such as Buddha and Mohammed sought for divine knowledge in order that they might impart it to the world, the Initiates believed that sacred mysteries should not be revealed to the profane but should remain exclusively in their own keeping. So although the desire for initiation might spring from the highest aspiration, the gratification, whether real or imaginary, of this desire often led to spiritual arrogance and abominable tyranny."[20]

Regarding the Illuminati, Webster discusses whether Adam Weishaupt had created the organization on his own accord, or whether he was working on behalf of others, and looks for the source of his inspiration. Early writers and researchers link Adam Weishaupt with a Jutland merchant

---

[19] Webster, Nesta – *Secret Societies and Subversive Movements* page 3-4
[20] Webster, Nesta – *Secret Societies and Subversive Movements* page 4

named Kolmer who had studied occultism in Egypt and later came to Germany. It is believed by some that Kolmer met Weishaupt and initiated him into the secret doctrine. Other researchers believe Weishaupt was commissioned by the Rothschild family to organize and modernize the goals of the Mystery schools.

Webster wrote, "It would therefore appear possible that Weishaupt, although undoubtedly a man of immense organizing capacity and endowed with extraordinary subtlety, was not in reality the sole author if Illuminism, but one of a group, which recognizing his talents and the value of his untiring activity, placed the direction in his hands."[21]

Webster also lists the original writings of the Illuminati for anyone questioning the authenticity of the quotes from Adam Weishaupt or other original Illuminati members. Those sources are:

1. Einige Originalschriften des Illuminatenordens (Munich 1787)
2. Nachtrag von weitern Originalschriften, etc. (Munich, 1787).
3. Die neuesten Arbeiten des Spartacus und Philo in dem Illuminaten-Orden (Munich, 1794).

She goes on to say, "All these consist in the correspondence and papers of the Order which were seized by the Bavarian Government at the houses of the members, Zwack and Bassus, and published by the order of the Elector. The authenticity of these documents has never been denied even by the Illuminati themselves; Weishaupt, in his published defense, endeavored only to explain away the most incriminating passages. The publishers, moreover, were careful to state at the beginning of the first volume: "those

---

[21] Webster, Nesta – *Secret Societies and Subversive Movements* page 203

who might have any doubts on the authenticity of this collection may present themselves at the Secret Archives here, where, on request, the original documents will be laid before them."[22]

Some have labeled Nesta Webster anti-Semitic for her writings about Judaism, the Talmud and the Cabala. This is indeed a sensitive subject and often simply addressing the Jewish component of the Illuminati is opposed with claims of anti-Semitism. Webster wrote, "It must not, however, be forgotten that to the Jewish mind the human race presents a dual aspect, being divided into two distinct categories—the privileged race to whom the promises of God were made, and the great mass of humanity which remains outside the pale."[23]

As was the case with Christianity during the Inquisition, and Islam in the 21st century, Judaism contains a radical faction of self-appointed leaders who use their theology to justify their beliefs and actions and place themselves and their religion above others and believe they are divinely ordained by God to carry out certain acts or to hold privileged positions in society. Jesus denounced such Jewish views, saying that God's love and promises were for everyone, but many Jews still hold such privileged views. Webster wrote, "the conception of the Jews as the Chosen People who must eventually rule the world forms indeed the basis of Rabbinical Judaism...it is in the Cabala, still more than in the Talmud, that the Judaic dream of world-domination recurs with the greatest persistence."[24]

Webster knew the dangers of making such statements, saying, "For it will be noticed that anyone who attempts to

---

[22] Webster, Nesta – *Secret Societies and Subversive Movements* page 208-209
[23] Webster, Nesta – *Secret Societies and Subversive Movements* page 229
[24] Webster, Nesta – *Secret Societies and Subversive Movements* page 370-371

expose the secret forces behind the revolutionary movement, whether he mentions Jews in this connexion [sic] or even if he goes out of his way to exonerate them, will incur the hostility of the Jews and their friends and will still be described as "anti-Semite." The realization of this fact has led me particularly to include the Jews in the study of secret societies."[25]

Occult Theocrasy

In 1933 a two volume set titled *Occult Theocrasy* was published in one book which consists of over 700 pages of information about secret societies, their histories, and their plans for world domination. The book was written by a woman named Edith Starr Miller, and published shortly after she died. Many people think the title is spelled *Occult Theocracy*, but it is actually spelled *Theocrasy*, with an "s" which has a different meaning. Theocrasy means the merging of several deities or gods into one, and a definition is provided in the beginning pages of the book. A theocracy means a government ran by priests who claim some kind of divine right to rule. It's likely Miller meant to have both meanings applied as a play on words, since the Illuminati is a religious group which believes that they hold the divine right to rule the earth.

It's incredible how much information is compiled in Edith Miller's book, although *Occult Theocrasy* is not mentioned that often when discussing the history of the Illuminati. While the impact of *Occult Theocrasy* wasn't as powerful as John Robison's work or Abbe Burruel's, it is still an important piece of history regarding the evolution of the information exposing the Illuminati, and is included in this book for that reason. *Occult Theocrasy* also contains chapters on Mormonism, the Jesuits, the Assassins, and a long list of occult societies and philosophies.

Throughout *Occult Theocrasy*, Edith Miller demonstrates a thorough understanding of even the most esoteric occult philosophies. She explains, "Luciferians never call their infernal master "Spirit of Evil" or "Father and Creator of Crime." Albert Pike even forbade the use of the word *Satan* under any circumstances...Luciferians or the initiates of kindred rites, while still labouring under a strange delusion, act deliberately and glorify Lucifer as the principle of good. To them he is the equal of the God of the Christians whom they describe as the principle of evil."[26]

Miller goes on to discuss Freemasonry and that at their core is a doctrine of Luciferianism. She explains that the letter G represents geometry to the outer level Masons, but Gnosticism to the inner circle. Miller also knew that the founding members of the Knights Templar had learned strange and mystical teachings from the Muslim Assassins. She wrote, "Having embraced Gnosticism while in Palestine, and in touch with the sect of the Assassins, the Templar order degenerated, and some of its members, under the influence of that sect, were said to practice Phallicism or sex-worship and Satanism and to venerate "The Baphomet," the idol of the Luciferians. The crime of Sodomy was a rite of Templar initiation."[27]

Edith Miller displays an impressive amount of knowledge about the histories and interconnections of occult societies that would later evolve into the Illuminati. She explains, "As the organization of the Illuminati developed, so did its ambitions, which ended in a plot to subvert Freemasonry to its aim of world dominion by any and all means...religiously, it was anti-Christian. Its members were

---

[26] Miller, Judth – *Occult Theocrasy* page 31-32
[27] Miller, Judth – *Occult Theocrasy* page 144

pledged to blind obedience to their superiors and this was insured by a strict system of secret confessions, and monthly reports checked by mutual espionage. Each individual used a pseudonym instead of his own name to help disguise his identity."[28]

On page 185 she explains the top priorities of the Illuminati as:

1. The destruction of Christianity and of all Monarchical Governments.

2. The destruction of nations as such in favour of universal internationalism.

3. The discouragement of patriotic and loyal effort branded as narrow minded prejudice, incompatible with the tenets of goodwill to all men and the cry of "Universal Brotherhood."

4. The abolition of family ties and of marriage by means of systematic corruption.

5. The suppression of the rights of inheritance and property.

Miller also retells a story that is difficult to verify, but continues to be told regarding how a collection of Illuminati writings were allegedly discovered. The story goes that on July 10th 1785 a man named Jacob Lang was struck by lightening and killed (some say while riding his horse, others say while walking with Adam Weishaupt) and when his remains were examined, a set of documents were discovered sewn into his clothes and were handed over to the Bavarian government. It is not clear whether this actually happened, and citing this story as a reference for how the Illuminati papers were discovered should be avoided. History has

---

[28] Miller, Judth – *Occult Theocrasy* page 372

documented clear and verifiable references for how and where the original writings of the Illuminati were discovered, therefore the tale of the lightening striking and killing one of their members should not be used as evidence of the Illuminati's discovery. Never the less, this is one story that has become part of the Illuminati legend, and the reader should be aware of the uncertainty about its authenticity.

Edith Miller has been labeled a "fascist supporter" because of her marriage to Almeric Hugh Pagent, 1st Baron Queenborough in 1921 and was said to be friendly with Brigadier General Robert Byron Drury Blakeney, who was the second president of the British Fascisti and was active in various fascist organizations such as the British Fascisti and the Imperial Fascist Club. She would later divorce Almeric claiming he was abusive. Regardless of her supposed connections to questionable political groups, Edith Miller's book, *Occult Theocrasy* must be included in the list of literature detailing the Illuminati and their occult philosophies as we trace the timeline of such material from its beginning up to today.

None Dare Call It Conspiracy

In 1972 a man named Gary Allen released a thin but powerful book titled *None Dare Call It Conspiracy*. A lot of time had passed since the works of John Robison and others, and the Illuminati had been hard at work the entire time. They had not only been able to continue their planned course of action, but over the last nearly two hundred years, they had made incredible progress and achieved a large portion of their goals.

The forward to Allen's book was written by a United States Congressman named John G. Schmitz, and the first printing in 1972 consisted of 350,000 copies which sold out, and was soon followed with 1,250,000 which also sold out, and was finally followed by another 4,000,000 in April of 1972.[29] That's more than five and half million copies in a year. Astonishing numbers. People back in the 1970s were obviously more informed and concerned about the political affairs of the country than they are today. Most books on the subject today would be lucky to sell 10,000 copies, with most of the public more interested in Harry Potter than the Illuminati. Members of the John Birch society were largely responsible for promoting and handing out copies of *None Dare Call It Conspiracy*.

Garry Allen doesn't use the term "the Illuminati" but rather *"the Insiders"* to describe the organizations and strategies he exposes. He was obviously aware of the Illuminati and while mentioning them in the book, he chose to label the conspirators the *Insiders* since it accurately describes the group without attaching a formal name to their network. Allen shows a tremendous amount of knowledge regarding the political climate and mechanisms of the day. He primarily focuses on how the elite banking cartels and families secretly finance Communism and specialize in getting governments in debt to them.

He writes, "It should be noted that the originator of this type of secret society was Adam Weishaupt, the monster who founded the Order of Illuminati on May 1, 1776, for the purpose of conspiracy to control the world. The role of Weishaupt's Illuminists in such horrors as the Reign of Terror is unquestioned, and the techniques of the Illuminati have long been recognized as models for Communist methodology. Weishaupt also used the structure of the Society of Jesus (the Jesuits) as his model, and rewrote his code in Masonic terms."[30]

Aside from exposing wealthy business titans and private

---

[29] These numbers were taken from the copyright page inside the book.
[30] Allen, Gary – *None Dare Call It Conspiracy* page 80

organizations like the Federal Reserve, he also knew the dangers of blaming the entire conspiracy on one group and warned that some people, "will take small fragments of legitimate evidence and expand them into a conclusion that will support their particular prejudice, ie., the conspiracy is totally "Jewish," "Catholic," or "Masonic." These people do not help to expose the conspiracy, but sadly play into the hands of those who want the public to believe that all conspiratorialists are screwballs."[31]

Allen demonstrated an understanding of the power of the media by explaining, "Because the Establishment controls the media, anyone exposing the *Insiders* will be the recipient of a continuous fusillade of invective from newspapers, magazines, TV and radio. In this manner one is threatened with loss of "social respectability" if he dares broach the idea that there is organization behind any of the problems currently wracking America."[32]

He also knew why so few people even cared about what was happening to the country and how the *Insiders* could get away with such things. "They believe that most business and professional men are too shallow and decadent, too status conscious, too tied up in the problems of their jobs and business to worry about what is going on in politics."[33]

Allen also lays out the case that similar groups have existed in the past, and that it is foolish to think such things don't continue to operate. "...there have been Hitlers and Lenins and Stalins and Caesars and Alexander the Greats throughout history. Why should we assume there are no such men today with perverted lusts for power?"[34]

Allen continues to detail how international bankers

---

[31] Allen, Gary – *None Dare Call It Conspiracy* page 10-11
[32] Allen, Gary – *None Dare Call It Conspiracy* page 15
[33] Allen, Gary – *None Dare Call It Conspiracy* page 16
[34] Allen, Gary – *None Dare Call It Conspiracy* page 18

financed Hitler as well as Communism from New York and London, and how the Council on Foreign Relations and the Federal Reserve have secretly maneuvered themselves into having a stranglehold over the government and economy. Allen even discussed the Bilderberg group and knew the organization was formed in 1954 and meets each year at elite resorts to discuss plans for the New World Order.

In recent years more and more people are starting to learn and care about the New World Order, and it is interesting to read Gary Allen's warnings from the early 1970s and to see how his analysis and warnings have unfortunately been accurate.

Bloodlines of the Illuminati

Bloodlines of the Illuminati is an over 600 page book first published in 1999 by Fritz Springmeier. The book is an exhausting analysis of the history of 13 families believed to be involved with the Illuminati. Those 13 bloodlines are: Astor, Bundy, Collins, Dupont, Freeman, Kennedy, Li, Onassis, Rockefeller, Rothschild, Russell, Van Duyn, and the Merovingian bloodline. A revised edition was released in 2002, but *Bloodlines of the Illuminati* is currently out of print. Used copies may still available from online booksellers.

In the introduction the author explains, "The goal of this book is to lay out the historical facts about these elite bloodlines; it is the reader's responsibility and prerogative to decide what he or she wants to do with this fascinating information. There is no doubt that this information has far reaching implications. For instance, once one understands these bloodlines, wars between kings no longer appear as wars between elite factions, but often can be recognized as contrived wars created to control the masses of both sides by their greedy Machiavellian masters."[35]

"The Illuminati themselves decided to elevate 13 bloodlines. The number 13 is extremely important magically, and these 13 occult tribes mock the 13 tribes of Israel (remember the 13th tribe, the Tribe of Joseph was split into Ephraim & Manasseh). This does not mean that only 13 Illuminati bloodlines are powerful. There are other families that have risen to prominence. Further, worldwide there are other families of great oligarchial power who have allied themselves to the Illuminati in the political and economic realms without having to intermarry into the Illuminati."[36]

Springmeier was a frequent speaker on the subject, and one of his most well known lectures is a two and a half hour talk titled *The Top 13 Illuminati Bloodlines* which was given at Prophecy Club ministries and can be viewed on Google Video and other online video sites. While much of the author's claims are sourced, some viewers are disturbed by what is considered to be a far fetched and unsubstantiated claim that the Illuminati had built and maintains a space station on Mars. While nothing in his book is mentioned about this, he does mention it in the video lecture. Many feel this single statement casts a shadow of doubt on Springmeier's body of work. Others are able to overlook this statement, and focus on the documentable and verifiable information that is compiled in Springmeier's book.

Another blow to Springmeier would come in March of 2001 when he was arrested for allegedly growing marijuana and then implicated in a bank robbery.[37] Information regarding this incident is conflicting, and what actually happened and why remains the topic of debate. A newspaper

---

[35] Springmeier, Fritz – *Bloodlines of the Illuminati* page 1
[36] Springmeier, Fritz – *Bloodlines of the Illuminati* page 1
[37] The Oregonian *Deputies, Feds arrest Corbett Couple* by Stuart Tomlinson March 2, 2001

in Oregon, *The Oregonian*, reported that on February 9th 2001, agents raided his home and seized what they called military-style weapons and allegedly fifty marijuana plants. The police would later admit that the weapons were not illegal guns. The article stated that authorities also allegedly seized a small amount of ammonium nitrate and fuel oil which they said could be made into an explosive. There is some confusion about this article, and it is believed that *The Oregonian* got their facts wrong, and that the marijuana was found at the residence of Tony Huntington, who would later claim that Fritz was involved with a bank robbery Huntington and his house mate, Forrest E. Bateman Jr. had allegedly committed.

In 2003 Springmeier was sentenced to nine years in prison for his alleged involvement in an armed robbery of a bank that had occurred in Portland, Oregon years earlier in 1997. Prosecutors claimed that he and an accomplice, Forrest E. Bateman Jr. detonated a homemade pipe bomb at an adult video store on the other side of town as a diversion, and then robbed the Damascus branch of the Key Bank of Oregon. His participation is disputed and both he and his wife maintain his innocence.

They say what happened is that Huntington and Bateman had actually committed the robbery, and had been acquainted with Fritz because they lived in the same area and had read his book, *Bloodlines of the Illuminati* sometime earlier and had sought Fritz out to talk about such issues. Allegedly unknown to Fritz, Huntington and Bateman were facing a lengthy prison sentence for committing the robbery in question, and had struck a deal with prosecutors that if they were to tell them of any other crimes they knew of or were connected with, that they would reduce their sentence. Since these men knew that Fritz had written extensively about the Illuminati, they figured he would be an easy target for prosecutors so they claimed that Fritz was involved with the robbery. Prosecutors then painted Fritz as a right wing anti-government nut because of his writings and lectures.

Fritz had done radio interviews shortly before his sentencing and still maintained he was wrongfully implicated by Huntington and Bateman. After being sentenced, Fritz told the judge and the courtroom, "I'm innocent. I'm looking forward to discovering the divine benefits of the sentence that you give me. If the Government is trying to ruin my life, they will have to try harder." Months later his wife Patricia spoke with radio host Alex Jones, and maintained that Fritz was used as a scapegoat for the actual perpetrator to get a reduced sentence and that no marijuana was found on Springmeier's property.[38]

The Lexicon of Freemasonry

The Lexicon of Freemasonry was first published in 1845 by Albert G. Mackey, a 33rd degree Freemason and one of the twentieth centuries most prominent scholars on the subject of Freemasonry. The book contains an alphabetized list of most Masonic terms and definitions. It is over five hundred pages thick and is one of the most respected reference guides on the fraternity.

While it is fully admitted that Adam Weishaupt infiltrated Freemasonry in 1786 and created a secret society within the secret society where his Illuminists could then use the cover and structure of Freemasonry for Illuminati goals, Freemasons have denied that any current association between the two exists, and insist Weishaupt and his "Illuminated masons" were eradicated upon their exposure several hundred years ago.

Albert Mackey's entry on the Illuminati is extremely interesting, in that it shows Adam Weishaupt was not just a freethinker who was looking to better mankind through his

---

[38] The Alex Jones Show (11-10-2004)

organization, as some scholars continue to claim to this day, but that he was in fact a man with severe moral shortcomings.

On page 201 and 202, Mackey's entry reads: "Illuminati. Illumines (Signifying in Latin enlightened.) This was a secret society instituted in Bavaria, in 1776, by Adam Weishaupt, Professor of Canon Law in the University of Ingolstadt. Weishaupt was a radical in politics, and an infidel in religion; and he organized this association, not more for purposes of aggrandizing himself, than overturning Christianity and the institutions of society. With the view of carrying his objects more completely into effect, he united himself with a lodge of Freemasons in Munich, and attempted to graft his system of Illuminism upon the stock of Freemasonry."

"Many Freemasons, misled by the construction of his first degrees, were enticed into the order, but the developments made in the higher degrees, so averse from all the virtuous and loyal principles of Masonry, soon taught them the error they had committed, and caused them to abandon Illuminism with greater rapidity than that which they had embraced it."

"Among those who had abandoned the order, some went so far as to betray its secret principles. The elector of Bavaria becoming alarmed at the political tenets which were said to be taught in their assemblies, instituted a judicial examination into the merits of the charges made against them, and the consequence was, that the Illuminati were completely extinguished in his territories."

"The serpent had, however, only been scotched, not killed; and the order afterwards made rapid progress in other parts of Germany, and especially in France, where it had been introduced in 1787, two years before the execution of Louis XVI. It was an institution created at the period, when the locust plague of infidelity and atheism was blighting, with its destructive influences, the peace and order of

Europe; with the return of sense and virtue, it ceased to exist. Illuminism belongs only to the history of the past."

What is even more interesting is a footnote in the entry in which Mackey praises the writings of John Robison and his work on the Illuminati, saying, "See Robison's *Proofs of a Conspiracy*, which, although the work of an enemy to our order, contains a very excellent exposition on the nature of this pseudo-Masonic institution."

The reason Mackey labels Robison an enemy of their order is because aside from exposing Weishaupt and his associates, he included an attack on Freemasonry in general, and believed that the organization even without Illuminated masons, was in fact a dangerous den which bred corruption and anti-Christian sentiment.

Morals and Dogma

Often considered to be the bible of Freemasonry, *Morals and Dogma* was written by a 33rd degree Freemason named Albert Pike and published in 1872. The book contains the thirty-three different levels of philosophical teachings that are found within the Scottish Rite branch of Freemasonry today. For many years the contents of the book was a closely guarded secret and was only given to a Mason after he had achieved the highest level of membership, the 33rd degree. The copy of *Morals and Dogma* that these men were given had printed on the cover that it was to be returned to the lodge upon the death of the Mason, in order to prevent the text from circulating and having its teachings discovered by non Masons, or those who had not risen to the 33rd degree.

The book is an exhausting read, but several passages give a revealing look into the philosophies of the most closely guarded secrets in Freemasonry. In the chapter dedicated to the 28th degree, titled *Knight of the Sun or Prince Adept*, Pike wrote, "The True Word of a Mason is to be found in the concealed and profound meaning of the Ineffable Name of Deity...and which meaning was long lost by the very precautions taken to conceal it. The true pronunciation of that name was in truth a secret, in which, however, was involved the far more profound secret of its meaning. In that meaning is included all the truth that can be known by us, in regard to the nature of God."[39]

What he is saying is that the Masons know the true name of God, and by knowing that name, it gives them access to unimaginable spiritual powers when one understands what he calls "the profound secret of its meaning."

Within the book Albert Pike also reveals that lying is morally acceptable and necessary in Freemasonry, saying "Masonry, like all the Religions, all the Mysteries, Hermeticism and Alchemy, *conceals* [emphasis in original] its secrets from all except the Adepts and Sages, or the Elect, and uses false explanations and misinterpretations of its symbols to mislead those who deserve only to be mislead; to conceal the Truth, which it [the Mason] calls Light, from them, and to draw them away from it."[40]

He goes on to write in the 19th degree of *Grand Pontiff*, "Lucifer, the Light-bearer! Strange and mysterious name to give to the Spirit of Darkness! Lucifer, the Son of the Morning! Is it he who bears the Light, and with its splendors intolerable, blinds feeble, sensual, or selfish souls? Doubt it not!"[41]

Earlier in the book, Pike has this to say about the subject, "...for Satan is not a black god, but the negation of God. The Devil is the personification of Atheism or Idolatry. For the Initiates, this is not a Person, but a Force,

[39] Pike, Albert – *Morals and Dogma* p. 697
[40] Pike, Albert – *Morals and Dogma* p. 104-105
[41] Pike, Albert – *Morals and Dogma* p. 321

created for good, but which may serve for evil. It is the instrument of Liberty of Free Will. They represent this Force, which presides over the physical generation, under the mythological and horned form of the God Pan; thence came the he-goat of the Sabbat, brother of the Ancient Serpent, and the Light-Bearer."[42]

Many defenders of Freemasonry insist that the organization is simply a men's fraternity and nothing more, but Pike explains, "Every Masonic Lodge is a temple of religion; and its teachings are instruction in religion."[43]

When one wonders why the discrepancies in what is told to the public versus what is actually practiced and believed, a better understanding can come from Pike himself who explains, "The people will always mock at things easy to be misunderstood; it must [and] needs [to] have imposters. A Spirit...that loves wisdom and contemplates the Truth close at hand, is forced to disguise it, to induce the multitudes to accept it...Fictions are necessary to the people and the Truth becomes deadly to those who are not strong enough to contemplate it in all its brilliance...In fact, what can there be in common between the vile multitude and sublime wisdom? The truth must be kept secret, and the masses need a teaching proportioned to their imperfect reason."[44]

The Secret Teachings of All Ages

There are some within the modern Mystery schools, such as the Freemasons, who feel that the knowledge and philosophical teachings contained within should be more widely available to the public. Manly P. Hall wrote about the symbolism, philosophies, and history of the Mysteries,

---

[42] Pike, Albert – *Morals and Dogma* p. 102
[43] Pike, Albert – *Morals and Dogma* p. 213
[44] Pike, Albert – *Morals and Dogma* page 103

not to "expose" them as part of some sinister plot against mankind, but to spread them to others seeking enlightenment teachings who were not directly connected with an organization.

Arguably the most popular of such books is *The Secret Teachings of All Ages* which was published by Manly P. Hall in 1928. The book is considered his magnum opus, and consists of 747 pages.

The Secret Teachings of All Ages contains a variety of chapters including explanations of the signs of the Zodiac, as well as esoteric explanations of countless mystical organizations, teachings, and ancient gods and goddesses. Manly P. Hall is considered to be one of Freemasonry's greatest philosophers and was a 33rd degree Mason.

While Hall doesn't disclose all of the teachings contained within the Mystery schools, he openly talks about quite a few, including a variety of topics and interpretations of symbols that frequently confirm the suspicions of so-called "conspiracy theorists."

One such confirmation comes regarding the mysterious pyramid with an eye as the capstone that is found on the back of the one dollar bill. While most Freemasons and others deny that the symbol is anything more than merely a symbol, Hall states, "European mysticism was not dead at the time the United States of America was founded. The hand of the Mysteries controlled in the establishment of the new government, for the signature of the Mysteries may still be seen on the Great Seal of the United States of America. Careful analysis of the seal discloses a mass of occult and Masonic symbols chief among them, the so-called American Eagle...only the student of symbolism can see through the subterfuge and realize that the American eagle upon the Great Seal is but a conventionalized phoenix..."[45]

---

[45] Hall, Manly P. – *The Secret Teachings of All Ages* p. 282

He continues, "Not only were many of the founders of the United States government Masons, but they received aid from a secret and august body existing in Europe which helped them to establish this country for a peculiar and particular purpose known only to the initiated few. The Great Seal is the signature of this exalted body—unseen and for the most part unknown—and the unfinished pyramid upon its reverse side is a teeterboard setting forth symbolically the task to the accomplishment of which the United States Government was dedicated from the day of its inception."[46]

From reading Hall's work, one doesn't get the impression that he harbors any ill motives, or sinister plans, but he does admit that in the ancient past philosophic and religious doctrines were divided into several levels, and that the teachings, symbols, and meanings given to the public do not contain the true essence of what they mean. This esoteric meaning is reserved for the inner circle or the elect. Hall is under the impression that the Mysteries are not evil and that the initiates and adepts were of high moral character, but that at some point in time, "With the decline of virtue, which has preceded the destruction of every nation of history, the Mysteries became perverted. Sorcery took the place of the divine magic."[47]

Many people remain suspicious of Hall, and point to a passage in another of his books where he states, "When the Mason learns that the Key to the warrior on the block is the proper application of the dynamo of living power, he has learned the Mystery of his Craft. The seething energies of Lucifer are in his hands and before he may step onward and upward, he must prove his ability to properly apply this

---

[46] Hall, Manly P. – *The Secret Teachings of All Ages* p. 283
[47] Hall, Manly P. – *The Secret Teachings of All Ages* page 40

energy."[48]

Let me make it clear that many, if not most men involved in esoteric schools such as the Freemasons, Rosicrucians, or other fraternal orders, harbor no ill motives, are not part of any evil conspiracy, and are just seeking to understand and expand their spiritual knowledge in their quest for enlightenment. With that said, it certainly is interesting how Manly P. Hall and others confirm many of the accusations by "conspiracy theorists" regarding secret symbols and history. The fact that Hall and others have introduced a large portion of the "secret teachings" to a wider audience doesn't reduce the possibility that within these schools of enlightenment operates a network of criminal enterprises who use their superior intelligence and wisdom, not for the betterment of mankind and self-actualization, but to ruthlessly take advantage of those less informed or in a lower socioeconomic level.

Let's remember that Hall himself states that the Mystery schools became perverted, and in all likelihood, this corrupt core continues to exist today and grew into what we now call the Illuminati.

Bohemian Grove: Cult of Conspiracy

In 2003 one of the first books on the Bohemian Grove was published by Mike Hanson after he and his friend Alex Jones secretly infiltrated the club in the summer of 2000 and were able to videotape the Cremation of Care ritual which was then released in Jones' film *Dark Secrets: Inside Bohemian Grove*. Hanson's book, *Bohemian Grove: Cult of Conspiracy* is, and probably will remain forever, the most extensive work on the club ever produced.

Since its publication in 2003, the topic of the Bohemian

---

[48] Hall, Manly P. – *The Lost Keys Of Freemasonry* page 124

Grove has found its way into other books on so-called "conspiracy theories" as secret societies such as the Freemasons and the Knights Templar were brought to mainstream awareness with the popularity of Dan Brown's *Da Vinci Code*, and the revelation during the 2004 presidential election year that George Bush and John Kerry are members of Skull and Bones. Practically every author to jump on the secret society bandwagon owes a debt of gratitude to Alex Jones and Mike Hanson.

Hanson's book is 420 pages long and contains interviews with Mary Moore of the Bohemian Grove Action Network, an organization that has monitored and infiltrated the club for decades, as well as interviews with Nebraska Senator John DeCamp and British journalist Jon Ronson. Hanson covers the history of the Grove, and details some of the political developments that were hatched from within the club. He also discusses the significance of the Cremation of Care ceremony, the annual human sacrifice ritual using an effigy which is symbolically sacrificed to Moloch, an ancient Canaanite god to whom children were sacrificed to. For over 100 years this same ritual has been reenacted inside the Grove using a life-size paper mache effigy. But this strange, seemingly harmless ritual is only the beginning of the dark activities that are believed to occur inside.

It has been known for decades that prostitution plays a fairly large role in the parties inside the Bohemian Grove. For years it had been rumored that the Mitchell Brothers O'Farrell Theatre in the Tenderloin red-light district of San Francisco was a primary source of strippers and high-class call girls for the club. Several prostitutes have gone public with claims they worked in the Grove, and these allegations come with no surprise to those familiar with it.

Mike Hanson interviewed four Mitchell Brothers dancers for his book, and they all confirmed that prostitution was the accepted "unofficial" policy at Bohemian Grove, and that the girls were expected to "perform" sexually for the men in attendance. One such interview by Hanson uncovered more startling allegations about the club.

Hanson details an account of strippers who had claimed to work at the Grove writing, "When the girls went up to change for the show, they noticed a briefcase in the room that had apparently been left behind by one of the Grovers. Curiosity got the better of them, and they peeked inside. What they found shocked them. Inside was an owl mask, a long black robe with a gold hood, ritual gear, and a long butcher's knife that was very old and rusty."[49]

Hanson quotes one of the girls saying, "The knife looked like it had been used to kill before. It was old and very ornate in its design, with old stains on the blade. Whether it was rust or blood stains, I don't know."[50] One stripper admitted to steeling a laptop computer because the attendees wouldn't pay her for dancing after she refused to have sex with them. She told Hanson that after she got the computer home, she found pictures and videos on the hard drive of children being raped and tortured. Former Senator John DeCamp and other well respected officials have made identical allegations about the kinds of activities which occur inside. (See The Franklin Cover-Up page 120) (See Sex Magic page 305) (See Snuff Films page 301)

Common Sense Renewed

In 1986 a little known book was published titled *Common Sense Renewed* that was written by a man using the pseudonym "Robert Christian," who admitted to being the man behind the mysterious Georgia Guidestones. The Guidestones are an enormous granite monument consisting of four stone slabs standing almost twenty feet tall which

---

[49] Hanson, Mike – *Bohemian Grove: Cult of Conspiracy* p. 194
[50] Ibid

have an inscription of ten different commandments engraved on the eight different sides of the stones in eight different languages. The commandments are bizarre, to say the least, and some are very unsettling. Number one is to maintain the world's population at 500 million people. Other commandments, or "guides" speak of creating a world court and a world language. The monument has been the topic of both mystery and controversy, as it sits on public property in the small town of Elberton, Georgia. The true identity of the man, "R.C. Christian" who represented the group who financed the project has remained unknown since the stones were erected in 1980.

The publication of *Common Sense Renewed* shed some light on the subject, but his real name, and that of the group he represented remains a mystery. The book explains, "Robert Christian" is the pseudonym of a private American citizen who is concerned about the growing evidence of a decline in the political and economic strengths of our country. It goes on to say that the first two printings of *Common Sense Renewed* were sent to several thousand political officials and shapers of public opinion throughout the world, and all members of the United States Congress.

Aside from admitting "Robert Christian" is the author of the Georgia Guidestones, he explains that he "has chosen to remain anonymous in order to avoid useless controversy and better focus attention on his thoughts rather than on himself."[51]

The book is dedicated to Thomas Paine (a Deist); author of *Common Sense*, hence the title. On page six, the author explains one of the purposes for the monument saying, "The hearts of our human family must be touched and warmed to welcome a global rule by reason."

---

[51] About the author section on inside cover of *Common Sense Renewed* (1986)

This mysterious man also alluded to the transhumanist combination of man and machine saying, "We suggest that scholars throughout the world begin now to establish new bases upon which later generations can develop a totally new universal language for men and machines. It will be adapted to our speech mechanism and to the language faculties and patterns impressed in our nervous systems. Its spoken and printed forms will be capable of accurate interchange by electromechanical means."[52]

It should be noted that when this man first approached the Elberton Granit Association with plans for the project, he identified himself as "R.C. Christian," which is a label used by members of the Rosicrucians, a secret society with connections to the Enlightenment and Illuminati. He also admitted that he had not come up with this project by himself, but that he merely represented the organization which did.

When one reads the "guides" engraved in the side of the monument and understands that the stones' creators desire the world's population to be reduced by six billion people, it can be unsettling. What's worse is the fact that reducing the world's population by 80 to 95% has been a goal of the Illuminati for quite some time. Ted Turner the founder of CNN, Prince Phillip from England, Dr. Eric Pianka, and other extremely powerful and influential men have openly stated that such a goal would be beneficial for the earth and its inhabitants.

The Guidestones were no small project to create. Its design, engraving, and installation was an extremely labor intensive venture with costs that must have exceeded tens of thousands of dollars or more. Their existence serves as a scary reminder that the Illuminati plan to one day eliminate the majority of the earth's population in order to conserve

---

[52] Christian, Robert – *Common Sense Renewed* p. 14-15

the planet's natural resources. Their rationale is that when the New World Order's infrastructure is complete, only a maintenance force of slaves will be needed, and the rest of humanity are simply useless eaters consuming the earth's resources that the Illuminati want to keep for themselves.

Tragedy and Hope

In 1966 an establishment insider published a book which openly admitted that elite secret societies, networks, and organizations did in fact exist and were being used as an engine for creating a world government and financial system. Carroll Quigley wrote *Tragedy and Hope*, not as an exposé of these activities, but as a way to teach others who would be inclined to participating in such things. After all, most of the public is distracted with videogames, television, and other novelties that are continuously presented to them which keep them busy and unconcerned with issues of any significance.

Quigley was no ordinary author. He studied history at Harvard and had a B.A., M.A., and PhD, and taught at Princeton and Harvard. He was also a consultant to the Department of Defense and the Navy.

In 1992 during his acceptance speech at the Democratic National Convention, Bill Clinton named Quigley as one of his most important influences in college. "As a teenager, I heard John Kennedy's summons to citizenship. And then, as a student at Georgetown, I heard that call clarified by a professor named Carroll Quigley," he said.

Tragedy and Hope contains over 1300 pages of what many may see as dry history, but within this volume are found multiple stunning admissions. Quigley wrote, "There does exist, and has existed for a generation, an international Anglophile network which operates, to some extent, in the way the radical Right believes the Communists act. In fact, this network, which we may identify as the Round Table Groups, has no aversion to cooperating with the

Communists, or any other groups, and frequently does so. I know of the operations of this network because I have studied it for twenty years and was permitted for two years, in the early 1960's, to examine its papers and secret records. I have no aversion to it or to most of its aims and have, for much of my life, been close to it and to many of its instruments. I have objected, both in the past and recently, to a few of its policies (notably to its belief that England was an Atlantic rather than a European Power and must be allied, or even federated, with the United States and must remain isolated from Europe), but in general my chief difference of opinion is that it wishes to remain unknown, and I believe its role in history is significant enough to be known."[53]

"At the end of the war of 1914, it became clear that the organization of this system had to be greatly extended. . . . Lionel Curtis . . . established, in England and each dominion, a front organization to the existing local Round Table Group...This front organization, called the Royal Institute of International Affairs, had as its nucleus in each area the existing submerged Round Table Group...in New York it was known as the Council on Foreign Relations, and was a front for J. P. Morgan and Company in association with the very small American Round Table Group. The American organizers were dominated by the large number of Morgan 'experts'... The Round Table for years (until 1961) was edited from the back door of Chatham House grounds in Ormond Yard, and its telephone came through the Chatham House switchboard."[54]

Not only does Quigley admit that a secret society is operating behind the scenes and created the Council on Foreign Relations as a front, but he also explains that the two party system in American government works in concert to

---

[53] Quigley, Carroll – *Tragedy and Hope* 950
[54] Quigley, Carroll – *Tragedy and Hope* 951-952

fulfill the goals of this secret agenda.

"The chief problem of American political life for a long time has been how to make the two Congressional parties more national and international...(therefore the) argument that the two parties should represent opposed ideals and policies, one, perhaps, of the Right and the other of the Left, is a foolish idea acceptable only to doctrinaire and academic thinkers...Instead the two parties should be almost identical, so that the American people can 'throw the rascals out' at any election without leading to any profound or extensive shifts in policy."[55]

While people still scoff at the idea that the Federal Reserve a privately owned banking cartel which was created in secret and is being used to get governments and citizens in debt to them, Quigley openly admitted, "The powers of financial capitalism had (a) far-reaching aim, nothing less than to create a world system of financial control in private hands able to dominate the political system of each country and the economy of the world as a whole. This system was to be controlled in a feudalist fashion by the central banks of the world acting in concert, by secret agreements arrived at in frequent meetings and conferences. The apex of the systems was to be the Bank for International Settlements in Basel, Switzerland, a private bank owned and controlled by the world's central banks which were themselves private corporations. Each central bank...sought to dominate its government by its ability to control Treasury loans, to manipulate foreign exchanges, to influence the level of economic activity in the country, and to influence cooperative politicians by subsequent economic rewards in the business world."[56]

Most of the books written about the Illuminati or similar

---

[55] Quigley, Carroll – *Tragedy and Hope* pages 1247-1248
[56] Quigley, Carroll – *Tragedy and Hope* page 324

secret societies that are part of the same network, are written from the perspective of an outsider trying to show how these organizations operate, what their beliefs are, and how they affect the world. With very few books written by insiders and supporters of such groups, the words of Carroll Quigley should be taken quite seriously, and they clearly confirm what many outsiders have been claiming for decades.

The New World Order

In 1991, Pat Robertson published a book titled *The New World Order* which is surprisingly accurate in regards to the Illuminati's plans for a global government and the physical, financial, and spiritual enslavement of the human race. Now, of course, Pat Robertson didn't sit down at a computer and type the book up himself, he obviously had a ghostwriter do the work for him, which is common among celebrities and politicians who publish books. The most interesting thing about this book is that it mentions the Illuminati by name and gives a few details about their goals and accomplishments.

On page 67, the book reads, "On May 1, 1776 (May Day is still considered to be the key annual holiday for Communists), a Bavarian professor named Adam Weishaupt launched a small secret society called the Order of the Illuminati. Weishaupt's aims were to establish a New World Order based on the overthrow of civil governments, the church, and private property and the elevation to world leadership of a group of hand-picked "adepts" or "illumined" ones."

It goes on to say, "In 1782 Weishaupt succeed at the international convention of Freemasonry held in Wilhelmsbad, Germany with his planned infiltration of the Continental Masonic Order and the creation of what he termed Illuminated Freemasonry."

So whoever did the ghostwriting for this book included

some factual yet obscure information about the Illuminati. This is extremely rare, if not unheard of, for a mainstream Christian author, especially one as well known as Pat Robertson. Robertson should have at least read the manuscript before approving it for publication, so he likely saw the entry about such things. This is puzzling because some believe that Pat Robertson is actually involved with the Illuminati himself. Whatever the case, Robertson is one of the most well known Christian evangelicals, and his show *The 700 Club* has aired on national television since 1966.

There was nothing mentioned about the Skull and Bones society or the Bilderberg group in the book, and the author shows sympathy for then President George H.W. Bush and seems to think that Bush simply wasn't aware he was aiding in the construction of the New World Order. In reality, and omitted from Robertson's book, is the fact that the Bush crime family has been active with the Illuminati for generations.

Some of Pat Robertson's actions expose him as a charlatan who has profited tremendously from selling Christianity, including his bizarre conversations with God, where on his broadcasts God tells him of people watching with various ailments and then he proclaims "God is healing that right now." Also at the end of each year he announces his "prophecies" for the next twelve months which he claims God tells him will happen. In reality, these "prophecies" are nothing more than the forecasts of political and economic trend analyzers, which can be read in newspapers, and in no way reflect any sort of Divine revelation by Robertson.

Never the less, it is surprising that he is the "author" of a book which contains information about the Illuminati. Perhaps he didn't even read the manuscript that his ghostwriter prepared for him, or perhaps he allowed it to be included thinking it would increase his market. Whatever the case, it is significant that such information was published with Robertson's name attached as the author and the information about the historical Illuminati is surprisingly accurate, although *The New World Order* is extremely limited regarding the key Illuminati organizations and operations.

America's Secret Establishment

In the early 1980's, someone anonymously delivered an 8-inch thick package of documents containing information and membership lists for the Skull and Bones society to a college professor named Antony Sutton. Sutton reports that he didn't understand exactly what the information was and it sat for almost two years before he looked through it again, and then noticed it read like a who's who of the establishment. "Glancing through the sheets it was more than obvious— this was no ordinary group. The names spelled Power, with a capitol P. As I probed each individual a pattern emerged...and a formerly fuzzy world became crystal clear," Sutton wrote.[57]

"After 16 books and 25 years in basic research I thought I'd heard it all...the world was a confused mess, probably beyond understanding and certainly beyond salvation—and there was little I could do about it." Sutton admits that prior to his discovery about Skull and Bones, that the world's events didn't make sense and created what he called an insolvable puzzle. "Why did we build the Soviet Union, while we also transferred technology to Hitler's Germany? Why does Washington want to conceal these facts? Why have we boosted Soviet military power? And simultaneously boosted our own?" he pondered.[58]

His book, *America's Secret Establishment: An*

---

[57] Sutton, Antony – *America's Secret Establishment* Author's Preface page vii
[58] Ibid

Introduction to the Order of Skull and Bones was originally published in 1983 and was the first book on the subject to come into print. In the preface to the 2002 edition, the author writes that his book, "has received little publicity, few reviews,—ignored by mainline distributors yet, it has sold steadily for the past 16 years at the rate of several hundred copies a month."

Antony Sutton was a Research Fellow at the Hoover Institution, Stanford University from 1968 to 1973. He is a former economics professor at California State University Los Angeles. He was born in London in 1925 and educated at the universities of London, Gottingen and California with a D.Sc degree from University of Southampton, England. He passed away in 2002 at the age of 77.

Sutton was not a Christian fundamentalist or a conspiracy theorist like many try to label those who are interested in subjects such as Skull and Bones or the Illuminati. His book is an entirely secular and scholarly approach to the subject. It includes reprints from old articles and pamphlets including one titled *The Fall of Skull and Bones*, which is a document detailing an illegal break-in by a rival secret society called the Order of the File and Claw, whose members broke into the Skull and Bones headquarters in 1876 for the purpose of investigating the club.

Another article reprinted in the book is one from the October 13, 1873 issue of *The Iconoclast,* which was a student newspaper that ran a story detailing the operations and dangers of the Skull and Bones society.

Sutton writes, "The activities of The Order are directed towards changing our society, changing the world, to bring about a New World Order. This will be a planned order with heavily restricted individual freedom, without Constitutional protection, without national boundaries or cultural distinction."[59]

"The selection procedure for new members of The Order has not changed since 1832. Each year 15, never more, never fewer, are selected. In the past 150 years about 2500 Yale graduates have been initiated into The Order. At any one time about 500-600 are alive and active. Roughly about one-quarter of these take an active role in furthering the objectives of The Order. The others either lose interest or change their minds. They are silent drop-outs. A Yale Junior cannot ask to join. There is no electioneering. Juniors are invited to join and are given two options: accept or reject. Apparently some amount of personal information is gathered on potential members."[60]

"Entry into The Order is accompanied by an elaborate ritual and no doubt by psychological conditioning. For Example: Immediately on entering Bones the neophyte's name is changed. He is no longer known by his name as it appears in the college catalog but like a monk or Knight of Malta or St. John, becomes Knight so and so. The old Knights are then known as Patriarch so and so. The outside world are known as Gentiles and vandals."[61]

Through his research Sutton realized the extent of the Skull and Bones influence on society in their quest to build a New World Order. "The Order has either set up or penetrated just about every significant research, policy, opinion-making organization in the United States, in addition to the Church, business, law, government and politics. Not all at the same time, but persistently and consistently enough to dominate the direction of American society. The evolution of American society is not, and has not been for a century, a voluntary development reflecting individual

---

[59] Sutton, Antony – *America's Secret Establishment* page 31
[60] Sutton, Antony – *America's Secret Establishment* page 6
[61] Sutton, Antony – *America's Secret Establishment* page 7

opinion, ideas, and decisions at the grass roots. On the contrary, the broad direction has been created artificially and simulated by The Order."[62]

It is impossible not to see striking similarities between the goals of the Bavarian Illuminati and those of Skull and Bones. Skull and Bones was founded in 1832 by William Huntington Russell and Alphonso Taft. Russell had returned from a trip to Germany immediately preceding his creation of Skull and Bones. This was also a short period of time after Adam Weishaupt had created the Illuminati in Germany, and it is no stretch of the imagination to think that Russell was granted permission and given instructions on how to expand the Illuminati in America. Many admit that this was in fact the case. Another piece of evidence supporting this is that the members of the File and Claw society who broke into the Skull and Bones headquarters in 1876 reported that they saw a card placed in a frame and hung on a wall which read, "From the German Chapter. Presented by Patriarch D.C. Gilman of D. 50."

Fleshing Out Skull and Bones

Another of the most comprehensive books ever written on the Skull and Bones society is *Fleshing Out Skull and Bones: Investigations into America's Most Powerful Secret Society* which was edited by Kris Millegan. This 700 page book was published in 2004 and contains an array of photos, documents, and membership lists from this elite Illuminati branch.

Several authors including Webster Griffin Tarpley, Antony Sutton, Howard Altman, Dr. Ralph Bunch, and Anton Chaitkin have contributed to the book.

One of the documents printed in the book is a letter by

---

[62] Sutton, Antony – *America's Secret Establishment* page 25

Shirley Green, who was the acting press secretary to the Vice President in 1983 denying George Bush was a member of any "sordid secret society." Someone had sent a letter to the White House inquiring about Bush 41's membership in Skull and Bones, and Green had artfully dodged the issue by adding the word "sordid" in her denial. Both Bush 41 and his son George W. Bush have publicly admitted being members of the society and wouldn't comment any further.

Some of the historical pictures printed in the book include photos of the Tomb (the group's headquarters) and various Skull and Bones members sitting around a table which contains a real human skull. Such photos are taken each year with the new fifteen members.

Aside from simply being a history of the organization, *Fleshing Out Skull and Bones* contains various articles detailing the criminal activities of the network. Such activities include opium smuggling in the 1800s by the club's founders, as well as modern narcotics trafficking that is done by Skull and Bones, as in the case of Barry Seal and the infamous Mena, Arkansas cocaine operation in the 1980s. (See The Clinton Chronicles page 281)

There are countless fascinating articles in the book, including discussions about the number 322 which is often used by the club as a sort of calling card or identifier. One analysis of the group's signature symbol, the skull and cross bones, shows that the organization is thoroughly interested in esoteric mysticism and the secret teachings of the ancient Mystery schools.

An article on page 413 explains, "The skull represented the Temple of Wisdom, which was later Christianized for concealment and referred to as the *upper room*. It is the room at the top of the 33 vertebra of the spine which represented the path to the upper room; the equivalent of the journey through life or the road to enlightenment. ... The crossed bones represents the two pillars, which stand at the threshold to the pathway to the Temple of Wisdom. One bone represents Knowledge the other represents Understanding. This Temple of Wisdom is believed by the occultists to be the structure within which the human consciousness resides. When the neophyte becomes the *dweller at the Threshold,* he symbolically stands at the intersection of the crossed bones. If he chooses to pass through the threshold, he no longer resides only in the outer, material world; but he has become a dweller in a land of new consciousness to grow in self-awareness through Knowledge and Understanding. The neophyte symbolically dies or falls asleep to the outer world as the consciousness turns from outward concerns to inner concerns, knowing when he arrives at the Temple of Wisdom he will awaken or become resurrected to a new world order."[63]

Secrets of the Tomb

In 2002, *Secrets of the Tomb: Skull and Bones, the Ivy League, and the Hidden Paths to Power* was published by a Yale graduate and member of a similar but less powerful secret society, Scroll and Key, Alexandra Robbins. She was a former writer for *The New Yorker* and interviewed around one hundred Skull and Bones members for her book. She acknowledges that most of the people she approached declined to be interviewed, or even threatened her for investigating the organization.

Several years later during the build up to the 2004 presidential election, both the book, and Skull and Bones started getting news coverage by the mainstream media because both opposing candidates George W. Bush and John Kerry are members of the society. Most cable news shows had a brief segment about the issue and *60 Minutes* on CBS aired a short interview with Alexandra Robbins, but labeled

---

[63] Millegan, Kris – *Fleshing out Skull and Bones* page 413

the society a fraternity, and used past tense terminology falsely explaining that Bush and Kerry *were* members, while failing to identify that members aren't recruited until spring of their junior year and that the organization is geared towards the post graduate network that these individuals will enjoy.

Robbins' book is a short read of just over 200 pages, but doesn't compare to the depth and quality of the information found in *America's Secret Establishment* or *Fleshing Out Skull and Bones*, which will remain the authoritative works on the organization, its membership, philosophies, and goals.

Out of the one hundred members that granted Robbins an interview, it is safe to say that all of them were on the outer levels, or not even actively involved with the organization. Sutton and Millegan have identified that only one quarter of the members take an active interest in the goals and workings of the organization and form the inner circle which contains secrets and practices that less committed members are oblivious to.

One of the most interesting aspects of Robbins' book are the names of Skull and Bones members that George W. Bush placed into positions of power after he became president.

Alexandra Robbins explains, "Also like his father, George W. Bush has used his presidential power to reward his fellow Bonesmen. One of the first social gatherings (possibly the first gathering) George W. held at the White House after his inauguration was a reunion of his Skull and Bones clubmates...In February of 2003, the Senate approved Bush's nomination of William H. Donaldson (Bones 1953) as chairman of the Securities and Exchange Commission. In November 2001, Bush appointed Edward McNally (Bones 1979) general counsel of the new federal Office of Homeland Security and a senior associate council to the president for national security."

"Frederick W. Smith (Bones 1966) was reportedly George W.'s top choice for secretary of defense until he withdrew from the running because of a heart problem. One of President Bush's first appointments was 1968 Bones clubmate Robert D. McCallum, Jr., to the $125,700-per-year position of assistant attorney general, civil division, the largest litigation component in the Justice Department."[64]

"Bush also nominated 1968 clubmate Roy Austin as ambassador to Trinidad and Tobago. His administration appointed Evan G. Galbraith (Bones 1950) as the secretary of defense's representative in Europe and as the defense adviser to the U.S. mission to NATO. In addition, Bush announced the appointment of Victor Ashe—who in April 2001 was one of four mayors to attend a private meeting with Bush in the Oval Office before Bush spoke to a group of thirty-five mayors—to the board of directors of the Federal National Mortgage Association (Fannie Mae), the country's largest source of financing for home mortgages."[65]

While Bush appointed so many of his fellow Skull and Bones members to such high positions, the mainstream media didn't take notice. Every mainstream media outlet that bothered to mention that both Bush and Kerry are members of the organization, played it off like it was only a college fraternity for rich kids and nothing more.

September 11th 2001 Terrorist Attacks

The most credible and well known books written exposing the lies surrounding the September 11th attacks don't mention the Illuminati or anything about secret societies. Its hard enough to understand that elements within the U.S. government would purposefully allow the country to be attacked, but after looking at the patterns of history and the evidence is pieced together, this is the only conclusion

---

[64] Robbins, Alexandra – *Secrets of the Tomb* p.181
[65] Robbins, Alexandra – *Secrets of the Tomb* p. 182

that makes any sense. Understanding the reality of the 9/11 attacks and the mechanisms involved in the event is one thing, but understanding the Illuminati's existence and involvement is on a whole other level, which is the reason many authors who have written about 9/11 keep their discussion focused on specific government agencies, procedures, and events involved in the attacks.

David Ray Griffin has become the most prominent author of books which support the idea that the attacks were an inside job, and that elements of the U.S. government aided in the attacks and blocked investigations to ensure that they happened. His books *The New Pearl Harbor* and the *9/11 Commission Report: Omissions and Distortions* are two of his most popular works.

Another author whose book is just as powerful, if not more so, is that of Paul Thompson. His 590 page book *The Terror Timeline* details only mainstream news reports about inconsistencies and lies found in the version of events that has been parroted by the government and the 9/11 Commission which investigated the attacks.

Unlike Griffin and others, Thompson doesn't ever take the stance that the attacks were an inside job or that elements within intelligence agencies knew they were coming and aided in their execution. Rather, he just lays out all the clear and undeniable evidence complete with their sources and leaves it up to the reader to decide for themselves what actually happened. After looking over just a fraction of the evidence, the only reasonable conclusion one can come to is that, at a minimum, the attacks were purposefully allowed to happen as a pretext for the War on Terror, or that intelligence agencies aided in their execution. Thompson leaves himself out of that equation, something that has perhaps earned him a little more credibility within certain circles. The film *9/11 Press for Truth* which featured numerous widows including the "Jersey Girls" who were instrumental in getting the government to investigate the attacks, was largely based on Thompson's book and included interviews with him.

Over time a variety of credible people who had achieved prominent positions in various government offices, including CIA analyst Ray McGovern, former program director of Advanced Space Programs Development Lieutenant Colonel Bob Bowman, former German Minister of Technology Andreas von Buelow, as well as large numbers of firefighters, engineers, and architects came forward asking tough questions about the events of September 11th or concluded that the attacks were allowed to happen on purpose, or were aided by elements of the CIA and Mossad (Israel's intelligence agency) to advance a political agenda.

Some of the first individuals to come forward and make headlines was the former chief economist for the Department of Labor during George W. Bush's first term, Morgan Reynolds, professor James Fetzer, and former British Intelligence agent David Shayler. All of them gave credibility to the idea that the 9/11 attacks were an inside job, and they were frequently referenced by individuals when trying to inform their family and friends about the truth behind the events. These three men would later change the topic of their focus to bizarre and fanciful theories which caused them to be shunned by almost all other researchers and individuals in the 9/11 Truth Movement.

Morgan Reynolds appeared on Fox News on September 10th 2006, one day before the fifth anniversary of 9/11, and started saying that the planes were cartoons and didn't really exist, and that someone used computer graphics to insert them on television screens. James Fetzer would support Morgan in his new "research" and came up with his own new explanation of why the Twin Towers collapsed, which he proposed was the result of some kind of energy beam weapon. David Shayler, the former British Intelligence agent who was seen as one of the most credible in the 9/11 Truth Movement due to his credentials, later claimed that there were no planes that hit the World Trade Center, and that missiles were used in combination with three dimensional holograms which gave the appearance of jets. Soon after he began dispensing this theory, he also claimed to be the messiah.

While one might simply write them off as insane, another explanation is more fitting. The government frequently employs people to break up and discredit organizations it feels are a danger to its operations, and the most likely explanation is that these individuals were paid Illuminati operatives whose ridiculous claims are used to discredit the work of serious researchers. When the uninformed public is told about the lies, cover-ups, and inconsistencies in the government's account of 9/11 from a concerned friend or family member, they can easily dismiss them because they had already heard about these "crazy conspiracy theories" on the news thanks to such people as Reynolds and Shayler. This tactic is known as "poisoning the well" and works by mixing in a small amount of fraudulent information with the facts, and then exposing the false information hence trying to debunk the entire group of claims that are attached to them.

Despite attempts by the Illuminati to focus attention on the disinformation agents and their ridiculous claims, more and more credible and legitimate politicians, military personnel, and scientists have publicly questioned the official account of events from that morning, or outright stated it was a false flag attack and key officials in the U.S. knew exactly what was coming our way and wanted it to jump-start the War on Terror and later invade Iraq.

The Creature from Jekyll Island

A book that is considered by many to be the definitive exposé on the Federal Reserve banking system is *The Creature from Jekyll Island*, which was first published in

1994 by G. Edward Griffin and has since been reprinted at least seventeen times due to continuous demand.

In 1972 Griffin produced a film titled *The Capitalist Conspiracy*, which presented the case that international bankers had taken control of the banking system and maintain their power by loaning money to governments at interest, a practice which was secured by the passing of the Federal Reserve Act in 1913 which created the Federal Reserve Banking System that remains in place to this day.

When one understands the circumstances surrounding the Federal Reserve Act of 1913, one understands why the title of Griffin's book is called *The Creature from Jekyll Island.* He explains, "The basic plan for the Federal Reserve System was drafted at a secret meeting held in November of 1910 at the private resort of J.P. Morgan on Jekyll Island off the coast of Georgia."[66]

Griffin goes on to explain how the creation of the private Federal Reserve Bank would eventually be the undoing of the gold standard, which meant that every dollar in circulation represented one dollar worth of gold. Once the gold standard was removed in 1971, money became fiat money and since the dollar is no longer backed by gold, the Federal Reserve can print as much of it as they desire to loan out to governments or other banks, thus increasing the money supply and inflation, which makes each dollar in circulation worth less and drives the cost of goods up.

"Fiat money is paper money without precious-metal backing and which people are required by law to accept. It allows politicians to increase spending without raising taxes. Fiat money is the cause of inflation, and the amount which people lose in purchasing power is exactly the amount which was taken from them and transferred to their government by this process. Inflation therefore is a hidden tax. This tax is

---

[66] Griffin, G. Edward – *The Creature from Jekyll Island* p. 23

the most unfair of all because it falls most heavily on those who are least able to pay: the small wage earner and those on fixed incomes. It also punishes the thrifty by eroding the value of their savings."[67]

If one is to truly understand the Illuminati and the New World Order, the history of money and banking must be studied. When one looks at the current financial system of private banks creating money out of nothing and loaning it to the people, as well as governments at interest, one begins to understand why a two income household is still barely able to make ends meet. One also begins to understand why so much secrecy went into creating the Federal Reserve system to begin with. The secretive money manipulation by the ancient Knights Templars is still being used today, only as society has advanced, so have the methods of the money changers. (See Economic Control page 37)

The Satanic Bible

The Satanic Bible was written by Anton LaVey and published in 1969, and is still widely available today in the occult section of bookstores around the world. The book is really just a way to introduce teenagers to the occult, and doesn't compare in any way to more sophisticated and esoteric satanic philosophy. The ideas presented within LaVey's book are basically social Darwinsistic and encourage one to simply do whatever he wants and to not worry about social norms or moral codes of conduct.

It is bizarre that many supporters of *The Satanic Bible* claim to be Satanists while at the same time saying they are atheists. They say they use the symbol of Satan because it represents rebellion and a challenge to authority. Thus, many "Satanists" will say that Satanists don't worship Satan,

[67] Griffin, G. Edward – *The Creature from Jekyll Island* p. 164-165

and are simply atheists. To clarify this, a distinction should be drawn between a Satanist, and a "LaVeyan Satanist." LaVey's view of atheistic Satanism has created some confusion among those not familiar with the occult or the differences between atheistic Satanism and theistic Satanism. Like Luciferians, theistic Satanists believe in, and worship Satan as a supernatural being or a god, while atheistic Satanists simply adopt the name as a form of social protest.

So when a supposed "Satanist" calls themselves a Satanist, but says they don't worship Satan and are really an atheist, their limited understanding of satanism becomes clear. They often will not distinguish a LaVeyan Satanist from a plain Satanist (a theistic Satanist). Atheistic LaVeyan Satanists are also frequently unaware that Satanism in another form exists, and they think that all "Satanists" are atheists who have read Anton LaVey's book.

It is odd that LaVey and his followers deny that God exists and profess to be atheist while using the label of a Satanist, but what is even more perplexing is the fact that in his authorized biography, *The Secret Life of a Satanist*, he talks at length about placing curses on people and believed that he had supernatural powers. LaVey actually prayed to Satan on one occasion hoping that he would heal a wounded child of his friend Jane Mansfield.[68] Many consider this hypocritical contradiction of atheistic Satanists to be foolish, but somehow such incompatible beliefs haven't spurred LaVeyan Satanists to re-examine their "faith."

Several years before *The Satanic Bible* was published, LaVey created the Church of Satan in San Francisco which consisted of parties, lectures, and satanic rituals which were held in his home. LaVey remained High Priest of the organization until his death in 1997 at the age of 67. His

---

[68] Barton, Blanche – *The Secret Life of a Satanist: The Authorized Biography of Anton LaVey* page 98

second wife, Blanch Barton, later wrote his authorized biography. LaVey has two daughters, Zeena and Karla, both of who were involved with the Church of Satan, and practicing Satanists themselves. He also has a son named Xerxes, who was born in 1993. The current High Priest, Peter H. Gilmore describes the Church as follows:

"The organization is a cabal, a shadowy, underground network of like-minded individuals who work to lever against the inertia of the world, towards ends favorable to Satanism. Dr. LaVey[69] used Orwell's 1984 as a model for a cell-system in which each member didn't have awareness of exactly who else might be involved."[70]

The Church of Satan promotes claims that every individual can be their own god and doesn't need to worry about sin or breaking any of society's rules, because a Satanist lives by their own rules. Satan is used as a symbol and metaphor rather than the name of the actual god or fallen angel, following in line with the philosophies of *The Satanic Bible*.

LaVey was instrumental in modernizing Satanism and bringing it public in the 1960s. When *The Satanic Bible* was released in 1969, three years after the Church of Satan was founded, they had claimed a membership of more than 10,000.[71]

Unlike ordinary Churches, the Church of Satan does not have tax-exempt status, and unlike other satanic organizations such as the Skull and Bones society, or Illuminati hierarchies like the Freemasons, the Church of Satan is largely for social misfits who have no power or influence in society and who feel compelled to denounce

---

[69] The title "doctor," in this case, comes from a tradition of calling whorehouse piano players "Doc" and does not refer to an academic title.
[70] Baddeley, Gavin – *Lucifer Rising* p. 226
[71] Barton, Blanche – *The Authorized Biography of Anton LaVey* p. 92

morality and social standards and find satisfaction in calling themselves "Satanists," because of the rebellious connotations.

The Book of the Law

The infamous 20th century Satanist Aleister Crowley published a book in 1904 titled *The Book of the Law* which he claimed was dictated to him by a demon who temporarily possessed his wife when they were visiting Egypt. Crowley claims he didn't write the book, and that he simply wrote down what the demon had told him. This book is where the satanic saying 'Do what thou wilt' comes from, which means to do whatever you want, and don't worry about how your actions affect others, and that you are the only one that matters in this world.

The Book of the Law is used as the bible at the Ordo Templi Orientis (O.T.O.) (*Order of the Temple of the East*, or the *Order of Oriental Templars*), an international satanic secret society which continues to exist in the shadows of society today.

Some occult and satanic defenders claim that Anton LaVey or Aleister Crowley's writings don't encourage or condone violence towards others, and that they are just a path to enlightenment and personal fulfillment. When one actually reads the works of such authors, these defenses prove to be blatant lies.

On page 31 of the *Book of the Law*, it reads, "Compassion is the vice of kings : stamp down the wretched & the weak : this is the law of the strong : this is our law and the joy of the world...Now let it be understood: If the body of the King dissolve, he shall remain in pure ecstasy for ever."

On page 40 of the book it instructs the reader to, "Worship me with fire & blood; worship me with swords & with spears. Let the woman be girt with a sword before me:

let blood flow to my name. Trample down the Heathen; be upon them, o warrior, I will give you of their flesh to eat! Sacrifice cattle, little and big : after a child."

The book continues on the following page to read, "Mercy let be off : damn them who pity! Kill and torture; spare not; be upon them! The Best blood is of the moon, monthly: then the fresh blood of a child, or dropping from the host of heaven: then of enemies; then of the priest or of the worshipers: last of some beast, no matter what."[72]

Finally, Crowley (or the demon who allegedly dictated the book to him) shows his utter hatred for Jesus saying, "I am in a secret fourfold word, the blasphemy against all gods of men. Curse them! Curse them! Curse them! With my Hawk's head I peck at the eyes of Jesus as he hangs upon the cross."[73]

Crowley's brutal philosophy gets even more sadistic in another of his books titled *Magick: In Theory and Practice.*

Magick: In Theory and Practice

In his 1929 book, *Magick: In Theory and Practice,* Aleister Crowley wrote some very unsettling instructions for black magic rituals. He and other so-called magicians used the spelling "magick" with a "k" on the end. In the chapter titled "Of the Bloody Sacrifice" on page 95 and 96, Crowley wrote, "But the bloody sacrifice, though more dangerous, is more efficacious; and for nearly all purposes human sacrifice is the best...The animal should therefore be killed within the Circle, or the Triangle, as the case may be, so that its energy cannot escape. An animal should be selected whose nature accords with that of the ceremony—thus, by sacrificing a female lamb one would not obtain any appreciate quantity of

---

[72] Crowley, Aleister – *The Book of the Law* page 41
[73] Crowley, Aleister – *The Book of the Law* page 47

the fierce energy useful to a Magician who was invoking Mars. In such case a ram would be more suitable. And this ram should be virgin—the whole potential of its original total energy should not have been diminished in any way."

"For the highest spiritual working one must accordingly choose that victim which contains the greatest and purest force. A male child of perfect innocence and high intelligence is the most satisfactory and suitable victim."

Crowley himself was a degenerate bisexual heroine addict and enjoyed participating in the most horrific and disgusting practices imaginable. Shortly before the Italian dictator Benito Mussolini had him deported, rumors spread that Crowley once had his lover Leah Hirsig have sex with a goat, which he sacrificed afterward. Hirsig then had a nervous breakdown and their child died soon afterward. L. Ron Hubbard, the founder of Scientology was friends with Aleister Crowley, and in an audio clip available on the Internet he called him his "very good friend."

The Secret Doctrine

In 1888 a two volume set titled *The Secret Doctrine* was released by a Russian mystic named Helena Blavatsky. The book would turn out to be one of Adolf Hitler's favorites and he reportedly kept of copy next to his bed. Aside from writing that the Fall of Man was a spiritual evolution towards godhood, Helena Blavatsky explains the mystical significance of the swastika, and of course, Satan. This book sits in the occult or New Age section of most bookstores.

Blavatsky repeats the common belief that the real mystical secrets regarding the powers of God and the origin of the earth and human race are being kept a secret within the Illuminati. "For no one, not even the greatest living adept, would be permitted to, or could—even if he would—give out promiscuously, to a mocking, unbelieving world, that which has been so effectually concealed from it for long eons and ages."[74]

While most other writings of Illuminati supporters will only make veiled references to Satan, Blavatsky's book has quite a bit to say on the subject, and openly presents the case that Satan is a hero and a teacher, and that the Christian Church is responsible for spreading lies about him.

"It was left with the early and ignorant Christian fathers to degrade the philosophical and highly scientific emblem (the Dragon) into the absurd superstition called the Devil."[75]

When this author (Mark Dice) had first began researching the Illuminati and the occult, I had read some of these quotes posted on various websites but doubted their authenticity. It was only after purchasing the two volume set and reading it for myself that I realized such quotes were authentic. The following quotes were read directly out of the copy that I own, and were typed by the same hands typing these words as I sat with the book in front of me.

"Thus Lucifer—the spirit of Intellectual Enlightenment and Freedom of Thought—is metaphorically the guiding beacon, which helps man to find his way through the rocks and sand banks of Life, for Lucifer is the Logos in his highest."[76]

"Blessed and sanctifies is the name of the Angel of Havas— Satan."[77]

"Satan will now be shown, in the teaching of the Secret Doctrine, allegorized as Good, and Sacrifice, a God of Wisdom."[78]

---

[74] Blavatsky, Helena – *The Secret Doctrine* v I. p. xvii
[75] Blavatsky, Helena – *The Secret Doctrine* v. I p. 73
[76] Blavatsky, Helena – *The Secret Doctrine* v. II p. 162
[77] Blavatsky, Helena – *The Secret Doctrine* v. II p. 235
[78] Blavatsky, Helena – *The Secret Doctrine* v. II p. 237

"It is the Lord God, evidently, who was the real cause of all the mischief, the "agent provocateur," and the Serpent—only a prototype of Azazel, "the scapegoat for the sin of (the God of) Israel," the poor Tragos having to pay the penalty for his Master's and Creator's blunder."[79]

"But in antiquity and reality, Lucifer, or Luciferus, is the name of the angelic Entity presiding over the light of truth as over the light of the day."[80]

"Lucifer is divine and terrestrial light, the "Holy Ghost" and "Satan," at one and the same time, visible Space being truly filled with differentiated Breath invisibly; and the Astral Light, the manifested efforts of two who are one, guided and attracted by ourselves, is the karma of humanity, both a personal and impersonal entity...The Fall was the result of man's knowledge, for his "eyes were opened." Indeed, he was taught Wisdom and the hidden knowledge by the "Fallen Angel"...And now it stand proven that Satan, or the Red Fiery Dragon, the "lord of Phosphorus" (brimstone was a theological improvement), and Lucifer, or "Light-Bearer," is in us: it is our Mind—our tempter and Redeemer, our intelligent liberator and Savior from pure animalism...Without this quickening spirit, or human Mind or soul, there would be no difference between man and beast."[81]

The Externalization of the Hierarchy

Alice Bailey was a mystic from the 1900's who worked as a spiritual and occult writer and teacher. A primary

---

[79] Blavatsky, Helena – *The Secret Doctrine* v. II p. 387
[80] Blavatsky, Helena – *The Secret Doctrine* v. II p. 512
[81] Blavatsky, Helena – *The Secret Doctrine* v. II p. 513

source of publishing and promoting such literature is found with the creation of Lucis Trust, originally named Lucifer's Trust in 1922 when it was founded. Lucis Trust (also called Lucis Publishing) continues to publish the numerous books written by Alice Bailey. Their headquarters is located at 120 Wall Street, New York, NY 10005, just blocks from the New York Stock Exchange. Anyone who knows anything about commercial real estate knows that the rent on such a prime property is astronomical, and the fact that such a little known New Age publisher is able to afford such absorbent costs is extremely suspicious.

One of Alice Bailey's most popular books is *The Externalization of the Hierarchy* which outlines detailed plans the Illuminati has for taking over the world and is likely mandatory reading for all high level Skull and Bones members, Freemasons, and young Illuminati recruits.

Let me just say that this author (Mark Dice) owns this book and the following quotes that I am going to list were not copied and pasted from some random website, but were in fact typed by me as I read them directly from the book which I own. To the researcher who wants to gain a fuller understanding about the Illuminati and their beliefs and their plans, may I suggest that you do not go and purchase books like *The Externalization of the Hierarchy* because it is not necessary to financially support such authors and publishers. Within *The Illuminati: Facts & Fiction*, and my previous book, *The Resistance Manifesto*, one will find enough information and documentation to gain a complete understanding of such issues.

Many of the books that I purchased in the course of my research, I was fortunate enough to find at an obscure used bookstore and obtained them for just a few dollars each, which brought money in for the bookshop owner, and not the New Age publishers who sell to Barnes and Noble or Amazon.com. With that said, several of the most telling quotes from *The Externalization of the Hierarchy* follow.

"Esoterically speaking, a point of contact, a moment of "spiritual intercourse," is imminent, and *out of that moment a new world can be born*...If this spiritual contact can be brought about, it means that the Hierarchy will no longer be hidden and unknown, but will be recognized as present upon the physical plane...Increasingly the new group of world servers will be active in every nation and found functioning throughout the entire world."[82]

On page 107 of *The Externalization of the Hierarchy*, Alice Bailey point blank says the ruler of planet Earth will be Lucifer once the Hierarchy's plans are completed.

Bailey explains that the secret hierarchy is working towards creating a new religion, saying, "It has therefore become possible to synchronize the Approach of the divine to the human and to instruct the masses of men in the technique of thus invoking the Approach. This attitude of humanity will lead to a new revelation, to the new world religion and to new attitudes in the relation of man to God (religion) and of man to man (government or social relationships)."[83]

She goes on to admit that while the secret hierarchy does in fact exist, it is denied by the masses, and she admits that some who know of it are dedicated to resisting it. She writes, "The fact of the existence of the Hierarchy is consciously recognized by hundreds of thousands today, though still denied by the orthodox; the general public are familiar with the idea of the existence of the Masters, and either gullibly accept the mass of futile and idiotic information handed out by many today or fight furiously against the spread of this teaching."[84]

She insists that resistance is futile because, "So many

---

[82] Bailey, Alice – *Externalization of the Hierarchy* p. 21
[83] Bailey, Alice – *Externalization of the Hierarchy* p. 409
[84] Bailey, Alice – *Externalization of the Hierarchy* p. 417

know the truth today; so many people of integrity and worth are cooperating consciously with Members of this Hierarchy that the very foundations of the ecclesiastical antagonism and the belittling comments of the concrete minded are of no avail."[85]

She even admits that there are secret Illuminati agents who are working within Christian Churches in order to prepare the way for the brotherhood's plans. "There will be the invocative work of the masses of the people, trained by the spiritually minded people of the world (working in the churches, whenever possible, under an enlightened clergy) to accept the fact of the approaching spiritual energies, focused through the spiritual Hierarchy...This work, when rightly carried forward, will evoke response from the waiting Hierarchy; through this response, the belief of the masses will gradually be changed into the conviction of the knower. In this way humanity will be transformed and spiritualized."[86]

Bailey, like many others also confirms that Freemasonry is at the heart of the Illuminati, explaining, "There is no dissociation between the One Universal Church, the sacred inner Lodge of all true Masons, and the innermost circles of the esoteric societies...It must not be forgotten that only those souls who are on the Probationary Path or the Path of Discipleship will form the nucleus of the coming new world religion."[87]

"The *Masonic Movement* when it can be divorced from politics and social ends and from its present paralyzing condition of inertia, will meet the need of those who can, and should wield power. It is the custodian of the law; it is the home of the Mysteries and the seat of initiation. It holds its

[85] Bailey, Alice – *Externalization of the Hierarchy* p. 417
[86] Bailey, Alice – *Externalization of the Hierarchy* p. 418
[87] Bailey, Alice – *Externalization of the Hierarchy* p. 513

symbolism the ritual of Deity, and the way of salvation is pictorially preserved in its work. The methods of Deity are demonstrated in its temples, and under the All-seeing Eye the work can go forward. It is a far more occult organization than can be realized, and is intended to be the training school for the coming advanced occultists. In its ceremonials lies hid the wielding of the forces connected with the growth and life of the kingdoms of nature and the unfoldment of the divine aspects in man."[88]

Bailey describes the extent to which the Illuminati has infiltrated society, saying, "they will appear in office of some kind or another; they will be the current politicians, business men, financiers, religious teachers or churchmen; they will be scientists and philosophers, college professors and educators; they will be the mayors of cities and the custodians of all public ethical movements. The spiritual forcefulness of their lives, their clear, pure wisdom, the sanity and the modern acceptableness of the proposed measures in any department in which they choose to function, will be so convincing that little impediment will be set in the way of their undertakings."[89]

Near the end of the book, Bailey brags that the Illuminati secretly shapes the very fabric of civilization. "The Hierarchy directs and controls, more than is realized, the unfolding cyclic cultures and their resultant civilizations. These can then provide adequate forms, temporarily useful for the emerging soul of humanity. The format of cultures and civilizations receives special attention."[90]

It's important to note that these are not just the ramblings of a New Age guru who is simply imagining that such things are underway. Somehow the Lucis Publishing

[88] Bailey, Alice – *Externalization of the Hierarchy* p. 511
[89] Bailey, Alice – *Externalization of the Hierarchy* p. 570-571
[90] Bailey, Alice – *Externalization of the Hierarchy* p. 519-520

company is able to afford real estate on Wall Street, and the small revenues which are taken in from book sales wouldn't even be able to pay a fraction of these costs. Lucis Publishing is either given huge donations in the range of millions of dollars, or is involved in other unknown business ventures which allow it to operate and maintain its prestigious location.

However it financially sustains itself, it continues to publish books such as *The Externalization of the Hierarchy* which is hidden in plain view and contains large portions of the Illuminati's goals for a New World Order and an Illuminati Christ to rule the earth as a supernatural king.

Codex Magica

One of the greatest modern resources for photographic evidence about the Illuminati is Texe Marrs' 620 page book *Codex Magica* which was published in 2005. Texe has compiled hundreds of photographs of Masonic handshakes, Illuminati symbols, occult illustrations and more. *Codex Magica* is the size of a large phonebook. Two years after its initial publication, Texe released a similar follow-up book focusing specifically on monuments and buildings called *Mysterious Monuments*.

Texe writes, "Why do the Illuminati do what they do? After many years of research and investigation into their behavior and conduct, and understanding their goals and ambition, I am persuaded these men fit the definition of psychopathic personalities. They are psychopaths and as such they are afflicted with the dangerous malady called megalomania."[91]

"In sum, the psychopath possesses a clear perception of reality—he knows full well what he's doing—but he refuses

---

[91] Marrs, Texe – *Codex Magica* page 25

to abide by society's morals. Instead, he pursues personal gratification in such things as criminal acts, drug addition and sexual perversion. Combined with feelings of megalomania, the psychopath has visions of his own omnipotence—he thinks he is a god—and has delusions of grandeur. Since he is persuaded he is divine and not bound by the rules that apply to other, less godly beings, the psychopath is a dangerous person indeed."[92]

Texe is one of the most reliable authors whose works have exposed the Illuminati, their symbols, philosophies, and goals. Within Texe's work there is little to no speculation or exaggeration of claims, and his work is always meticulously documented with sources and references. Where some other authors simply make claims and cite alleged quotes from occult books, Texe's bibliographies provide the reader with original sources, of which almost all are from mainstream publications and political or Masonic authors own books.

Interestingly, Texe is the pastor who performed the wedding ceremony of radio host and film maker Alex Jones and his wife Violet. Both Texe and Alex Jones live in Austin, Texas.

Jim Tucker's Bilderberg Diary

In 2005 Jim Tucker finally published his long awaited *Bilderberg Diary*, recounting 25 years of his investigations into the ultra elite and secret Bilderberg group. This book and Daniel Estulin's *True Story of the Bilderberg Group* are the two most credible books that will ever be written on the subject. Since Tucker discovered the Bilderberg group in the 1970s, he has made it his life's mission to infiltrate and report on the group's annual conference. Anyone who wants to fully understand the Bilderberg group and their

---

[92] Marrs, Texe – *Codex Magica* page 26

accomplishments should avoid scowering the Internet for random information without sources, and instead just read one of these two books.

Tucker's Diary begins with a brief description and history of the Bilderberg group, and then each following chapter chronicles year after year where the meetings are held, who has attended them, and what was discussed. The book reads, "The Bilderberg group is an organization of political leaders and international financiers that meets secretly every spring to make global policy. There are about 110 regulars—Rockefellers, Rothschilds, bankers, heads of international corporations and high government officials from Europe and North America. Each year, a few new people are invited and, if found useful, they return to future meetings. If not, they are discarded. Decisions reached at these secret meetings affect every American and much of the world."[93]

While some reporters and so-called whistle blowers who attempt to expose the Illuminati or New World Order operations mix fact with fiction in order to create a buzz with the hopes of selling books and lectures, Jim Trucker is the real deal. He is a legitimate journalist whose work is practically flawless. Someone new to this kind of information may find it hard to believe the Bilderberg group exists, and consists of such powerful and well known men, but Tucker's information has been verified by other qualified researchers, and there is no doubt among those who follow New World Order news that Jim Tucker's Bilderberg research is truthful and he has the best intentions.

British journalist Jon Ronson chronicled Jim Tucker's investigation of the 1999 Bilderberg meeting which took place at the Hotel Caesar Park in Sintra, Portugal. Ronson was skeptical and appeared to even ridicule Tucker but was

---

[93] Tucker, Jim – *Jim Tuckers Bilderberg Diary* preface

later shocked to find limos and private cars arriving at the hotel and was able to identify several influential people who were in attendance. Video of his time with Tucker can be seen in the Bilderberg segment of his *Secret Rulers of the World* series.

Tucker is also featured in Alex Jones 2007 film *Endgame: Blueprint for Global Enslavement* where Tucker, Jones, and others tracked the Bilderberg group to Ottawa, Canada and were able to get clear photographs and video footage of many of the high profile guests arriving as they stepped out of their limos at the entrance of the Brookstreet Hotel. Several individuals spotted were Queen Beatrix of the Netherlands, David Rockefeller, Richard Hass who is the president of the Council on Foreign Relations, Henry Kissinger, and others.

An anonymous source from within the Bilderberg group has secretly provided Tucker with attendee lists and talking points for several years. Tucker has also reported that he has paid staff and waiters at the hotels where the conference is held to listen closely to conversations and later inform him what they overheard.

Despite the Bilderberg group meeting annually every year since 1954, virtually no news coverage is given to the event. Year after year the most powerful politicians, business men, royalty and media moguls meet for several days of secret talks, yet it is never covered on television or in print. This shows how much control the group has over the media, particularly in America. Operation Mockingbird has been extremely effective in preventing any reporters from covering the event. Many attendees of Bilderberg meetings are owners and CEOs of major newspapers and television studios.

Many Bilderberg attendees may also be in violation of the Logan Act which is a United States federal law that prohibits unauthorized citizens from negotiating with foreign governments. The law was passed in 1799 and is still in effect today. A violation of the Logan Act is a felony and punishable with imprisonment. Similar violations likely occur annually at the Bohemian Grove, as well. (See Dark Secrets: Inside Bohemian Grove page 269)

The True Story of the Bilderberg Group

Continuing on the trail that Jim Tucker had blazed exposing the Bilderberg group is Daniel Estulin, who next to Jim Tucker, is seen as the world's foremost expert on the organization. Estulin has been doing his own investigations into the club and wrote *The True Story of the Bilderberg Group*, which has been translated into twenty four languages and became an international bestseller.

Estulin explains how he got involved in investigating the Bilderberg group, "I'm a Russian ex-patriot who was kicked out of the Soviet Union in 1980. My father was a dissident who fought for freedom of speech who was jailed, and tortured by the KGB. When these people got tired of us they threw us out. We moved to Canada and 12 years ago I came to Spain. My grandfather was a colonel in the KGB and the counter-intelligence in the 1950s, so I am privileged somewhat to get a lot of the information from the secret service which are our best sources of information. Not only the KGB people but the MI-6 people, the CIA because most of the people who work for the secret service as you probably know are patriots and they love their country and they're doing it for the good of the nation and they're the first ones absolutely terrified of the plans of the Bilderbergers."[94]

Estulin's writing is extremely accurate. He refrains from speculation or theorizing about the activities of the

---

[94] *The Alex Jones Show* May 27, 2005 on the Genesis Communications Network

THE ILLUMINATI: FACTS & FICTION

organization, and instead asks compelling questions and documents the facts. He writes, "Any modern democratic system protects the right to privacy, but doesn't the public have a right to know what their political leaders are talking about when they meet the wealthiest business leaders of their respective countries? What guarantees do citizens have that the Bilderberg Group isn't merely a center for influence trafficking and lobbying if they aren't allowed to know what their representatives talk about at the Group's secret gatherings? Why are the Davos World Economic Forums and G8 meetings discussed in every newspaper, given front-page coverage, with thousands of journalists in attendance, while no one covers Bilderberg Group meetings?"[95]

"We are at a crossroads. And the roads we take from here will determine the very future of humanity. We have to wake up to the true objectives and actions of the Bilderberg Group and its parallel kin if we hope to retain the freedoms fought for by our grandfathers in World War II."

"Its not up to God to bring us back from the "New Dark Age" planned for us. It is up to us! Whether we emerge from this century as an electronic global police state or as free human beings *depends on the actions we take now.*"[96]

Like Jim Tucker, Estulin is featured in Alex Jones' 2007 documentary film *Endgame: Blueprint for Global Enslavement*, which documents their investigations into the Bilderberg group as they track them to the Brookstreet Hotel in Ottawa, Canada in 2006 and capture members on video as they enter the hotel under enhanced security.

In December 2007, Estulin reported that elite members of the Bilderberg group had discussed the effects of having Congressman Ron Paul assassinated. Estulin emphasized that his source said they were not planning to do it at the

---

[95] Estulin, Daniel – *The True Story of the Bilderberg Group* page xiv
[96] Estulin, Daniel – *The True Story of the Bilderberg Group* page xv

time, but were openly discussing it as a possibility, and were trying to determine whether it would be an effective strategy to silence the Congressman.

Ron Paul is known for speaking out about the Federal Reserve system and for publicly chastising Federal Reserve Chairman Ben Bernanke on live television regarding the monetary policies of the bank. Paul ran for president on the Republican ticket for the 2008 election, but did not win the Republican nomination. He revitalized true conservatives who want a return to sound monetary principles, the end of big government, and a non intervention foreign policy. Paul is one of the few, if not only Congressman who has no strings attached to him by special interest groups or the Illuminati, and by him speaking to a national audience about what was really happening in the country, he was a tremendous thorn in the side of the Bilderberg group and posed a danger to them by exposing their actions.

Daniel Estulin and his family have received death threats and worse as a result of his investigations into the Bilderberg group.

The Search for the Manchurian Candidate

While some may be familiar with the fictional film titled *The Manchurian Candidate* about a secret government program that experimented on soldiers using brainwashing and mind control techniques, what many do not know is there is a non-fiction book that was released in 1979 which details the actual existence of such programs and the horrendous crimes and abuse that were committed during those experiments.

John D. Marks, a former State Department Officer wrote *The Search for the Manchurian Candidate: The CIA and Mind Control,* based off of thousands of newly released documents, behavioral science studies, as well as interviews with victims.

His findings are disturbing, not only because of the goals of such programs, but the inhumane and unethical ways that such experiments were carried out. The MK-ULTRA program was an umbrella name for these kinds of experiments, which often involved hallucinogenic drugs, hypnotism, and torture.

While the existence of MK-ULTRA was admitted by the government, the official stance on the program is that it was abandoned and is no longer in operation. It doesn't even take a skeptic to think that such statements are false, and in reality identical programs have secretly continued operating with extra safety measures taken to prevent their exposure from happening again.

Marks explains, "This book has grown out of the 16,000 pages of documents that the CIA released to me under the Freedom of Information Act. Without these documents, the best investigative reporting in the world could not have produced a book, and the secrets of the CIA mind-control work would have remained buried forever, as the men who knew them had always intended. From the documentary base, I was able to expand my knowledge through interviews and readings in the behavioral sciences. Nevertheless, the final result is not the whole story of the CIA's attack on the mind. Only a few insiders could have written that, and they choose to remain silent. I have done the best I can to make the book as accurate as possible, but I have been hampered by the refusal of most of the principle characters to be interviewed and by the CIA's destruction in 1973 of many of the key documents."[97]

The Search for the Manchurian Candidate covers the evolution of the CIA's sinister experiments beginning in the 1950s. Unknowing subjects were often given powerful hallucinogenic drugs including LSD, so the CIA could learn

---

[97] Marks, John – *The Search for the Manchurian Candidate* page xix

of the effects. One man, Dr. Frank Olson ended up committing suicide by jumping out of a ten story building in 1953. Olson worked as a chemist with the U.S. Army and it wasn't until decades later that his widow and family learned the true circumstances surrounding his death. The CIA had hoped that they could develop various techniques that could be used to extract information from people, as well as "program" them to be assassins. The ultimate goal of MK-ULTRA was to use a combination of drugs and hypnosis to transform any person the CIA desired into an assassin who would carry out any orders they were given, regardless of the consequences.

In his book, John D. Marks explains one such experiment. "On February 19, 1954, Morse Allen simulated the ultimate experiment in hypnosis: the creation of a "Manchurian Candidate," or programmed assassin. Allen's "victim" was a secretary whom he put into a deep trance and told to keep sleeping until he ordered otherwise. He then hypnotized a second secretary and told her that if she could not wake up her friend, "her rage would be so great that she would not hesitate to kill." Allen left a pistol nearby, which the secretary had no way of knowing was unloaded. Even though she had earlier expressed a fear of fire-arms of any kind, she picked up the gun and "shot" her sleeping friend. After Allen brought the "killer" out of her trance, she had apparent amnesia for the event, denying she would ever shoot anyone."[98]

Anyone who knows anything about hypnotism knows that it is actual science and has very real applications. Many people are also aware of post-hypnotic suggestions which involve using a word or phrase to put a person back into a hypnotic trance days or weeks after they had been originally hypnotized. Using post-hypnotic suggestions, a person can

---

[98] Marks, John – *The Search for the Manchurian Candidate* page 195

be fully conscious and going about their day when a key word or phrase is uttered out loud, and when they hear that word or phrase, they will automatically respond with whatever command they were given when they were originally hypnotized.

Anyone who has ever seen a stage hypnotist perform knows how easily someone under hypnosis can be manipulated. People see things that aren't there, they hear things they are told to hear, and they can be tricked into believing or doing practically anything. It is no wonder the CIA experimented to harness this amazing power.

One of the key figures involved in MK-ULTRA was Dr. Ewen Cameron who worked at the Allan Memorial Hospital in Canada where many of the experiments took place. With such sinister activities, one would suspect that the Illuminati had their hand in the program, and one would be correct. The Rockefeller Foundation had donated money to set up this psychiatric facility at the McGill University Healthcare Center which operated the Allan Memorial Institute.

The Reappearance of the Christ and the Masters of Wisdom

In 1982 a man named Benjamin Crème began running advertisements in newspapers around the world which read "The Christ is now here" and claimed he would soon announce himself to the world on an international television broadcast. Crème refers to this "Christ" as Maitreya, which he says is the long awaited messiah and world teacher that all religions have been waiting for. He says this man is the "Avatar for the Aquarian Age."

Crème describes in his book, *The Reappearance of the Christ and the Masters of Wisdom*, "This will lead to the Day of Declaration, when He will appear on the radio and television networks of the world linked by satellite. On that day Maitreya will mentally overshadow the whole of humanity simultaneously. All will hear His words inwardly in their own language. This telepathic communication will reach everyone, not only those watching or listening, and hundreds of thousands of miraculous healings will take place throughout the world. On that day, there will be no doubt that Maitreya is the Christ, the Imam Mahdi, Maitreya Buddha, Kalki Avatar: the World Teacher. His open worldwide mission will have begun."[99]

While some may dismiss Crème's predictions as the rantings of a lunatic, upon a closer examination it becomes clear that Crème casually confirms the suspicions of those who point the finger at Freemasonry as being involved in the creation of the New World Order and working in conjunction with the Illuminati. He writes, "The new religion will manifest, for instance, through organizations like Masonry. In Freemasonry is embedded the core or secret heart of the occult Mysteries—wrapped in number, metaphor and symbol."[100]

Crème also reveals he understands the forces behind Communalism saying, "Marx was indeed a member of the Hierarchy, of a certain degree. Looking at the effect of his work over the years — that could only have been the work of a disciple of some degree, an initiate of some level: first to have the vision, and secondly to have the capacity to embody that vision so that the work could spread."[101]

While most who point out such connections do so to help others understand the larger forces behind Communism, such as the international banks, and expose such connections with hopes of preventing the banking cartels from creating

---

[99] Crème, Benjamin – *The Reappearance of the Christ and the Masters of Wisdom* p. 25
[100] Crème, Benjamin – *The Reappearance of the Christ and the Masters of Wisdom* page 82
[101] Crème, Benjamin – *The Reappearance of the Christ and the Masters of Wisdom* p. 190-191

their one world financial system, Crème does so by praising those behind such actions. Let's be clear that it is no conspiracy theory that Karl Marx was working for a secret organization when he wrote *The Communist Manifesto*. In the preface to the 1872 German edition it is made clear that Marx and Engels were chosen basically as secretaries to write and publish the manifesto.

It reads, "The Communist League (formerly called the "League of Just Men")…which could of course only be a secret one…commissioned the undersigned [Karl Marx and Friedrich Engels], at the Congress held in London in November 1847, to draw up for publication a detailed theoretical and practical program of the Party. Such was the origin of the following Manifesto, the manuscript of which traveled to London to be printed, a few weeks before the February Revolution."

Crème's claims of the coming mystical Christ were enthusiastically received within many New Age circles, but as more time went by and Maitreya didn't appear, Crème's supporters began to dwindle.

It remains unclear what connections if any Crème has with the Illuminati. It is possible that his writings and lectures are just those of a man who supports such ideas, but the enormous amounts of money that Crème has spent by taking out newspaper ads and posting billboards should make one take a closer look at Benjamin Crème and his connections.

It should be clear that Crème was not referring to Jesus as the Christ who would appear, but instead a leader that would come forth from the secret hierarchy of the Illuminati who have been working behind the veil of secrecy to prepare for this "leader's" arrival.

The Franklin Cover-Up

The most disgusting and disturbing book ever written is

possibly *The Franklin Cover-Up* which was first published in 1992 and later released with revisions in 2005. The book was written by former Nebraska Senator John DeCamp, and uncovers a scandal so large and perverted, that most people simply do not want to hear about it, let alone believe it actually happened.

The Franklin Cover-Up began with the Franklin Community Federal Credit Union in Omaha, Nebraska which had thirty-eight million dollars embezzled from it by its manager Laurence E. King. As the investigation proceeded, it was learned that those involved in siphoning millions from the credit union were involved in far more sinister activities. It turns out that the money was being used by Laurence E. King to pay off politicians and to operate a child pornography and prostitution ring. As if this wasn't bad enough, allegations of kidnapping, snuff films, and government mind control experiments would also haunt those connected to the case.

While money laundering, organized crime, bribes, and illegal businesses are common in politics, we will briefly go over some of the darker and more unique aspects of this case.

One of the central victims of this scandal was a boy named Paul Bonacci who gave investigators unsettling details about his involvement in child pornography and aiding in kidnapping other children who would be sold into sex slavery. Besides being involved in such unthinkable acts, the story gets even stranger and more unsettling. Bonacci told his lawyer that at one time when he was involved in such activities he was taken into a forest in Northern California which contained a huge moss covered statue that looked like an owl, and that men wearing robes performed some kind of ceremony there. This was around 1984, he says.

Later, after the Franklin credit scandal began to unfold, Bonacci drove with his lawyer, John DeCamp, to the place he said this occurred. Bonacci had navigated to a place which turned out to be the entrance of the Bohemian Grove. (See Dark Secrets: Inside Bohemian Grove page 269) At the time, John DeCamp had no idea that each summer a human sacrifice type of ritual was performed in the club by men wearing colored robes, and that Bonacci was describing Moloch, the 40 foot tall stone idol which is the focus of such ritual. All DeCamp knew at the time was that Bonacci had lead him to the club and said that was where he was taken. Later, other children would identify the Bohemian Grove as the place they were taken and sexually abused as well.

Bonacci says that when he was inside this campground in 1984 (later identified as the Bohemian Grove), he was forced to participate in child pornography videos. As he participated in these videos he was allegedly an eyewitness to the rape and ritualistic murder of another young boy there who he was forced to have sex with on video. In Bonacci's own words in his journal he wrote "After that the men grabbed Nicholas and drug him off screaming. They put me up against a tree and put a gun to my head but fired into the air. I heard another shot from somewhere and then saw the man who killed the boy drag him like a toy. Everything including when the men put the boy in the trunk was filmed. The men took me with them and we went up in a plane. I saw the bag the boy was in. We went over a very thick brush area with a clearing in it. Over the clearing they dropped the boy. One said the men with the hoods would take care of the body for them."

Furthermore, Bonacci says that a man named "Hunter Thompson" was the one who took video of this entire ordeal. Later, a man named Rusty Nelson, who was connected to the Franklin Cover-Up claimed that Hunter S. Thompson, the famous gonzo journalist offered him $100,000 to produce a snuff film when the two had met at a party.[102] (See Fear and Loathing in Las Vegas page 318) Rusty Nelson was the personal photographer for Lawrence E. King, the key perpetrator in the Franklin Cover-Up. Nelson admits that it was his job to secretly take photos of people who attended King's parties when they were in "compromising positions with children." Nelson denies taking any pornographic photos, but does admit that he would often witness and photograph grown men "making out with boys." The men who attended these parties were often politicians who King would then blackmail with the photos.

Senator DeCamp left out details of the gigantic owl statue in the forest and men in robes in the initial printing of his book because at the time he thought it was, "too far fetched for people to believe." At the time Bonacci's testimony was recorded by DeCamp, he was unaware of Bohemian Grove, the activities surrounding an owl statue, and the mysterious rituals that were performed inside. Only in the passing years did Senator DeCamp learn about the details of Bohemian Grove and the chilling revelations of the moss covered idol in the redwood forest of Sonoma County California. The revised edition of DeCamp's book includes all the information about Paul Bonacci's alleged horrendous experiences in the Bohemian Grove.

The former head of the CIA, Bill Colby, told DeCamp to forget everything he knew and to, "Get as far away from this thing as you can. Forget you ever saw it or know it, heard it or anything else."[103] He also said that there were forces too dark for DeCamp to handle. Only after saying he couldn't walk away, did Colby tell DeCamp he better get his story out before the perpetrators would have him murdered. He then

---

[102] *A Closer Look* with Michael Corbin April 12, 2005
[103] Alex Jones Show July 21, 2004 *Alex Jones Interviews John DeCamp, Author of "The Franklin Cover-up"*

wrote and published his book, *The Franklin Cover-Up*.

On April 27, 1996 Colby died in what was called a canoeing accident. The incident happened at night which is strange, because Colby wouldn't go canoeing after dark. He was alone when the incident happened, and had not told his wife that he was going canoeing. He was not wearing a life jacket, which his friends said he usually wore, and many believe he was murdered for aiding DeCamp or for knowing to much about such things.

Some of the things found in DeCamp's book are even worse than what is mentioned in this brief summary. John DeCamp has had nothing to gain from being involved in exposing the Franklin Cover-Up and when this author (Mark Dice) spoke with him on the phone, he said that he wished he would have never heard about the Bohemian Grove, or the Franklin Credit Union scandal, and that he has lived in a constant state of fear for his life, and that of his family ever since he became involved in investigating it.

Learning about such horrific and perverted activities leads one to wonder why would anyone want to do such disgusting and inhumane things, especially to children. How could a group of men possibly find enjoyment in such things? The answers are found in the deepest and darkest secrets regarding Satanism and the occult. Such activities are a form of sex magic and the practitioners believe that such activities are the only way to achieve a particular level of altered consciousness and communicate with entities from other dimensions or to open their minds up to become possessed by these entities, or alter their brain chemistry in an attempt to "super-charge" their mind and metaphysically alter reality. (see Sex Magic page 305)

David Rockefeller's Memoirs

In his 2002 book, *Memoirs*, Illuminati kingpin David Rockefeller wrote on page 405, "For more than a century ideological extremists at either end of the political spectrum have seized upon well-publicized incidents such as my encounter with Castro to attack the Rockefeller family for the inordinate influence they claim we wield over American political and economic institutions. Some even believe we are part of a secret cabal working against the interests of the United States, characterizing my family and me as "internationalists" and conspiring with others around the world to build a more integrated global political and economic structure—one world, if you will. If that's the charge, I stand guilty, and I am proud of it."

"The anti-Rockefeller focus of these otherwise incompatible political positions owes much to Populism. "Populists" believe in conspiracies, and one of the most enduring is that a secret group of international bankers and capitalists and their minions control the world's economy."

David Rockefeller is one of the grandchildren of John D. Rockefeller, the founder of Standard Oil, and at the time when he lived, John D. was the richest man in the world. David Rockefeller has had his hands in nearly every major New World Order organization in existence in the twentieth and twenty first centuries. In fact, he is the founder of the Trilateral Commission and is the former Chairman of the Council on Foreign Relations. He also attends nearly every Bilderberg meeting. At the time of this writing, David Rockefeller (senior) is 93 years old.

Outside of Rockefeller Center in New York City stands a huge gold colored statue of Prometheus holding fire in one hand as he flies through the air. The mythological Greek story of Prometheus stealing fire from the Gods and giving it to mankind despite the punishment he will face is seen by occultists as identical to the story of Lucifer giving mankind the knowledge of good and evil that God had forbid us to have. So essentially this statue which stands outside of Rockefeller Center is a tribute to Lucifer, which goes unnoticed by the average person not familiar with Illuminati symbolism.

Foreign Affairs

The Council on Foreign Relations (CFR) is part of the triad of power that has been openly constructing the New World Order with regards to American foreign policy for decades. The CFR is often used in succession with the Trilateral Commission and the Bilderberg group, and their elite members have rapidly been achieving their goals of global government.

The CFR is a privately owned and operated organization whose members include many elite politicians and media moguls. Most of their meetings are not secret, but instead are used to generate and spread propaganda regarding what policies and courses of action the United States government should take concerning foreign policy. Because of their name, the Council on Foreign Relations sounds like a government committee that would meet in Congress to discuss and formulate policies on international affairs. The CFR is similar to the Federal Reserve in this manner, but both organizations are privately owned and operated by the Illuminati. The Council on Foreign Relations publishes a quarterly journal titled *Foreign Affairs*, which is used to steer the US into the directions that this private organization desires.

In the May/June 2007 edition of *Foreign Affairs* there was an essay by Benn Steil, the Director of International Economics at the CFR, titled *The End of National Currency*, where the Council appeared to endorse the end of economic sovereignty.

Steil argued, "The right course is not to return to a mythical past of monetary sovereignty, with governments controlling local interest and exchange rates in blissful ignorance of the rest of the world. Governments must let go of the fatal notion that nationhood requires them to make and control the money used in their territory. National currencies and global markets simply do not mix; together they make a deadly brew of currency crises and geopolitical tension and create ready pretexts for damaging protectionism. In order to globalize safely, countries should abandon monetary nationalism and abolish unwanted currencies, the source of much of today's instability."

Steil went on to say, "The lessons of gold-based globalization in the nineteenth century simply must be relearned... Since economic development outside the process of globalization is no longer possible, countries should abandon monetary nationalism. Governments should replace national currencies with the dollar or the euro, or, in the case of Asia, collaborate to produce a new multinational currency over a comparably large and economically diversified area.... Most of the world's smaller and poorer countries would clearly be best off unilaterally adopting the dollar or the euro, which would enable their safe and rapid integration into global financial markets. Latin American countries should dollarize; eastern European countries and Turkey, euroize."

Steil's essay concludes by warning that if governments fail to take the CFR's advice that, "the market may privatize money on its own."

One of the Illuminati's ultimate goals is to have the entire world use the same currency and then abandon that currency for a completely electronic one. The use of cash and coins as money will likely be obsolete in the New World Order and replaced with an RFID (Radio Frequency Identification Device) such as the VeriChip or similar device. This way all purchases can be tracked, traced, and taxed. Such a device is believed to be what the Bible calls the mark of the Beast. The path to an electronic currency must first accomplish several regional currencies and then later merge those currencies into one global unit. The Council on Foreign Relations has been pushing the agenda of creating what they call a "North American Union" which would merge the currencies of Canada, the United States, and Mexico into one regional currency. The economic collapse in the United States stemming from the mortgage bubble bursting in 2008 spurred calls for a regional currency, and even a global currency as a "solution" to the economic disaster that ensued.

The CFR usually gets what it wants, and if one desires to have an advanced look into the future of American foreign policy, the *Foreign Affairs* journal will give you that insight. It's interesting to note that the logo for the *Foreign Affairs* journal is a man riding a white horse who is holding a bow. In the Book of Revelation, the Bible describes the first horseman of the apocalypse as a man riding on a white horse while holding a bow in one hand and is considered the horseman of conquest. Since the CFR is an Illuminati created organization, such a symbol was chosen to reflect the dark forces that are behind the council as they work to construct the New World Order.

Purported Illuminati Texts

Over the centuries several books have been published, or rumored to exist, which are allegedly ancient books that the Illuminati and occult hierarchies have kept secret and only allowed certain initiates to learn the contents of. Some of these alleged texts are quite old, as in the case of the *Emerald Tablet of Hermes* and the *Book of Thoth*. Others such as *The Necronomicon* and *The Illuminati Manifesto* are more recent.

Upon even a glance, the fraudulent nature of some of these supposed Illuminati texts is obvious, while the existence of others remains ambiguous and unclear. In the following pages you will find an examination of the most popular alleged Illuminati texts including their history and contents.

The Necronomicon

The Necronomicon is the name of a book that horror writer H.P. Lovecraft incorporated into several of his stories in the early 1900s. In Lovecraft's novels, the book was said to contain magic spells and ancient occult knowledge. The interesting thing is that some individuals took this concept and tried to cash in on it by publishing what they marketed as real versions of *The Necronomicon*.

In 1973, a book that was said to be *The Necronomicon* was published by Owlswick Press which consisted a made-up language. The book contains a preface by L. Sprague de Camp who was a popular science fiction writer.

In the late 1970s a man named John Todd claimed to be a former Illuminati member and told audiences that he had seen one of the only three copies in existence of *The Necronomicon* and that the Illuminati were using it to practice black magic. In H.P. Lovecraft's writings, he said that only five copies of the mystical book were in print. The locations of these five books was said to be: the British Museum, the National Library of France, Widener Library of Harvard University, the University of Buenos Aires, and a fictional library Lovecraft called Miskatonic University. The story of John Todd is lengthy and fascinating and is expanded in more detail in another section of this book which covers alleged Illuminati defectors (See John Todd page 157)

Another writer trying to cash in on gullible occultists was George Hay who released a version of the book in 1979 titled *The Necronomicon: Book of Dead Names.* Several years later Colin Wilson, who wrote the introduction for the book, would admit it was a hoax.[104]

Then in 1980 a man known only as "Simon" who was said to have been a student of the occult since the 1960s published a book called *The Necronomicon* which was marketed as a real English translation of the supposed ancient text. The *"Simon Necronomicon"* as it has been called, is reported to have sold several hundred thousand copies and is still found on shelves in the occult section of most bookstores. It consists of typical mystical ramblings and magic spells.

The publisher claimed, "Simon was a young man drawn to the mysterious world of the occult through his association with several Eastern Orthodox religions and his friendship with the owner of an occult bookstore in Brooklyn. In 1972 he stumbled upon a stolen text in a friend's apartment, unaware that what he held in his hands was the real Necronomicon—something long thought to be a creation of Lovecraft's brilliant mind and deft pen. After an arduous translation, done in the utmost secrecy (since the tome was

---

[104] Wilson, Colin – *Crypt of Cthulhu* magazine issue #23 (1984) The Necronomicon—The Origin of a Spoof

in fact stolen), Simon and his close circle of friends unveiled the now–infamous grimoire to a clamoring public."

Only the most foolish occultists, mainly young teenagers, believed (or continue to believe) "Simon's" book is an authentic ancient mystical text.

In 1998 "Simon" released *The Necronomicon Spell Book* in another attempt to cash in on the subject from the gullible occultists who believe the book to be authentic. Then again in 2006, the same author published *Gates of the Necronomicon* which was described as a companion to the original book. That same year "Simon" also published *Dead Names: The History of the Necronomicon* as an answer to critics who claim he and his book are frauds. Despite serious occultists and critics claims that the book is a complete fraud, "Simon" must be overjoyed and laughed all the way to the bank as he earned possibly hundreds of thousands of dollars from royalties from sales of the books.

In 1998 Daniel Harms and John Wisdom Gonce III published *The Necronomicon Files: The Truth Behind the Legend* and traced the origins of the various supposed authentic books and showed how they were in fact fictions based H.P. Lovecraft's mentioning of the book and incorporating occult principles and mysticism into books that were then marketed as legitimate, like the "Simon Necronomicon."

In 2004, yet another occultist named Donald Tyson published *The Necronomicon: The Wanderings of Alhazred*, and similarly tried to cash in on the controversy surrounding the supposed ancient text.

Some of those who are aware that the concept for *The Necronomicon*, as well as the title, was the creation of Lovecraft's novels, still think such a book actually exists. These people believe that Lovecraft had knowledge of such a book, and simply incorporated it into his fictional stories.

Emerald Tablet

Another supposed ancient text that some believe contains esoteric wisdom about the nature of reality and the secret of our existence is the *Emerald Tablet of Hermes*. Legend has it that the Greek god Hermes (also called Hermes Trismegistus) created the text. Alchemists see the tablet as a foundational work of Hermeticism. While popular opinion is under the impression that Alchemy involved ancient scientists who hoped of creating gold out of lead by means of a chemical reaction, Alchemy in the esoteric enlightenment circles refers to a mystical practice which would purify the soul, uncover valuable wisdom, and possibly allow one to achieve immortality. The metaphor of turning lead into gold is meant to describe a person's transformation into an enlightened being.

Although it is called the Emerald Tablet, some believe if the tablet did in fact exist, that the writings were carved into a slab of jade stone which is green in color.

According to Alchemists, there are various explanations and theories as to its authorship. One is that Hermes was a son of Adam and wrote the tablet to help mankind redeem themselves from his father's sins in the Garden of Eden. Another popular legend regarding the tablet's origin says the object was found in a cave or a secret chamber under the pyramid of Cheops around 1350 BC by a man named Balinias who then wrote down the text in a Syriac language, which has since become the source of various translations.

The central theme to the writings on the supposed tablet is that our own mind determines and influences physical reality and that one can learn to manifest their desired reality through knowledge of God and his principles.

In the opening sequence of *The Secret* (2006) by Rhonda Byrne, a brief scene shows someone making a rubbing of the tablet in ancient times, and it is alluded that its contents make up some or all of "the secret" which the DVD teaches. This "secret" or "law of attraction" is supposedly that our mind can create any reality we desire and is directed by our thoughts and beliefs. Like a magnet, whatever you think about, good or bad, is manifested in your life. The film's opening sequence explains that the "Secret" had been carried on through the centuries and kept for the benefit of only those who were aware of it. Another shot in the opening scene shows several business men sitting around a table, likely referring to the Illuminati. These men apparently knew the "Secret" and were having a meeting to discuss how they could keep it from getting out into the public. There are several translations of the supposed contents of the *Emerald Tablet,* including one said to be by Isaac Newton. This translation was not something that Newton had publicized, and was supposedly discovered in his papers after his death. It is believed that Isaac Newton was a member of the Invisible College, which was a secret group of scientists and philosophers in Europe, and through this group he would have been aware of such mystical and occult ideas.

The *Emerald Tablet* is sometimes associated with, or believed to be the philosopher's stone, which according to alchemical legends can give the owner enlightenment or eternal life. Some occult legends say that the *Emerald Tablet* came from Lucifer himself, and contained the knowledge of good and evil that was given to Adam and Even in the Garden of Eden. Most historians consider the tablet a legend, and no historical artifact has ever been discovered and released to the public. Whatever the *Emerald Tablet* is, or if it even actually exists remains a mystery.

The Book of Thoth

The Book of Thoth is believed to be an ancient book containing secret knowledge and magic, according to some mystics and occultists. Its actual existence is often considered only a legend, but there are those who claim and believe the book to be authentic and kept hidden by the Illuminati. The tale following the *Book of Thoth* says that the book was buried with an Egyptian Prince named Neferkaptah. This is not to be confused with a book Aleister Crowley published in the mid 1900s titled the *Book of Thoth*, which is a philosophical description of a deck of Tarot cards that Crowley designed called Thoth Tarot.

The respected mystic and philosopher Manly P. Hall wrote, "Nothing definite is known concerning the contents of the Book of Thoth other than its pages were covered with strange hieroglyphic figures and symbols, which gave to those acquainted with their use unlimited power over the spirits of the air and the subterranean divinities. When certain areas of the brain are stimulated by the secret processes of the Mysteries, the consciousness of man is extended and he is permitted to behold the Immortals and enter into the presence of the superior gods. The Book of Thoth described the method whereby this stimulation was accomplished. In truth therefore it was the Key to Immortality."[105]

"The book is still in existence and continues to lead the disciples of this age into the presence of the Immortals. No other information can be given to the world concerning it now, but the apostolic succession from the first hierophant initiated by Hermes himself remains unbroken to his day, and those who are peculiarly fitted to serve the Immortals may discover this priceless document if they will search sincerely and tirelessly for it."[106]

Could such a book actually exist, and could the Illuminati be in possession of it? If so, could the knowledge

---

[105] Hall, Manly P. — *The Secret Teaching of All Ages* page 96
[106] Hall, Manly P. — *The Secret Teaching of All Ages* page 97

contained within its pages be the source of the Illuminati's wisdom and power? It's not absurd to think that such a text does exist and that they are in possession of it. The Illuminati's power comes largely from their ruthlessness and the extent which they go to ensure their goals are achieved, but could they actually have certain information about the nature of reality that aids them in their lives?

While it certainly is possible that such a book contains secrets to reality that were once discovered and documented, another possible scenario, perhaps more likely, is that the myth of such material is used as a way to entice members of the Illuminati and the promise of one day learning the forbidden contents of such a book is constantly dangled as a carrot in front of them and used as a motivator to keep them working in accordance with the organization's goals.

Perhaps the highest levels of the Illuminati are given access to the book if it exists, or perhaps they are the only ones who know that rumors of the book are nothing more than myths, and perpetuate them to their advantage.

The Book of Shadows

The *Book of Shadows* is a popular text in the religion of Wicca which contains various philosophies, rituals, and magical teachings. There are various versions of the book, with the most popular coming from Gerald Gardner, who is considered by most to be the father of Wicca. His 1954 book, *Witchcraft Today* was largely responsible for bringing the religion of Wicca to the public's awareness.

Gardner claimed that he had been initiated into a group, or a coven as they are called, which carried on the tradition of paganism and witchcraft. He said that sections of the book had been passed down through the ages and included writings of witches who were persecuted and killed for their beliefs. Many writings are believed to be inspired from or interpretations of Aleister Crowley's work, or taken from the

Gospel of Witches which was a book published in 1899 written by Charles Godfrey Leland, who claimed to have discovered the book in the 1890s after it had been handed down from an underground tradition of witchcraft in Italy.

Of course almost every scholar doubts these claims, and both Leland and Gardner were frauds and opportunist who wanted to cash in on sales of these supposed authentic underground books and use such claims to increase their prestige among occultists. Gardner explained that students from the past would copy the *Book of Shadows* by hand from a copy allegedly owned by their witchcraft teacher.

In today's fairly educated and modern society such claims appear laughable, and the economic motives clear, but the tradition of occultists claiming to have discovered an ancient text continues to be believed by many as in the case of the *Book of Mormon*, and by the more modern *Necronomicon.*

The Book of Shadows has found its way into various films and television plots, including the fanciful series *Charmed* which stars Shannen Doherty, Allyssa Milano, and Holly Marie Combs, and the 1996 film *The Craft* about a group of four teenage girls who become involved in witchcraft.

The Illuminati Manifesto

In 2001 a man named Solomon Tulbure released a book titled *The Illuminati Manifesto*, claiming to be the Illuminati's goals and philosophy which was now being made public. Only a handful of the most ignorant and gullible individuals actually believed these claims, and unlike similar books claiming to be secret or ancient texts like *The Necronomicon* and *Book of Shadows, The Illuminati Manifesto* failed to catch on and was a miserable dud, with little to anyone believing it was an authentic Illuminati text.

Solomon Tulbure is also the author of *Christianity*

Exposed (2001) which claims that most Christian beliefs are unbiblical and modern Christians follow the teachings of Paul and not Jesus, and that Jesus' teachings are not worthy of our attention and that an alternative to religion is needed. In 2002 he also published, *President G.W. Bush is a Moron: Islam Is NOT Peace*; not exactly a title that would be chosen by an ascended Illuminati master, especially since George W. Bush is in the Illuminati.

The preface for the manifesto reads, "Our vision and goals are clearly spelled out in this abridged version of our Manifesto, the core principles of what we represent. We had hoped to publish an unabridged version of our Manifesto, however, due to recent events and other reasons we have decided it is not yet the proper time to publish all our protocols and perspectives. Perhaps in 50-100 years the rest of our protocols will find a more fertile ground and at such time we will publish an unabridged Manifesto. Nevertheless, in order to squash the many lies that have been written about our organization we thought it necessary to put forth our imprint on the world scene once more."[107]

While it is obvious that *The Illuminati Manifesto* is a poor and unconvincing fraud, the story surrounding Solomon Tulbure does get more interesting though, albeit tragic. In November of 2004 he was found dead after jumping off an interstate overpass in Knoxville, Tennessee. He was 35 years old and apparently he had made a posting on the Internet two years earlier threatening suicide. But Tulbure's sister, Lidia Zotoiu, didn't believe it and claimed he was murdered. "His right hand is bruised. His left hand is full of scratches," she said. "Somebody kill him and bring him under the bridge."[108]

---

[107] Tulbure, Solomon – *The Illuminati Manifesto* page ix-x
[108] Knoxville News Sentinel *Police ID dead man found on interstate* November 19, 2004 by Randy Kenner

When his brother was asked by police if Solomon was mentally disturbed, his brother Israel answered, "I don't know. He could have been because he was very private."[109]

When asked if he thought his brother committed suicide, Israel said, "We don't know how he get from the bridge down there."[110] English was obviously not the family's native language.

Solomon Tulbure had claimed in the past that his life was in danger because of the information he had disclosed on the Internet and in his books.

The more the story unraveled surrounding Tulbure, the more clear it became that he was nothing more than a man trying to hustle up a few dollars using a variety of schemes. Allegedly he was the creator of MyMatchmaker.com, a website attempting to raise money from investors claiming it hoped to have 55 million members within three years. The site, which is no longer online, offered little information other than reading, "We will be more than happy to provide a detailed business plan upon request."

According to his brother, Tulbure made money from day trading and from running various websites and that a month before his death someone from "some type of agency" had been calling the family looking for Solomon and said they were investigating him for Internet fraud. This could have possibly caused or contributed to his decision to commit suicide.

While there are numerous people who are murdered, die in unusual circumstances, or who allegedly commit suicide but are in fact murdered by the FBI, CIA or other agency in order to silence them from telling what they had witnessed in regard to corruption and crime, the case of Solomon Tulbure is a sad case of a man trying to make money off the hysteria

---

[109] Ibid
[110] Ibid

that is often associated with the Illuminati, and perhaps in other illegal and underhanded ways. Upon reading just a few sentences in *The Illuminati Manifesto* it becomes apparent that this individual did not possess any literary skills whatsoever and his fragmented thought patterns clearly reflect a mentally unstable person.

One of the most bizarre, and somewhat amusing things found in Tulbure's book is his talk about how the Illuminati had set up an online dating site for Illuminati swingers. He wrote, "You must also have available documentation proving that you and/or your spouse or lover does not have any STDs. To find other Illuminati or non-Illuminati swingers visit *www.IlluminatiMatchMaker.com* or Swingers.com."[111]

The book is 303 pages long, and is full of random and sometimes incoherent statements. What can be understood from the book is that the author had no compassion for anyone. Found within his fanciful Illuminati Constitution, it reads, "Title V. Requires parents who give birth to disabled people to provide for all the needs of the disabled individual for as long as the disabled has the needs. Requires that government do not provide any financial aids/welfare to the disabled, just because he/she is disabled. Society does not have any obligation to support, raise and feed disabled people."[112]

Tulbure also shows his contempt for all religions, saying "We seek to eliminate all the churches, synagogues and mosques and all those whom brainwash our young with mystical baloney and enslave the minds of men and women with religion and false virtues."[113]

---

[111] Tulbure, Solomon – *The Illuminati Manifesto* page 267
[112] Tulbure, Solomon – *The Illuminati Manifesto* page 266
[113] Tulbure, Solomon – *The Illuminati Manifesto* page xviii

The Book of Dzyan

Another alleged book that is being kept hidden away by the Illuminati is *The Book of Dzyan* which is said to originate from Tibet. Several prominent occult authors claimed to have seen the book and have included various information purporting to come from it in their own works. *The Secret Doctrine* written by Helena Blavatsky is said to be based on the *Book of Dzyan*. Blavatsky claimed to have seen the actual book when she was studying in Tibet and that it was guarded from the "profane" by the Great White Brotherhood. The term "profane" is often used by occultists to describe people who are not a part of an occult hierarchy or secret society.

The Book of Dzyan is said to have been written in the language of Senzar, which is unknown to linguists and said to be a secret language of enlightened masters. Blavatsky wrote in *The Secret Doctrine*, "This first installment of the esoteric doctrines is based upon Stanzas, which are the records of a people unknown to ethnology; it is claimed that they are written in a tongue absent from the nomenclature of languages and dialects with which philology is acquainted; they are said to emanate from a source (Occultism) repudiated by science; and, finally, they are offered through an agency, incessantly discredited before the world by all those who hate unwelcome truths, or have some special hobby of their own to defend. Therefore, the rejection of these teachings may be expected, and must be accepted beforehand. No one styling himself a "scholar," in whatever department of exact science, will be permitted to regard these teachings seriously."[114] (See The Secret Doctrine page 102)

In Alice Bailey's 1925 book *A Treatise on Cosmic Fire*,

---

[114] Blavatsky, Helena – *The Secret Doctrine* Volume 1 page xxxvii

she writes several verses from *The Stanzas of Dzyan* (another name for the *Book of Dzyan*) which she claims were psychically dictated to her by a Tibetan Master named Djwal Kul, who some New Age thinkers believe is an "ascended master" who lives in another dimension outside of human perception. These "ascended masters" are believed by some to be working with and directing the Illuminati.

Some people in New Age circles believe that the *Book of Dzyan* was originally written by the inhabitants of the lost city of Atlantis. Swiss author Erich von Daniken, who believes that aliens from other planets have influenced culture on earth, has said that the *Book of Dzyan* came from extraterrestrials and predates Earth. Fictional writer H.P. Lovecraft, who died on March 15, 1937 at the age of 46, also made references to the *Stanzas of Dzyan* in his novels.

Whether the *Book of Dzyan* actually exists or not is open to debate. Certainly it is possible such a book exists, although its authorship would be uncertain. It is also possible, and perhaps more likely, that the *Book of Dzyan* is the creation of the over-active imaginations of occultists and New Age authors such as Helena Blavatsky and Alice Bailey. Some also believe that these "ascended masters" who such authors claimed to be telepathically in communication with were in reality, idealizations of the mentors of the very occultists who wrote about such beings.

The Report From Iron Mountain

In 1967 a book was published titled, *The Report from Iron Mountain* which was allegedly a leaked document containing the analysis of a government funded think tank which argued the case that perpetual war was needed to fuel the United States economy, and that if a state of world peace would ensue, that it would be devastating for the economy and society. If peace were to happen, the document suggested several actions to ensure a constant state of war would continue. Shortly after *The Report from Iron Mountain* was published in the form of a book, it made the *New York Times* bestseller list and created quite a stir particularly within militia groups and those suspicious of corruption within the government. *The Pentagon Papers,* which were a top-secret history of the United States involvement in Vietnam, were released shortly after which added to peoples fears.

U.S. News and World Report wrote that an unnamed government official had confirmed the authenticity of the documents, and that President Johnson had "hit the roof" when word of the report was made public. The article reported that orders were sent to U.S. embassies around the world saying that the book had nothing to do with U.S. government polices.[115]

Several years later in a 1972 edition of the *New York Times Book Review*, Leonard Lewin took credit as the actual author, saying, "I wrote the "Report," all of it. (How it came about and who was privy to the plot I'll have to discuss elsewhere.) But why as a hoax? What I intended was simply to pose the issues of war and peace in a provocative way. To deal with the essential absurdity of the fact that the war system, however much deplored, is nevertheless accepted as part of the necessary order of things. To caricature the bankruptcy of the think-tank mentality by pursuing its style of scientistic thinking to its logical ends. And perhaps, with luck, to extend the scope of public discussion of "peace planning" beyond its usual, stodgy limits."[116]

Decades later in 1996 Jon Elliston published a book titled, *Report from Iron Mountain: Highbrow Hoax Mocks*

---

[115] U.S. News and World Report *Hoax or Horror? A Book that Shook the White House* November 20, 1967
[116] NY Times Book Review *The Guest Word* Mach 19, 1972 by Leonard Lewin

National Security Speak, which detailed the evolution of the report and the ensuing speculation after its publication.

Some believe the idea for writing it came from Victor Navasky who was the editor of the left wing magazine *The Nation* from 1978 until 1995. Navasky was also the editor of a satirical newspaper called the *Monicle* until it ceased publication in the mid 1960s.

Harvard professor John Kenneth Galbraith added fuel to the controversy when he wrote a book review for the *Washington Post* using the pseudonym "Herschel McLandress," where he said, "As I would put my personal repute behind the authenticity of this document, so would I testify to the validity of its conclusions. My reservations relate only to the wisdom of releasing it to an obviously unconditioned public."[117]

While it is officially classified as a hoax, *The Report from Iron Mountain* contains some chillingly accurate information and predictions about what the future would hold. Keep in mind, the book was published in 1967. If it actually is a hoax, the author had a tremendous amount of knowledge and foresight as you can see by reading an excerpt below which talks about creating a fake alien threat to unite the world, and to push the idea of ecological destruction as a terrible danger and threat to mankind.

The Report reads, "It has been hotly argued that such a menace would offer the "last, best hope of peace," etc., by uniting mankind against the danger of destruction by "creatures" from other planets or from outer space. Experiments have been proposed to test the credibility of an out-of-our-world invasion threat;...nevertheless, an effective political substitute for war would require "alternate enemies," some of which might seem equally farfetched in

---

[117] The Washington Post *News of War and Peace You're Not Ready For* by Herschel McLandress November 26, 1967, p. 5.

THE ILLUMINATI: FACTS & FICTION

the context of the current war system. It may be, for instance, that gross pollution of the environment can eventually replace the possibility of mass destruction by nuclear weapons as the principle apparent threat to the survival of the species. Poisoning of the air, and of the principal sources of food and water supply, is already well advanced, and at the first glance would seem promising in this respect; it constitutes a threat that can be dealt with only through social organization and political power. But from the present indications it will be a generation to a generation and a half before environmental pollution, however severe, will be sufficiently menacing, on a global scale, to offer a possible basis for a solution."[118]

While the idea of an actual alien threat may be far fetched, or the idea of manufacturing one to appear as if it is real equally far fetched, the technology of Project Blue Beam would allow just that to happen using high-tech projection systems to create enormous three dimensional holograms in the sky.[119] Also, decades after *The Report from Iron Mountain* was published, President Ronald Reagan would make a similar remark. On September 21, 1987, he told the United Nations General Assembly, "In our obsession with antagonism of the moment, we often forget how much unites all the members of humanity. Perhaps we need some outside, universal threat to make us recognize this common bond. I occasionally think how quickly our differences worldwide would vanish if we were facing an alien threat from outside this world."

If *The Report from Iron Mountain* is indeed authentic, then the best and pretty much only strategy the government would have to counter its release would be to pay someone

---

[118] Lewin, Leonard – *The Report from Iron Mountain* page 66-67
[119] Washington Post *When Seeing and Hearing Isn't Believing* By William M. Arkin Feb. 1, 1999

to claim authorship and say it was a hoax.

If the document is a hoax, the author had the rare knowledge of the use of false flag terrorist attacks and the strategy of creating enemies and events so that political or military actions may be taken. The report reads, "However unlikely some of the possible alternate enemies we have mentioned may seem, we must emphasize that one must be found, of credible quality and magnitude, if a transition to peace is ever to come about without social disintegration. It is more probable, in our judgment, that such a threat will have to be invented rather than developed from unknown conditions."[120]

Leonard Lewin, who claimed authorship and said it was a hoax, sued several individuals who believed the report was authentic and had reprinted it and were selling it themselves as a way to make money and spread the word about this diabolical plan. Lewin technically had the copyright and was legally entitled to the ownership of the text. Such an action is suspicious if in fact the document was authentic because one may think Lewin would want the document to become public domain and spread to as many people as possible. However, some suspect that the legal action was taken as a way to intimidate patriots who were spreading awareness of the report and that Lewin's supposed admission that he was the author was not the truth, and was instead an attempt at damage control to disarm the public and persuade them the report was a hoax, when in reality it was authentic.

In 1996 the book was released again with an Afterward written by Leonard Lewin where he discussed how he was surprised that word continued to spread about the report decades after its initial release. This new edition also includes several articles that were written about the report when it was first released. The Forward to the 1996 book

[120] Lewin, Leonard – *The Report from Iron Mountain* page 67

was written by Victor Navasky where he explains how he and Lewin allegedly concocted the idea for money, believing the book would sell due to the controversy it would cause.

Whatever the truth is regarding *The Report from Iron Mountain*, some its contents turned out to be chillingly accurate in regards to what the future would hold even though it was written over forty years ago. There are already plenty of authentic declassified documents, government white papers, and mainstream reports which confirm similar or even more sinister operations than the ones found in *The Report from Iron Mountain*. So the authenticity of the report isn't that important, but when one is presenting information about false flag terrorism or fear mongering surrounding climate change, one is best advised to use confirmed and reputable sources, instead of *The Report from Iron Mountain*.

Protocols of the Elders of Zion

Another document that is classified as a hoax yet has elements which clearly reflect reality is *The Protocols of the Elders of Zion*. The document surfaced in 1903 in Russia and was written to make it seem as if it was a plan drawn up by a powerful group of Jews who had formulated strategies to take over the world and maintain dominance. The document is still believed to be authentic by some, including anti-Semites, and is referenced as evidence of Jewish control of the New World Order. (See Why are the Jews Always Blamed? page 25)

While many of the Protocols are seemingly accurate with regards to their strategies to maintain control over economies, media, and politics, it appears the author went to great lengths to include wording that overtly illustrates the diabolical nature of the document and its supposed creator, the Jews, in an attempt to demonize them. It gratuitously emphasizes several points to give the impression to the reader that the document outlined malicious intentions by Jews. Even documents which are 100% legitimate that outline diabolical schemes such as Operation Northwoods, use a very matter of fact language and do not brag in excess about the brilliance of the plans, or their insidious nature. Such language in the Protocols can clearly be seen as a way to brand the Jews as the ones pulling the strings in a conspiracy.

When first published in Russia in 1903, the Protocols rapidly made their way around the world and continue to be circulated in print and on the Internet today. The supposed original manuscript never surfaced, which cast a shadow of doubt on the authenticity of the Protocols. While some have claimed to see the original document, the material is classified as a literary forgery deliberately designed to smear the Jews as the puppet masters behind a conspiracy to rule the world. During the rise of Adolf Hitler, the Protocols were used to enflame hatred against the Jews, and lent more support for the Third Reich by the Germans.

When the Protocols are read and the word "Jew" is replaced with "the Illuminati" the plans and the methods found in the document still ring true today. Several excerpts from the 24 different Protocols are listed below to illustrate this point. The original author of the Protocols was most likely inspired from John Robison's *Proofs of a Conspiracy* which was published in 1798. (See Proofs of a Conspiracy page 47)

Excerpt from Protocol 1

"It must be noted that men with bad instincts are more in number than the good, and therefore the best results in governing them are attained by violence and terrorization, and not by academic discussions...Behold the alcoholised animals, bemused with drink, the right to an immoderate use of which comes along with freedom. It is not for us and ours to walk that road. The peoples of the goyim are bemused with alcoholic liquors; their youth has grown stupid on classicism and from early immorality, into which it has been inducted by our special agents—by tutors, lackeys, governesses in the houses of the wealthy, by clerks and others, by our women in the places of dissipation frequented by the goyim. In the number of these last I count also the so-called "society ladies," voluntary followers of the others in corruption and luxury."

Excerpt from Protocol 2

"Through the Press we have gained the power to influence while remaining ourselves in the shade; thanks to the Press we have got the gold in our hands, notwithstanding that we have had to gather it out of oceans of blood and tears."

Excerpt from Protocol 3

"We shall create this crises by all the secret subterranean methods open to us and with the aid of Gold, which is all in our hands: a universal economic crises whereby we shall throw upon the streets whole mobs of workers simultaneously in all the countries of Europe."

"These mobs will rush delightedly to shed the blood of those whom, in the simplicity of their ignorance, they have envied from an early age, and whose property they will then be able to loot."

"Ours they will not touch, because the moment of attack will be known to us and we shall take measures to protect our own."

Excerpt from Protocol 4

"Gentile masonry blindly serves as a screen for us and our objects, but the plan of action of our force, even its very abiding-place, remains for the whole people an unknown mystery."

"...it is indispensable for us to undermine all faith, to tear out of the minds of the goyim the very principle of Godhead and the spirit, and to put in its place arithmetical calculations and material needs. In order to give the goyim no time to think and take note, their minds must be diverted towards industry and trade. Thus, all the nations will be swallowed up in the pursuit of gain and in the race for it will not take note of their common foe."

Excerpt from Protocol 5

"In place of the rulers of today we shall set up a bogey which will be called the Super-Government Administration. Its hands will reach in all direction like nippers and its organization will be of such colossal dimensions that it cannot fail to subdue all the nations of the world."

Excerpt from Protocol 6

"We shall soon begin to establish huge monopolies, reservoirs of colossal riches, upon which even large fortunes of the goyim will depend to such an extent that they will go to the bottom together with the credit of the states on the day after the political smash."

Excerpt from Protocol 7

"The intensification of armaments, the increase of police forces—are all essential for the completion of the aforementioned plans."

Excerpt from Protocol 8

"Our directorate must surround itself with all these forces of civilization among which it will have to work. It will surround itself with publicists, practical jurists, administrators, diplomats and, finally, with persons prepared by a special super-educational training in our special schools. These persons will have cognisance of all the secrets of the social structure, they will know all the languages that can be made up by political alphabets and words; they will be made acquainted with the whole underside of human nature, with all its sensitive chords on which they will have to play."

Excerpt from Protocol 10

"We are destroying the causes of your torment—nationalities, frontiers, differences of coinages....we shall destroy among the goyim the importance of the family and its educational value and remove the possibility of individual minds splitting off, for the mob, handled by us, will not let them come to the front nor even give them a hearing; it is accustomed to listen to us only who pay it for obedience and attention. In this way we shall create a blind, mighty force which will never be in a position to move in any direction without guidance of our agents set at its head by us as leaders of the mob. The people will submit to the regime because it will know that upon these leaders will depend its earnings, gratifications and the receipts of all kinds of benefits."

Excerpt from Protocol 11

"There is another reason also why they will close their eyes: for we shall keep promising them to give back all the liberties we have taken away as soon as we have quelled the enemies of peace and tamed all parties."

Excerpt from Protocol 12

"Not a single announcement will reach the public

without our control. Even now this is already being attained by us inasmuch as the news items are received by a few agencies, in whose offices they are focused from all parts of the world. These agencies will then be already entirely ours and will give publicity only to what we dictate to them."

Excerpt from Protocol 13

"When we come into our kingdom our orators will expound great problems which have turned humanity upside down in order to bring it at the end under our beneficent rule. Who will ever suspect then that all these peoples were stage-managed by us according to a political plan which no one has so much as guessed at in the course of many centuries?

Excerpt from Protocol 14

"Our philosophers will discuss all the shortcomings of the various beliefs of the goyim, but no one will ever bring under discussion our faith from its true point of view since this will be fully learned by none save ours, who will never dare to betray its secrets."

The Holy Grail

The Holy Grail is frequently believed to be a cup that was used by Jesus at the Last Supper, which was the final meal he had before being taken into custody by the Romans and crucified. Aside from people believing it is an ancient artifact, some believe that it contains supernatural powers and can bestow them onto whoever possesses the Grail. Others believe that the Holy Grail is not a cup, but that it is an ancient parchment containing writings which explain the mysteries of the Universe and God. Others still insist that the Holy Grail actually refers to a bloodline of Jesus and

THE ILLUMINATI: FACTS & FICTION

Mary Magdalene and believe the two were married and had a child, and that the bloodline remains to this day and is hidden and protected by secret societies. No definitive information is available about any such theories, and there is a continuing debate about what the Grail is, or if it even exists at all.

Such legends often include the Knights Templar, and some suspect that whatever the Grail is, that the Knights Templar obtained it from their excavations under Solomon's Temple during their time there, and it continues to be in the possession of the modern day Illuminati.

Whatever the Holy Grail actually is, and if it still exists today remains a mystery. However, the Knights Templar learned their strange occult rituals from somewhere after they had established themselves in Jerusalem in the 12th century. And the same is true with their knowledge of banking and collecting interest, a practice which is still used today by the Federal Reserve Bank which was created by the Illuminati. (See The Creature from Jekyll Island page 95) Therefore it is not baseless speculation that the Templars did indeed find some ancient scrolls where they learned such things from. The discovery of the Dead Sea Scrolls between 1947 and 1956 verify the fact that similar information had been written down and hidden, only to be found hundreds of years later.

The Knights Templar are known as a military order of supposed Christian warrior monks who protected Christian peasants as they traveled to the Holly Land in Jerusalem starting around 1196. They were called the Knights Templar because they used the site of Solomon's Temple as their headquarters.

As a closer look was taken at the Templars, many believe that they had an ulterior motive for staying at the temple. Evidence proves that they were secretly excavating under the temple for treasure. Many believe what they were after was not only gold, but some hidden documents as well.

152

Some believe that these documents contain the family tree and a bloodline of Jesus, a fraud that was popularized by Dan Brown's book *The Da Vinci Code*. (See Angels and Demons page 312)

Others believe that these documents held some kind of mystical secrets about life and the nature of reality and the spiritual laws of the world and the workings of God. This is what many occultists believe is actually the Holy Grail.

The king of France, King Philip IV, eventually accused the Templars of being Satanists and had their leadership and as many Templars he could find arrested in 1307. While many people today defend the Templars, and believe the king had simply made up the accusations as a reason to confiscate their wealth, most prominent occultists openly admit that the Templars had learned magic rituals, and were indeed in possession of esoteric mystical knowledge.

Eliphas Levi, a prominent 19th century occultist writes, "What was actually this secret and potent association which imperiled Church and State, and was thus destroyed unheard? Judge nothing lightly; they are guilty of a great crime; they have exposed to profane eyes the sanctuary of antique initiation. They have gathered again and have shared the fruits of the tree of knowledge, so they might become masters of the world."[121]

Among the accusations, the Templars were said to have done satanic rituals involving a person's decapitated head, called Baphomet. Levi admits, "Yes, in our profane conviction, the Grand Masters of the Order of the Templars worshipped the Baphomet, and caused it to be worshipped by their initiates."[122]

Manly P. Hall writes, "The famous hermaphroditic Goat of Mendes was a composite creature formulated to

[121] Levi, Eliphas – *Transcendental Magic* p. 7-8
[122] Levi, Eliphas – *Transcendental Magic* p. 307

symbolize this *astral light*. It is identical with Baphomet, the mystic *pantheos* of those disciples of ceremonial magic, the Templars, who probably obtained it from the Arabians."[123]

Christopher Knight and Robert Lomas explain in *The Book of Hiram*, "Hence it follows that the mysteries of the craft are in reality the mysteries of religion. The Knights were, however, careful not to entrust this important secret to any whose fidelity and discretion had not been fully proved. They therefore invented different degrees to test their candidates, and gave them only symbolical secrets without explanation, to prevent treachery and solely to enable them to make themselves known to each other. For this purpose it was resolved to use different signs, words and tokens in each degree, by which they would be secured against the Saracens, cowans or intruders."[124]

Eliphas Levi confirms this in his 1913 book *The History of Magic*, writing, "The Templars had two doctrines; one was concealed and reserved to the leaders, being that of Johannism; the other was public, being Roman Catholic doctrine. They deceived in this manner the enemies that they hoped to supplant. The Johannism of the adepts was the Kabalah of the Gnostics, but it degenerated speedily into a mystic pantheism carried even to idolatry of Nature and hatred of all revealed dogma...They went even so far as to recognize the pantheistic symbolism of the grand masters of Black Magic, and the better to isolate themselves from obedience to a religion by which they were condemned before, they rendered divine honors to the monstrous idol Baphomet."[125]

The Knights Templar are believed to have created Freemasonry and incorporated their mystical teachings into

---

[123] Hall, Manly P. – *The Secret Teachings of All Ages* p. 316
[124] Night & Lomas – *The Book of Hiram* p. 434
[125] Levi, Eliphas – *History of Magic* p. 211

the organization, which, like the Templars, contains a secret doctrine for the inner circle of elite adepts and dispense lies to lower level members about the true meanings of symbols and about the teachings and occult beliefs hidden at the core. (See Morals and Dogma page 70)

Alleged Defectors and Victims

In the fairly recent past several individuals have come forward and made claims that they were former members of the Illuminati and have left the organization and decided to write books and give lectures exposing them. Others have made similar claims, only instead of saying they were members, they say that they were victims of experiments and mind control techniques that were directed by the Illuminati. As bizarre or far fetched as some of their claims may seem, if one is familiar with declassified government programs, some allegations are not unrealistic. Despite what some may consider fanciful tales, or even delusions, some of these alleged defectors and victims have made headlines and developed a fair amount of supporters.

Others have had many of their claims exposed as exaggerations or blatant lies upon further examination. Others yet, remain in the realm of possibly being true. These stories have become a part of the folklore surrounding the Illuminati and the occult, and warrant mentioning and being analyzed as we sift through the facts and fiction of the Illuminati.

John Todd

John Todd, also known as "John Todd Collins" or "Lance Collins" was one of the first, if not the first person to claim to be a former member of the Illuminati in modern times.

In the late 1970s Todd began a series of speaking engagements at various evangelical Churches and organizations in what he said was his mission to expose the workings and plans of the Illuminati. He claimed to be a high level member who decided to become a Christian in 1972, and leave the organization. At this time there were several others who were claiming to be former Satanists turned Christians and were now trying to warn people about the occult, but Todd actually claimed to be a high level Illuminati member himself, and not just someone who dabbled in the occult.

By listening to the recorded speeches he gave, he did know a fair amount about the Illuminati, their symbolism, and their organizations and operations. Several hours of his lectures are available on the Internet in mp3s. John Todd is actually a fairly dynamic and confident speaker. He speaks with authority, and sounds like he is extremely knowledgeable on the Illuminati. It's important to note that in the 1970s, hardly anyone knew anything about the Illuminati or the New World Order. There was no Internet that anyone could use to quickly look up his claims and very few books had been published on such material. As we dissect John Todd's claims and cross examine them with what we now know to be true about Freemasonry and the Illuminati, most of them completely fall apart and are undoubtedly a series of fabrications and lies. Despite being a fraud, the legend of John Todd is fascinating to explore and he proves to be a very talented story teller or possibly a very persuasive compulsive liar.

John Todd appeared on the scene in the late 1970s shortly after Gary Allen's book, *None Dare Call It Conspiracy* was published in 1972 which brought the Illuminati conspiracy out in the open again after it had laid dormant since the 1920s and 30s with the publication of *Secret Societies and Subversive Movements* by Nesta Webster, and *Occult Theocrasy* by Edith Miller. These books were the primary sources of Todd's information, and he made reference to Allen during one of his speeches which can be heard on the Internet. (See None Dare Call It Conspiracy page 62) (See Secret Societies and Subversive Movements page 56) (See Occult Theocrasy page 59)

The other source John Todd had learned about the

Illuminati from was Myron Fagan's audio recordings which were released in the late 1960s. (See Myron Fagan page 208) Todd basically regurgitated information about the Illuminati that he learned from Allen and Fagan's work, but presented it as if he had first hand knowledge of it from being personally involved.

One of Todd's claims that deviated from the typical Illuminati takeover plan was that he alleged when he was in the Illuminati he oversaw eight million dollars that was given to Pastor Chuck Smith, founder of Cavalry Chapel, for the purpose of launching the Christian Rock industry. Todd claimed that the lyrics didn't matter, and that the music had a demonic beat that was being used to brainwash the listeners. He also claimed that Jerry Falwell had been bought off by the Illuminati with a fifty million dollar donation.

Another bizarre claim unique to Todd was that the novel *Atlas Shrugged* by Ayn Rand was supposedly written in code specifically for Illuminati members as a blueprint for their world takeover, and that only Illuminati members were supposed to read the book and the publishers were concerned that the book had become so popular since it would give away the Illuminati's plan.

More red flags continue to come up the more one listens to Todd. He referred to *The Necronomicon* as being a real book that he once saw and held in his hand when he was an Illuminist. *The Necronomicon* is a fictional book that was mentioned several times in the writings of 1920's horror writer H.P. Lovecraft. Todd kept calling the Necronomicon, the Necro*mon*icon. Several times during his speech, he mispronounced the name of this book. One would think that a high level Illuminati member would know the proper pronunciation of this sacred book. He called it the original occult bible.

"There are only three copies in existence today. One is in the town…in the Saint Petersburg cathedral in the USSR. One is in New York City, no I'm sorry. One is in Glasgow and one is in London. I saw....the one from the London museum was in New York for a while and I got to look at it and hold it when I was in the occult," he said as he stumbled over his words quite extensively when trying to explain his alleged contact with the book.

In H.P. Lovecraft's novels it is said that there are only five copies in existence, an idea that Todd essentially parroted as he tried to describe the book to one of his audiences. No such book was ever at the London museum, or any museum for that matter, and Todd's claims of holding it in his hand was completely unpractical. In 1973, several years before John Todd began speaking about the Illuminati, a man claiming that he had discovered the real Necronomicon published what was an obvious hoax and an attempt to cash in on the legend of the book. (See The Necronomicon page 129)

Aside from not seeming very clear on several aspects of the Illuminati, and claiming to have seen an actual copy of *The Necronomicon*, Todd also claimed to have been a Green Beret in the Vietnam War. As more people investigated Todd's allegations, it was discovered that he was a general clerk/typist. When confronted with this discovery, he claimed that the Illuminati must have altered his records in an attempt to discredit him. He would frequently claim his life was in danger and that numerous attempts had been made to have him killed.

John Todd had pieced together various quotes and secret society history, and organized it into what sounded like an honest confession, but any modern student of the Illuminati can clearly see Todd for the fraud that he was. In one of his speeches he said, "I'm going to read you the initiation to become a member of the council of 33, the 3rd, or actually the second highest council within the Masons, I mean within the Illuminati." He then goes on to read, "When the Mason learns that the key to the warrior on the block is the proper application of the dynamo of living power, he has learned the mystery of his Craft. The seething energies of Lucifer are in his hands and before he may step onward and upward, he must prove his ability to properly handle energy." This is not the initiation into any level of Freemasonry or the Illuminati, but rather a quote from page 124 of Manly P. Hall's book *The Lost Keys of Freemasonry.*

In a recording titled *John Todd explains the Illuminati,* that can be heard on YouTube, he says, "When I was saved I complained....or not when...(mumbling) what am I saying, what am I saying, when I was saved? I didn't find this out until I was saved. When I was in the occult, I complained at our council meeting because the 33rd council had so much power and I felt it was unjust because I had proven myself so greatly to Lucifer."

In this same speech he also claims to read a passage from the Masonic book *Morals and Dogma*, but actually reads an alleged letter from Albert Pike to the 33rd degree inspectors generals which is not found anywhere in *Morals and Dogma.* He also uses the terms "The Trilateral Council," and the "Council of Foreign Affairs," to refer to Illuminati organizations, when their actual names are the Trilateral Commission, not council, and the Council on Foreign Relations, not affairs.

Another bizarre statement that can be heard on the Internet postings of his lectures are his claims that the credit card was the mark of the Beast, and almost all license plates in Israel start with the number 666.

He said that the Illuminati had planned to confiscate all guns within a year and a half and were going to remove the tax exempt status of churches unless they belonged to the World Council of Churches, and that all church members would have their name, address, and phone number published in post offices in their town so that everyone would know who and where all the Christians were so they could eventually be rounded up and killed. Also, he warned that people will soon be charged with murder if they convert someone to Christianity, and that the New World Order would be created by 1980.

While it is still common, and a good idea to have a food supply in your home that will sustain you and your family for several weeks in case of an emergency, Todd claimed that an anti-hording act would soon be passed saying people couldn't store more than one month's supply of food or they will go to prison for a year.

One of the most blatant lies that anyone who has studied the Illuminati would see as preposterous was that Todd repeatedly said he was a member of the ultra elite Council of 13, which is actually comprised of the 13 heads of the top 13 families of the Illuminati. A broke nobody like John Todd, even if he were actually a member of the Illuminati, would not be anywhere close to such a prestigious level of the hierarchy. Such positions are filled by wealthy titans like the Rockefellers and Rothschilds.

In the 1970s when Todd was giving his speeches, not only was little known about the Illuminati to the public, but there was no Internet for anyone to use to investigate his claims, so since some of what he was saying sounded plausible to his audience, a thorough examination of his claims would prove extremely difficult during that time period.

Jack Chick, one of the most published comic book artists in the world ended up creating a comic book called *The Broken Cross* which was based on Todd's allegations, and in 1980 Jacob Sailor also published a comic book based on Todd's supposed knowledge of the Illuminati. Chick had publicly defended Todd as others began to question his truthfulness.

A Christian Identity group called The Covenant, The Sword, and the Arm of the Lord (CSA) published a book titled *Witchcraft and the Illuminati* which used some of Todd's claims as evidence of the Illuminati. The book also incorporated and supported the serpent seed theory and attacked Jews and African Americans as being spawn of Satan. (See Why are the Jews Always Blamed? page 25)

In 1973 allegations were being made that John Todd had sex with two teenage girls he met while working at a coffeehouse, carried a .38 handgun into church meetings, and was using drugs.[126] After he and his claims came under more fire, some Christian leaders who once promoted him started to distance themselves or outright denounced him.

While not actually being a member of the Illuminati, apparently Todd was involved with Wicca, and in 1976 he temporarily held a charter of Watchers Church of Wicca, but after it was discovered that he had been charged with having oral sex with a minor in Dayton, Ohio, Gavin Frost revoked the charter he had granted to Todd's coven of Frost's Church and School of Wicca.[127]

In 1979 Todd was arrested and later convicted for statutory rape and transporting a minor across a state line. Of course, he claimed he was innocent and set up by the Illuminati as payback for him exposing them, and that they used the charges as a way to silence him.

Several Christian ministries investigated Todd's claims of his background and discovered gaping discrepancies and fantastic lies. The magazines *Christianity Today*, and *Cornerstone* did their own investigations and published articles exposing him.[128]

John Todd often spoke with such conviction that he was able to fool a fair amount of people into believing him. His charisma overshadowed his claims, some of which even in the 70s should have seemed ridiculous to his audience. By reading some of the comments on YouTube videos featuring audio of Todd's speeches, it sadly shows that still today

---

[126] *Christianity Today* February 2,1979 The Legend(s) of John Todd
[127] Ibid
[128] Cornerstone Magazine *The John Todd Story* by Gary Metz [Issue 48]

some gullible listeners believe his story to be true.

In closing this analysis of John Todd, I will add several more preposterous claims to his long list of lies, just in case anyone still thinks he was telling the truth about being a former member of the Illuminati. For example he claimed that the highest degree in Freemasonry was the 35th degree, when in fact it is the 33rd degree. He said that the entire cast of the film *Star Wars,* which had just been released at the time, were all witches and that one million people joined witchcraft as a result of the film. He said he knew this because he was friends with the "head of publicity" for the film. Also, "the entire cast" of the popular soap operas at the time, *The Young and the Restless,* and *All My Children,* were witches. He told his audience that the Illuminati bought Smith and Weston and purposefully made the guns poor quality so they would "blow up in your face" because they didn't want the people to be armed. Aside from saying that both the secular and Christian music industries were controlled by Satan, he said that before an album was mass produced, that a group of 13 witches would cast a spell on the master copy and that all copies made from it would be possessed with demons.

Bill Schnoebelen

Another man claiming to be a former member of the Illuminati is William Schnoebelen as he recounts in his 1993 book *Lucifer Dethroned.* He is the author of seven books, including *Masonry Beyond the Light* (1991), *Wicca: Satan's Little White Lie* (1990), *Space Invaders* (2003) which is only 120 pages and talks about UFOs, *Blood on the Doorposts: An Advanced Course in Spiritual Warfare* (1994) which was written with his wife Sharon, and *Mormonism's Temple of Doom* (1987) which is only 79 pages. He has also appeared in several films including *Riddles In Stone,* and *Interview with an Ex-Vampire.*

Schnoebelen is an interesting character with white hair and a long white beard, looking somewhat like a wizard out of the *Lord of the Rings* movies, which is perhaps a deliberate style he adheres to for reasons that will become obvious as you learn more about him. He claims to be a former 32nd degree Freemason and a Shriner. He shows a photo of himself in the Shriner hat, where he looks much younger, and he has what he claims to be his certificate showing he had achieved the 32nd degree level of Freemasonry. This could very well be true. He says he was a former member of the Church of Satan and also shows a letter signed by Anton LaVey welcoming him to the group. This is also possible, as the Church of Satan does have an application that people fill out and send in to become a member. Since someone familiar with the occult would know the true possibilities of the teachings found within Freemasonry, it is certainly not far fetched that a member of the Church of Satan would want to join the Masons to further his occult knowledge. Now let's examine the more far fetched claims that Schnoebelen has been making.

One of the most popular speeches Schnoebelen has given which includes his testimony on why he allegedly left the Illuminati and became a born again Christian, is in the video *Exposing the Illuminati from Within* which can be viewed on Google Video and YouTube. In his nearly three hour lecture, Schnoebelen goes through his supposed credentials when he was climbing the ranks in witchcraft and satanic circles, until ultimately he claims he was inducted into the Illuminati.

Schnoebelen is a very knowledgeable speaker. Most of what he talks about has been essentially considered factual by researchers of the Illuminati and the New World Order. He talks about how there is an agenda to demoralize society and indoctrinate the youth into a culture of immortality. He details some of the philosophy of Freemasonry and its connection to the web of secret societies and mentions the usual suspects such as the Knights Templars and Aleister Crowley.

But just when you start thinking that this is a legitimate guy, his credibility starts to rapidly erode. One of the growing list of far fetched claims he makes is that at one point in time in order to join the Illuminati, he had to have sex with a demon as part of his initiation into the second highest level.

Schnoebelen says, "What this means is you have to have sex with a fallen angel. And this is a very appalling and bizarre process, and it really nearly destroys every human being who has to go through it. It nearly killed me. I went through a formal marriage with a fallen angelic being. And of course you understand there is a Biblical principle at work here which Satan is using. And that is when you have sex with someone, you become one flesh with that person. And what happens at that point is, you become so demon possessed that it's like burbling up here around your eyeballs. I had more demons per cubic centimeter than the entire city of Indianapolis, let me tell you. And the result of that is you just become a pretty vile, evil person."[129]

Now, there are four different ways to look at this claim. One is that he is making this up in order to create a unique point in his story and get people talking about him so he can sell more books and make more money off of his lecture circuit. Two, he is an insane person and actually believes that he had sex with the demon in his own mind. Three, the organization he was a part of actually concocted a bizarre ritual in which he was given a hallucinogenic drug (LSD or peyote) and had sex with a woman who was dressed up in a costume, and he was so high that he thought he actually was having sex with a demon. Or four, one might believe that he

---

[129] Schnoebelen, William – *Exposing the Illuminati from Within* (1:26:10)

actually did have sex with a demon and that he is telling the truth.

His claims of having sex with a demon are actually quite tame compared to what he says in another video titled *Interview with an Ex-Vampire*, where he states that within in the vampire subculture, human vampires exist and indeed grow fangs to feed off of human blood. A small subculture of "vampires" actually does exist, but they are not walking dead who turn into bats and sleep in coffins. They are a small minority of the gothic subculture who do drink animal or human blood as part of their lifestyle. Usually they do not kill people for this blood, but they have friends and fellow "vampires" willingly give up a pint of blood for consumption, or they purchase animal blood from butcher shops and consume it. But Schnoebelen takes this idea to an absurd extreme, claiming that to become a "real" vampire, he drank the blood of a fallen angel and was then able to grow fangs which would retract when he was not "feeding." He says as a result of "becoming a vampire" that he couldn't go outside during the day because his skin would blister, and that he had to get a third shift job because he could only go outside at night.

Now, this author (Mark Dice) certainly has an open mind. Many things that I now know as indisputable facts, I would have considered exaggerations or paranoid delusions in the past before I had seen enough evidence that came from reliable sources. While it is certainly possible that Schnoebelen was a Satanist and high level Freemason, or even a member of the Illuminati, one has to see his claims of becoming a vampire as completely 100% fraudulent, and his claims of having sex with a fallen angel as highly suspicious and unlikely.

While it is my conviction that the Illuminati continues to exist today, that they follow a satanic philosophy complete with rituals and on some levels murder, human sacrifice, and child rape, none of the so-called former Illuminati members have offered much evidence of their alleged involvement, other than information that has been circulating in anti New World Order literature for decades.

One motive is always that of money. Another is the purpose of spreading disinformation by mixing facts with fiction in order to make those who believe in the Illuminati seem like they are all conspiracy theorists or science fiction nuts. Perhaps some who make false claims about being a former Illuminati member actually believe that they are helping *The Resistance*, in that they are getting people's attention and educating them about other real issues involving the New World Order and the occult. Another motive is simply that of attention. And yet another is that of personal entertainment on behalf of some and their friends by fooling people into believing their claims and watching the news spread on the Internet like an urban legend.

The fact that Schnoebelen is the author of seven different books on the subject of the occult, one may have a better understanding of his motives for exaggerations and outright lies about his involvement in such activities. In his video *Interview with an Ex-Vampire*, Schnoebelen admits that he never had a steady career and that most of his adult life he moved from one dead end job to another. After college, he began working as a music teacher at a Catholic school, but was fired and then, in his own words says he "had numerous, basically menial jobs until, really after I got saved. I never really had a super duper job. I worked in a foundry for a while, I was as a security guard, I worked for the *Milwaukee Sentinel* as a person who went around and filled up the boxes at night with newspapers, so that was basically my wonderful career."[130] He also admits that he was a cocaine addict and later worked as a drug counselor when he got clean. So in his own words, he never had a

---

[130] Schnoebelen, Bill – *Interview with an Ex-Vampire* (part 1, 23:33)

career until he got saved, which means, until he became a Christian. As you now know, this new career he had discovered was that of writing books about the occult, while fabricating and exaggerating large portions of his life in order to create a compelling and attention-getting story.

While large portions of his lecture *Exposing the Illuminati from Within* are based on historic facts and philosophies, which Schnoebelen then mixes with his own fantasies and distortions, his *Interview with an Ex-Vampire* begins with a series of absurdities which even the most gullible and uneducated person should see as fictions. The interview starts with him recounting numerous supposed experiences from his past as he studied the occult, all of which get more absurd than the next. He begins with tales of haunted houses and ghosts throwing silverware in the kitchen, and later claims that a friend of his disappeared before his eyes in a magic circle during an occult ritual performed in a garage and never returned.

One can't help but see a pathetic old man telling ghost stories as if they had actually happened to him, or a delusional schizophrenic who was once so absorbed with such stories, that now his mind can't distinguish them from reality. There is also an eerie look of joy and excitement on his face when he tells his stories, probably from his own amusement that his audience is listening to him as if his fantastic tales were real, but instead the man is a walking, talking fictional novel.

While a completely honest and well meaning person may unknowingly exaggerate or inaccurately convey details from personal experiences from their past, Schnoebelen's claims far exceed any standard of objectivity or credibility and upon even the brief examination found here it should be clear that he is not an authentic Illuminati defector and is a complete fraud.

THE ILLUMINATI: FACTS & FICTION

Mike Warnke

In the 1970s a man named Mike Warnke became one of the most popular experts on Satanism after having claimed to be a former satanic high priest who converted to Christianity. He detailed his alleged satanic activity in his 1978 book, *The Satanic Seller*. Warnke ended up working with the traveling evangelist Morris Cerullo as he taught Christians the dangers of Satanism.

In 1991 the Christian magazine *Cornerstone* investigated his claims, the same magazine which had shown John Todd to be a fraud. Mike Hertenstein and Jon Trott interviewed over one hundred personal friends and acquaintances of Warnke's and looked over his ministry's tax receipts. Just as many suspected, they discovered dramatic inconsistencies, and the publication of their article would be the undoing of Warnke's career.

Warnke had claimed that while he was a satanic high priest, that he had waist-length hair and long fingernails, but *Cornerstone* magazine obtained pictures of him from that time period and his appearance wasn't anything like he claimed. The article labeled him a typical "square" of the 1960s.

Warnke also claimed that when he was a Satanist he had attended a satanic ritual with Charles Manson, but it turns out Manson was in prison during that time period for a crime preceding and unrelated to the infamous Tate/LaBianca murders in 1969. Hertenstein and Trott also discovered that Warnke was involved with the college Christian group Campus Crusade for Christ, although he claimed he had never been involved with Christianity until years later when he joined the Navy.

Mike Hertenstein, one of the writers for the 1991 *Cornerstone* article, later published a book titled *Selling Satan: The Evangelical Media and the Mike Warnke Scandal* which exposed Warnke in more detail, and analyzed how he was able to uphold his charade for as long as he did.

While Warnke didn't claim to be a member of the Illuminati, he serves as an example of someone who had successfully, for a period of time, fooled segments of the Christian community that he was involved in Satanism, and duped them into believing his stories of rituals and mysticism.

In today's "anything goes" morally bankrupt society, people wouldn't be surprised by someone being a satanic priest. In fact many people would think it was cool, but back in the late 1970s and early 80s a "satanic panic" had spread across America and many people feared that secret societies of Satanists were sexually abusing and sacrificing children.

Cathy O'Brien

In 1995 a woman named Cathy O'Brien published a book titled *Trance Formation of America*, where she claimed to be a victim of the government's mind control program, MK-ULTRA, and was essentially a sex slave for wealthy politicians. While MK-ULTRA was (and probably still is) a top secret program involving sexual abuse, torture, drugging, and hypnotism as methods for brainwashing and mind control techniques, her allegations come under a cloud of suspicion.

Trance Formation of America is quite strange and disturbing, and is written in the form of almost a narrative, including long passages of dialog that O'Brien claims to have remembered. She says that during the mind control sessions she developed dissociative identity disorder, which used to be classified as multiple personality disorder, and that one of her "alters" had a photographic memory and could recall every conversation that occurred in her presence during the years of her captivity and abuse.

O'Brien claims that some of her abusers were George H.W. Bush, Ronald Reagan, Gerald Ford, Jimmy Carter,

Dick Cheney, and Hillary Clinton. She says that she was rescued in 1988 by a man named Mark Phillips who claims to be a former CIA operative. Also a part of the story is O'Brien's daughter Kelly who was also said to be a victim of this program.

What makes O'Brien's allegations seem believable to some, is the fact that mind control programs like MK-ULTRA have been exposed, and that the aims of such experiments included some unthinkable practices including torture, mind-altering drugs, sexual abuse, and hypnotism. Some of the actual goals of this program were to create mind controlled slaves or Manchurian Candidates, who would willingly accept and carry out any order given to them regardless of what it was. There are authentic declassified documents which outline these horrific practices and several victims have been awarded financial settlements for their abuse, so some believe that Cathy O'Brien could be another actual victim of such programs. During a press conference, President Bill Clinton publicly admitted that, "thousands of government sponsored experiments did take place, at hospitals, universities and military bases around our nation. Some were unethical, not only by today's standards, but by the standards of the time in which they were conducted."[131]

Adding to the controversy over O'Brien's claims is that in her book she recalls that she was taken to the Bohemian Grove and sexually abused inside the resort. Similar allegations have been made by Senator John DeCamp as he wrote in his book, *The Franklin Cover-Up*. Numerous children have come forward saying that they were sexually abused in the Bohemian Grove and were forced to participate in child pornography and snuff films, allegations that Ted Gunderson, former Senior Special Agent In Charge of the Los Angels FBI confirms. So such abuse has been alleged to

---

[131] YouTube: *Bill Clinton Admits Government Mind Control Experiments*

occur in the past, and by young children with no books to sell, and who are not even aware of what the Bohemian Grove is, or who its membership consists of. So one must carefully consider whether O'Brien herself was a victim as well, or if she is just another in a line of frauds making such claims in an attempt to sell books and lectures.

In her speeches, O'Brien has claimed that a smiley face was carved on the inside of her vagina using an X-Acto knife for the pleasure of her abusers. In a documentary film called *The Most Dangerous Game*, produced by the Guerilla News Network in 2002, the film makers took her to a gynecologist and had her examined, and to the doctor's surprise, there did appear to be such a thing. The film showed extremely graphic video and photos of the examination in an attempt to prove her allegations. Skeptics may view the existence of such a thing as a natural anomaly that was discovered by one of her lovers, which she then included in her story of being a victim of MK-ULTRA. We may never know.

Cathy O'Brien says that her father Earl O'Brien was a pedophile and had been involved in selling her into child pornography when she was a little girl. In her book she includes a photo of him, along with her family and names them all, including her siblings. While the claims she makes are extremely disturbing and far fetched, similar activities have been uncovered by congressional hearings and declassified documents. Serious investigations need to be made into O'Brien's claims and her background. While others such as John Todd and Bill Schnoebelen have little to lose if and when they are exposed as frauds, O'Brien making such damning claims about her father would be disastrous if he, or any other family members would find out, if she was fabricating the allegations.

Perhaps O'Brien was a victim of sexual abuse and child pornography by her father and exaggerated her abuse by spinning tales of being a victim of MK-ULTRA instead of her father. Perhaps emotionally scarred from such abuse, she justified her exaggerations and hoped to earn a living by selling books and lectures. The copy of *Trance Formation of America* that this author has in my possession is from the fourteenth printing. Generally, the bare minimum book printings are 2,000 copies, which would mean the book could have sold 30,000 copies reasonably, or perhaps three times that many, which could have earned O'Brien a healthy profit of close to $100,000 if just over $1 was earned per book. These are extremely conservative estimates.

Perhaps Cathy O'Brien and Mark Phillips concocted the entire thing, and out of financial desperation, have tried to earn a living by telling such tales. They may have been familiar with the anti-New World Order literature and the existence of the Bohemian Grove, MK-ULTRA, and elite pedophiles and sex trafficking. Or, perhaps she is telling the truth and is a survivor of such activities, which actually do happen. There are very real victims of such programs, and there are elite perpetrators who are involved in such things, so it is possible that a victim would write a book about them and have nobody believe her.

Whatever the truth is surrounding Cathy O'Brien, no matter how unbelievable her story seems, there are bits and pieces of verifiable information that seem fictional to someone who is unfamiliar with the Illuminati, so one must not dismiss the reality of such things even if O'Brien and Phillips are proven to be frauds.

In 1999 a woman named Brice Taylor published, *Thanks For The Memories: The Truth Has Set Me Free! The Memoirs of Bob Hope's and Henry Kissinger's Mind-Controlled Slave* which she alleges is her account of being a victim of MK-ULTRA, as well. In 2003 a woman named Kathleen Sullivan released a similar book titled, *Unshackled: A Survivor's Story of Mind Control.*

Johnny Gosch

The story of Johnny Gosch, a paperboy from Iowa who went missing in 1982, has perhaps the most credible yet disturbing ties to the Illuminati and their affiliates. Gosch disappeared while delivering papers on September 5th, 1982, and as details emerged in the case, a very dark picture began to come into focus. Evidence pointed to the idea that a pedophile sex slavery ring had taken the boy, but this would be just the tip of the iceberg surrounding the case. The kidnapping of Johnny Gosch was huge news in the 1980s, and the boy's picture was the first to appear on milk cartons as a campaign to help find missing children. The TV show *America's Most Wanted* had also aired a segment hoping viewers could help find the boy. The case remained unsolved, and there were no arrests and Johnny wouldn't be found.

Seventeen years later in 1999, Johnny's mother, Noreen Gosch, testified during a lawsuit against Laurence E. King which had been brought forth by John DeCamp on behalf of his client Paul Bonacci. (See Conspiracy of Silence page 287) During this testimony Noreen stated for the first time publicly that in March of 1997 (15 years after Johnny went missing) she was awakened at 2:30 in the morning by someone knocking on her door who she said was her son Johnny. She immediately recognized the man as her son, and the two talked for several hours in her living room where Johnny began to tell her about what had happened to him since he was kidnapped. Noreen says that Johnny was forced into child pornography and had become an unwilling victim of a CIA sponsored mind control program called Project Monarch.

According to Noreen, Johnny also said that a man named Colonel Michael Aquino was the central perpetrator in his kidnapping. Aquino was a former member of the Church of Satan, who had started his own satanic organization called the Temple of Set. He is an educated man with a Ph.D. and a Green Beret who was a Lieutenant Colonel in the Army. He authored a paper titled *From PSYOP to MindWar* for the U.S. Army, which detailed various mind control methods. He was an admitted Satanist with a high level security clearance and an expert in mind control. In the 1980s, Aquino, his wife, and another were accused of ritual child sexual abuse involving a daycare center at the Presidio military base in San Francisco. On August 14, 1987, the FBI and the San Francisco Police served a search warrant and seized videotapes, 29 photos, and two plastic gloves from the kitchen. (Case #870910025, 8114/87) No charges were filed against Aquino, although he was titled by the army.[132] A cloud of controversy and suspicion still surrounds Aquino.

Rusty Nelson, a personal photographer for Laurence E. King, the central figure in the Franklin Cover-Up scandal, would later come forward as a witness who saw children being abused by powerful men at King's pedophile parties and it was his job to photograph the men in compromising situations with the children so the photos could be used as blackmail to persuade the politicians to vote certain ways or to keep their mouth shut regarding various criminal activities they may become aware of. Nelson says that, "there was one instance where Michael Aquino, Colonel Michael Aquino came to a motel room and he got from Larry King a suit case and it was filled with bearer bonds and cash, and there was millions of dollars in that thing. And it was for the Iran Contras."[133]

Another boy, named Paul Bonacci, admitted he was forced to help kidnap Johnny Gosch into sex-slavery, and

---

[132] Miami Herald *Army Re-Opening Probe Against Officer in Child Sex Case* December 24, 1988
[133] Interview with Michael Corbin, host of *A Closer Look*

told Franklin Committee investigators he toured the White House at midnight on July 3, 1988 with Craig Spence, a lobbyist who operated an underage male homosexual prostitution ring in the Washington D.C. area with an elite client list. Spence turned up dead from what police called a suicide, three months after the June 29, 1989 edition of the *Washington Times* ran a front page headline reading, "Homosexual Prostitution inquiry ensnares VIPs with Reagan, Bush."

Bonacci says he was used to lure Johnny near a vehicle so that men could then grab him. He was used in this manor for several kidnappings. Bonacci is the witness/victim who allegedly witnessed the making of a snuff film in Bohemian Grove in 1984, after he and other children were taken to the club. Bonacci's testimony also filled in the missing pieces of the Gosch kidnapping, and tied it, and those involved, to the infamous Omaha, Nebraska Franklin Cover-Up. This information is exposed in detail in Senator John DeCamp's book of the same title. (See The Franklin Cover-Up page 120) Noreen Gosch also detailed her own account in her book titled *Why Johnny Can't Come Home*.

What's important to understand about the Johnny Gosch case is that numerous witnesses with absolutely nothing to gain have come forward and made identical allegations about the same group of people and the same kinds of activities. Unlike other supposed witnesses who come forward with information and write books and make money off the lecture circuit, witnesses like Paul Bonacci and Rusty Nelson have only embarrassment and legal persecution to gain from coming forward with the allegations they have made. How is it possible that Paul Bonacci described the inside of the Bohemian Grove and took his lawyer, a former United States Senator to the entrance of the club in the late 1980s? How is it possible that Bonacci knew intimate details surrounding the Johnny Gosch kidnapping? Why is it that Michael Aquino's name keeps getting mentioned by people involved in this case?

When one understands that a certain segment of the Illuminati enjoys pedophilia and sadomasochism as a way of exercising the ultimate power over another human being, answers start to emerge in the Johnny Gosch kidnapping case. Powerful men, child sex slaves, Satanism, and mind control are all intertwined at the dark core of the Illuminati. (See Sex Magic page 305)

MK-ULTRA Victims Testimony

UNITED STATES OF AMERICA ADVISORY COMMITTEE ON HUMAN RADIATION EXPERIMENTS (PUBLIC MEETING)

Executive Chambers
The Madison Hotel
15th and M Streets, NW
Washington, D.C.
Wednesday, March 15, 1995
1:00 p.m.
Statement of Chris DeNicola, Valerie Wolf and Claudia Mullen, New Orleans, Louisiana

MS. WOLF: Okay. I'm going to start. My name is Valerie Wolf. In listening to the testimony today, it all sounds really familiar. I am here to talk about a possible link between radiation and mind-control experimentation that began in the late 1940s.

The main reason that mind-control research is being mentioned is because people are alleging that they were exposed as children to mind-control radiation drugs and chemical experimentation, which were administered by the same doctors who are known to have been involved in conducting both radiation and mind-control research.

Written documentation has been provided revealing the

names of people and the names of research projects in statements from people across the country.

It is also important to understand that mind-control techniques and follow-ups into adulthood may have been used to intimidate these particular research subjects into not talking about their victimization in government research. As a therapist for the past 22 years, I have specialized in treating victims and perpetrators of trauma and their families. When word got out that I was appearing at this hearing, nearly 40 therapists across the country, and I had about a week and a half to prepare, contacted me to talk about clients who had reported being subjects in radiation and mind-control experiments.

The consistency of people's stories about the purpose of the mind-control and pain-induction techniques, such as electric shock, use of hallucinogens, sensory deprivation, hypnosis, dislocation of limbs and sexual abuse, is remarkable.

There is almost nothing published on this aspect of mind-control used with children, and these clients come from all over the country, having had no contact with each other.

What was startlingly was that therapists reported many of these clients were also physically ill with auto-immune problems, thyroid problems, multiple sclerosis, and other muscle and connective tissue diseases as well as mysterious ailments for which a diagnosis cannot be found.

While somatization disorder is commonly found in these clients, many of the clients who have been involved in the human experimentation with the government have multiple medically-documented physical ailments, and I was really shocked today to hear one of the speakers talk about the cysts and the teeth breaking off, because I have a client that that's happening to.

Many people are afraid to tell their doctors their histories as mind-control subjects for fear of being considered to be crazy. These clients have named some of the same people, particularly a Dr. Green, who was associated with clients' reports of childhood induction of pain, mind-control techniques, and childhood sexual abuse.

One of my clients, who had seen him with a name tag, identified him as Dr. L. Wilson Green. A person with this same name was the scientific director of the Chemical and Radiological Laboratories at the Army Chemical Center, and that he was engaged in doing research for the Army and other intelligence agencies.

Other names that have come to light are Dr. Sidney Gottlieb and Dr. Martin Orne, who, it is reported, were also involved in radiation research.

It needs to be made clear that people have remembered these names and events spontaneously with free recall and without the use of any memory-retrievable techniques, such as hypnosis. As much as possible, we have tried to verify the memories with family members, records and experts in the field.

Many attempts have been made through Freedom of Information Act filings to gain access to the mind-control research documentation. These requests have generally been slowed down or denied, although some information has been obtained, which suggests that at least some of the information supplied by these clients is true.

It is important that we obtain all of the information contained in the CIA and military files to verify or deny our clients' memories. Although many of the files for MK-ULTRA may have been destroyed, whatever is left, along with the files for other projects, such as Bluebird and Artichoke, to name only two, contain valuable information.

Furthermore, if, as the evidence suggests, some of these people were used in radiation experiments, there might be information in the mind-control experiment file on radiation experiments.

We need this information to help in the rehabilitation and treatment of many people who have severe psychological and medical problems which interfere with their social, emotional and financial well-being. Finally, I urge you to recommend an investigation into these matters. Although there was a commission on mind-control, it did not include experiments on children because most of them were too young or still involved in the research in the late 1970s to come forward. The only way to end the harassment and suffering of these people is to make public what has happened to them in the mind-control experiments. Please recommend that there be an investigation and that the files be opened on the mind-control experiments as they related to children. Thank you.

DR. FADEN: Thank you.

MS. DeNICOLA: Good afternoon. I'm Christine DeNicola, born July 1962, rendering me 32 years of age.

I was a subject in radiation as well as mind-control and drug experiments performed by a man I knew as Dr. Green.

My parents were divorced around 1966, and Donald Richard Ebner, my natural father, was involved with Dr. Green in the experiments. I was a subject from 1966 to 1976. Dr. Green performed radiation experiments on me in 1970, focusing on my neck, throat and chest in 1972, focusing on my chest and my uterus in 1975.

Each time I became dizzy, nauseous and threw up. All these experiments were performed on me in conjunction with mind-control techniques and drugs in Tucson, Arizona.

Dr. Green was using me mostly as a mind-control subject from 1966 to 1973. His objective was to gain control of my mind and train me to be a spy assassin. The first significant memory took place at Kansas City University in 1966. Don Ebner took me there by plane when my mom was out of town. I was in what looked like a laboratory, and there seemed to be other children. I was strapped down, naked, spread-eagle on a table, on my back.

Dr. Green had electrodes on my body, including my head. He used what looked like an overhead projector and repeatedly said he was burning different images into my brain while a red light flashed aimed at my forehead.

In between each sequence, he used electric shock on my body and told me to go deeper and deeper, while repeating each image would go deeper into my brain, and I would do whatever he told me to do.

I felt drugged because he had given me a shot before he started the procedure. When it was over, he gave me another shot. The next thing I remember, I was with my grandparents again in Tucson, Arizona. I was four years old.

You can see from this experiment that Dr. Green used trauma, drugs, post-hypnotic suggestion and more trauma in an effort to gain total control of my mind. He used me in radiation experiments, both for the purposes of determining the effects of radiation on various parts of my body and to terrorize me as an additional trauma in the mind-control experiments.

The rest of the experiments took place in Tucson, Arizona, out in the desert. I was taught how to pick locks, be secretive, use my photographic memory, and a technique to withhold information by repeating numbers to myself.

Dr. Green moved on to wanting me to kill dolls that looked like real children. I stabbed a doll with a spear once after being severely traumatized, but the next time, I refused. He used many pain-induction techniques, but as I got older, I resisted more and more.

He often tied me down in a cage, which was near his office. Between 1972 and 1976, he and his assistants were sometimes careless and left the cage unlocked. Whenever physically possible, I snuck into his office and found files with reports and memos addressed to CIA and military personnel.

Included in these files were project, sub-project, subject and experiment names with some code numbers for radiation and mind-control experiments, which I have submitted in your written documentation. I was caught twice, and Dr. Green ruthlessly used electric shock, drugs, spun me on a table, put shots in my stomach and my back, dislocated my joints, and hypnotic techniques to make me feel crazy and suicidal. Because of my rebellion and growing lack of cooperation, they gave up on me as a spy assassin. Consequently, the last two years, 1974 to 1976, Dr. Green used various mind-control techniques to reverse the spy assassin messages, to self-destruct and death messages. His purpose. He wanted me dead, and I have struggled to stay alive all of my adult life. I believe it is by the grace of God that I am still alive.

These horrible experiments have profoundly affected my life. I developed multiple personality disorder because Dr. Green's goal was to split my mind into as many parts as possible so he could control me totally. He failed. But I've had to endure years of constant physical, mental and emotional pain even to this day.

I've been in therapy consistently for 12 years, and it wasn't until I found my current therapist two and a half years ago, who had knowledge of the mind-control experiments, that I finally have been able to make real progress and begin to heal.

In closing, I ask that you keep in mind that the memories I have described are but a glimpse of the countless others that took place over the 10 years between 1966 and 1976, that they weren't just radiation but mind-control and drug experiments as well.

I have included more detailed information of what I remember in your written documentation. Please help us by recommending an investigation and making the information available so that therapists and other mental health professionals can help more people like myself.

I know I can get better. I am getting better, and I know

others can, too, with the proper help. Please help us in an effort to prevent these heinous acts from continuing in the future. Thank you very much.

DR. FADEN: Thank you.

(Applause)

MS. MULLEN: Good afternoon. Between the years of 1957 and 1974, I became a pawn in the government's game, whose ultimate goal was mind-control and to create the perfect spy, all through the use of chemicals, radiation, drugs, hypnosis, electric shock, isolation in tubs of water, sleep deprivation, brain-washing, verbal, physical, emotional and sexual abuse.

I was exploited unwittingly for nearly three decades of my life, and the only explanations given to me were that "the end justifies the means," and "I was serving my country in their bold effort to fight communism."

I can only summarize my circumstances by saying they took an already-abused seven-year old child and compounded my suffering beyond belief. The saddest part is I know for a fact that I was not alone. There were countless other children in my same situation, and there was no one to help us until now.

I've already submitted as much information as possible, including conversations overheard of the agencies responsible. I'm able to report all this to you in such detail because of my photographic memory and the arrogance of the doctors—the arrogance of the people involved. They were certain they would always control my mind.

Although the process of recalling these atrocities is not an easy one, nor is it without some danger to myself and my family, I feel the risk is worth taking.

Dr. L. Wilson Green, who claimed to have received $50 million from the Edgewood Chemical and Radiology

Laboratory as part of a TSD or technical science division of the CIA, once described to Dr. Charles Brown that "children were used as subjects because they were more fun to work and cheaper, too." They needed lower profile subjects than soldiers or government people. So, only young willing females would do. Besides, he said, "I like scaring them. They and the agency think I'm a god, creating subjects experiments for whatever deviant purposes Sid and James could think up." Sid being Dr. Sidney Gottlieb, James, Dr. James Hamilton.

In 1958, I was to be tested, they told me, by some important doctors from the society or the Human Ecology Society, and I was instructed to cooperate. I was told not to look at anyone's faces, and not—try hard not to ignore—to try hard not to ignore any names as this was a very secret project, but I was told that all these things would help me forget.

Naturally, as most children do, I did the opposite, and I remembered as much as I could, but Dr. John Gittinger tested me, Dr. Cameron gave me the shots, and Dr. Green the x-rays. Then I was told by Sid Gottlieb that "I was ripe for the big A" meaning Artichoke. By the time I left to go home, just like every time from then on, I would remember only whatever explanations Dr. Robert G. Heath of Tulane Medical University gave me for the odd bruises, needle marks, burns on my head, fingers, and even the genital soreness. I had no reason to believe otherwise. They had already begun to control my mind.

The next year, I was sent to a lodge in Maryland called Deep Creek Cabins to learn how to sexually please men. I was taught how to coerce them into talking about themselves, and it was Richard Helms, who was deputy director of the CIA, Dr. Gottlieb, George White, Morris Allen, were all planning on filming as many high government agency officials and heads of academic institutions and foundations as possible, so that later, when the funding for mind-control and radiation started to dwindle, projects would continue.

I was used to entrap many unwitting men, including themselves, all with the use of a hidden camera. I was only nine years old when this sexual humiliation began. I overheard conversations about a part of the agency called Ord, which I found out was Office of Research and Development. It was run by Dr. Green, Dr. Steven Aldridge, Martin Orne, and Morris Allen.

Once a crude remark was made by Dr. Gottlieb about a certain possible leak over New Orleans involving a large group of retarded children who were being given massive doses of radiation. He asked why was Wilson so worried about a few retarded kids, after all, they would be the least likely to spill the beans.

Another time, I heard Dr. Martin Orne, who was the director then of the scientific office, and later head of the Institute for Experimental Research state that, "In order to keep more funding coming from different sources for radiation and mind-control projects, he suggested stepping up the amounts of stressors used and also the blackmail portion of the experiments." He said it needed to be done faster and to get rid of the subjects or they were asking for us to come back later and haunt them with our remembrances.

There's much more I could tell you about government-sponsored research, including project names, cell project numbers, people involved, facilities used, tests and other forms of pain induction, but I think I've given more than enough information to recommend further investigation of all the mind-control projects, especially as they involve so much abuse of the radiation.

I would love nothing more than to say that I had dreamed the whole thing up and need just to forget it, but that would be a tragic mistake. It would also be a lie.

All these atrocities did occur to me and to countless other children, and all under the guise of defending our country. It is because of the cumulative effects of exposure to radiation, chemicals, drugs, pain and subsequent mental and physical distress that I've been robbed of the ability to work and even to bear any children of my own.

It is blatantly obvious that none of this was needed nor should it ever have been allowed to take place at all, and the only means we have to seek out the awful truth and bring it to light is by opening whatever files remain on all the projects and through another presidential commission on mind-control.

I believe that every citizen of this nation has the right to know just what is fact and what is fiction. It is our greatest protection against the possibility of this ever happening again. In conclusion, I can offer you no more than what I've given you today, the truth, and I thank you for your time. (Applause)

Activists and Eyewitnesses

Aside from individuals claiming to be former members of the Illuminati or victims of satanic rituals or mind control, there are also an array of people who claim to have witnessed such things first hand, or who have acquired evidence and information regarding such activities. Far from being attention seekers or liars, most of the individuals in this section are completely honest and their claims are legitimate and verifiable. Others such as Hal Turner, as you will read, are not only liars, but likely paid disinformation agents whose purpose is to publicize false and misleading information which aims to discredit serious research and vital information.

One reliable eye witness is Chris Jones who worked in the Bohemian Grove, who this author got to know personally. When we met for lunch in 2006 he showed me pictures and video taken from inside the secretive compound which was still on his camera. Another eyewitness, to many people's surprise, is that of President John F. Kennedy, who as you will read gave a chilling warning about what he called a monolithic and ruthless conspiracy that the world was facing.

William Morgan

A man in the early 19th century named William Morgan would become the spark that would ignite a third political party in the United States for the first time in the country's history. A party, solely against Freemasonry, and called the Anti-Masonic Party. Morgan was a Freemason in New York who decided to publish a book exposing many of the secrets of Freemasonry, including their hand signals, symbols, and rituals. In 1826 he was kidnapped and murdered by Freemasons who took very seriously the life threatening oaths Masons commit to.

His disappearance and death was the catalyst for a large public backlash against Freemasonry, which ultimately lead to the Anti-Masonic Party being formed in 1828. Suddenly Freemasonry had become an enemy of the public, and membership in the United States was quickly cut in half as large numbers of men left the fraternity.

A man named David Cade Miller, who owned a local newspaper, was going to publish William Morgan's book, and before Morgan was killed there were several attempts to burn down Miller's office after word had spread about their plans.

Prior to his murder, Morgan had been harassed by several Freemasons and put in jail based on allegations that he owed them money and that he had stolen some clothing from them. After he was released he disappeared the next day and a month later his dead and decomposing body was discovered on the shores of Lake Ontario.

Three men, all Freemasons, were charged and convicted for kidnapping. They were Loton Lawon, Nicholas Chesebro, and Edward Sawyer. Many Freemasons deny that Morgan was killed, and instead claim he was paid by them to leave the country.

As a result of Morgan's murder, New York politician Thurlow Weed formed the Anti-Masonic Party. John Quincy Adams supported this new party and in 1847 released a book titled *Letters on the Masonic Institution* which criticized Freemasonry.

Morgan's widow would later become one of Joseph Smith Jr.'s multiple wives after he created the cult of Mormonism. The Mormon church performed a baptism for the dead for Morgan where Mormons baptize a living person on behalf of someone who is dead, and think that the dead person is then baptized by proxy and can then possibly get into Heaven if they were denied for not being baptized themselves. (*The Resistance Manifesto* by Mark Dice has a detailed analysis of the cult of Mormonism.)

The newspaper publisher, David Miller, would later publish Morgan's book which became a best seller. Morgan's murder is often referred to as the "William Morgan incident" and left a stain on Freemasonry which remains to this day. (See Morals and Dogma page 70)

JFK Warns Against Secret Societies

President John F. Kennedy once made a profound statement about secret societies when speaking to the American Newspaper Publishers Association. While not singling out any specific group, his statements are extremely chilling. Kennedy clearly had intimate knowledge of the workings of the Illuminati and didn't want to go along with them. Audio of his statements are widely available on the Internet. He said, "The very word "secrecy" is repugnant in a free and open society; and we are as a people inherently and historically opposed to secret societies, to secret oaths and to secret proceedings."

He continued, "We decided long ago that the dangers of excessive and unwarranted concealment of pertinent facts far outweighed the dangers which are cited to justify it...For we are opposed around the world by a monolithic and ruthless conspiracy that relies primarily on covered means for expanding its sphere of influence, on infiltration instead of invasion, on subversion instead of elections, on intimidation instead of free choice, on guerillas by night instead of armies by day."

"It is a system which has conscripted vast human and material resources into the building of a tightly knit highly efficient machine that combines military, diplomatic, intelligence, economic, scientific and political operations, its preparations concealed not published its mistakes are buried not headlined, it's dissenters are silenced not praised, no expenditure is questioned, no rumor is printed, no secret is revealed."

Several months prior to his assassination, John F. Kennedy had signed Executive Order No. 11110, which attempted to strip the Federal Reserve of their power to loan money to the United States government at interest. Many see this act as the major motive for the Illuminati orchestrating his assassination.

Chris Jones

In the summer of 2005, an individual who went by the pseudonym "Kyle" obtained a job in the Bohemian Grove with the sole purpose of investigating the activities within the club. Over the course of the summer he brought his digital camera to work and was able to shoot several close up photos of the effigies which are used in the Cremation of Care ritual. He also obtained video footage of Moloch, and the electronic systems used to control the music, lights, and fireworks for the ceremony.

His photos clearly show that the item being burned on the altar is a life-size human effigy. The pictures, and his personal testimony reveal that the effigy is a metal skeleton which is then wrapped with paper. Prior to the Cremation of Care, he was able to inspect the effigy to see if there was a small child or infant's body stuffed inside, or a vile of blood, but the effigy seemed to contain only paper. While the modern Cremation of Care ritual uses a paper effigy, it is believed that in the past, the ritual used a real human or child as did ancient sacrifices to Moloch.

The photos he took, as well as video, is featured in Alex Jones' film *The Order of Death* (2005) and can be viewed on the Internet. This author, Mark Dice, has met "Kyle" on several occasions and I have seen the photos and video on his camera with my own eyes. Aside from taking video and photos from inside the club, he was able to obtain a 2005 membership list and program guide, as well.

THE ILLUMINATI: FACTS & FICTION

"Kyle" whose real name is Chris Jones, would later be imprisoned due to trumped up charges surrounding showing some kids in his neighborhood the video footage and educating them about the club. Police claimed he was showing kids snuff films, and a series of charges were filed against him for allegedly wanting to harm children. It's likely these charges were to punish him for his investigations into the Bohemian Grove, and his imprisonment was ordered by the Illuminati. The entire case and the trial stunk of corruption, and despite no evidence or testimony from the children in his neighborhood that he had any ill motives, he was found guilty in 2008 and sentenced to several years in prison.

Chris hadn't written a book, nor ever discussed plans to do so, and made no money off any lectures about the Bohemian Grove. Until his incarceration, he had remained an anonymous informant. It was only after his imprisonment that others who knew him spoke openly about his true identity to let others know what had happened to him. He was simply a man who was appalled with what the elite were involved in, and spent his own time, money, and energy to gather evidence to expose them. He asked for no money from Alex Jones in return for sending him the video footage and photos he had taken from inside the Grove when he had worked there. He granted Alex full permission to use the photos and videos in his film, and only asked for some free copies in return that he could give to family and friends.

Unlike others who write books about such things or talk about them on radio shows or even make films about the Illuminati, Chris crossed a line few dare to even approach by becoming an eye witness and physically gathering evidence from an Illuminati meeting place and then releasing it to the public.

For those who fear a fate of Chris Jones, you may relax a little with the understanding that simply reading books and talking about the Illuminati is a totally different thing than going to one of their meeting places and taking video and photos. While *The Resistance* owes Chris our utmost respect and sympathy for the repercussions from his actions, let them also serve as an example of the strings the Illuminati may pull to enact revenge upon those who cross them. Anyone willing to risk their freedom and their life to expose the crimes and perversions of the Illuminati is a brave soul, and we can only hope that there are others like Chris Jones out there who are infiltrating the Illuminati and gathering credible and verifiable evidence against them.

Ted Gunderson

One of the highest ranking government officials to publicly talk about the Illuminati and admit that organized child kidnapping rings were active in the United States is Ted Gunderson. Gunderson is a retired FBI agent who worked as the Senior Special Agent-in-Charge of the Los Angeles office who retired in March of 1979 and then became a private investigator.

Gunderson has worked closely with the families and victims of several of the most well known cases of child abuse involving the Illuminati, such as the Johnny Gosch case and Paul Bonacci, who was involved in the Franklin Cover-Up scandal and is just one of many children who say they were taken into the Bohemian Grove in the 1980s and forced to participate in child pornography and pedophilia parties involving powerful politicians and business men.

Gunderson openly states that the Illuminati exists and that they are an elite Luciferian pedophile group with goals of creating a New World Order and turning most of society into a financially bankrupt group of peasants, while they enjoy the fruits of society's labor and hold all wealth and key political positions.

While numerous public officials have spoken out about the 9/11 attacks being an inside job, few have specifically mentioned the Illuminati. Gunderson's once prestigious position in the Los Angels bureau of the FBI adds tremendous credibility to his claims. Surely other well-meaning prominent law enforcement officials and politicians are aware of the Illuminati, but keep silent on the issue for the sake of their career or their family's safety. Those individuals understand the dangers of speaking about such topics, and we can only hope that other high level respected FBI or law enforcement agents can one day come forward and speak about such things.

Benjamin Fulford

A Canadian journalist living in Japan named Benjamin Fulford, who was the Asian bureau chief for *Forbes* magazine from 1998 to 2005, came to the attention of many in 2008 when he reported that a Chinese secret society was threatening to assassinate high level Illuminati members due to their pro white and racist agendas.

While many would dismiss such allegations as another hoax by a publicity seeking unknown author, Fulford has a list of respectable credentials, including his work at *Forbes* magazine, the *Nihon Keizai Shimbun* (the Japan Economic Times), the *South China Morning Post*, and other well respected publications. In November of 2007 he conducted a sit down interview with David Rockefeller which can be viewed on YouTube.

Fulford says he was approached by a representative of a secret society called the Green and Red society after he made a speech in Tokyo, Japan where he talked about the Bush regime's plans to develop race-specific bio weapons. He describes the society as having six million members, including 1.8 million Asian gangsters and 100,000 trained assassins. According to Fulford, the society was particularly upset with the Illuminati after discovering plans to reduce the world's population by 90% as is described on the

Georgia Guidestones. (See Common Sense Renewed on page 77) The Green and Red society believe that a large number of Asians will be exterminated when such plans are put into action.

Fulford says that he provided the society with a list of 10,000 names of the highest profile people involved in the Illuminati, such as Bilderberg, Skull and Bones, and Council on Foreign Relations members.

"I have been promised that not a single person will die if they negotiate in good faith," Fulford said.[134]

"Think about it, the Illuminati and their top servants have a total membership of about 10,000 whereas the Chinese group has over 6 million members. That is 600 to one odds. Furthermore, the 6 million have the names and addresses of the 10,000 while the 10,000 do not know who or where the 6 million are."[135]

"They [the Illuminati] are also neo-Nazis who want to reduce the amount of colored people in the world by at least half through disease, starvation and war. The Chinese secret society got wind of this and is preparing to stop them."[136]

"So far, I have told the Illuminati that they are no longer allowed to murder Japanese politicians. I now plan to extend this protection to all politicians in the West. If the Illuminati assassinate or attempt to assassinate Ron Paul, Barack Obama or any politician, may God have mercy on their souls."[137]

"Since I am a peace-loving, laid-back Canadian suddenly put in a situation of great responsibility, I feel I must act as a servant of the weakest people and creatures on the planet. I have also been negotiating in secret with the

---

[134] Makow, Henry *Chinese Secret Society Challenges Illuminati* Rense.com 6-30-07
[135] Ibid
[136] Ibid
[137] Ibid

Illuminati in the hopes of arranging for them to cede power without any bloodshed in exchange for a general amnesty."[138] Fulford insists that the Green and the Red societies can be read about in history books. He says that when the Manchus invaded China in 1644, that it caused the Ming army to organize as an underground society aimed at overthrowing the Qing (Manchu) and restoring the Ming. Later, he says, the society overthrew the last Emperor and installed Sun Yat Sen in his place. They were called the Green Gang and the Red Gang who fought Communism in Shanghai in the 1940s but after being defeated in 1949, they went underground.

It certainly is understandable if a secret society with no affiliation with the Illuminati were to see the organization as a threat to their country, especially if they are under the impression that their population is going to be eliminated as part of the population reduction agenda that elite globalists and the Illuminati clearly have.

The sheer numbers of the alleged members in the Green and Red societies are staggering, and cast doubts on Fulford's claims. If this society exists, and if they did tell their plans to Fulford, perhaps they exaggerated their numbers as a way to intimidate the Illuminati or perhaps, just like there are millions of Freemasons, with only a small fraction composing the inner circle, perhaps this is the case with the Green and Red society as well. Or, perhaps, Fulford is just another fraud on a long list of people who have claimed to have intimate knowledge of the Illuminati's activities or goals. While this certainly is possible, unlike almost all of the people making fraudulent claims concerning these issues, Fulford doesn't have a book he is peddling, (at least at the time of this writing) but could possibly be

---

[138] Ibid

making money by giving lectures. Having reached a fair amount of success as a writer and working for prestigious, well respected companies, Fulford has a lot to lose by making such claims, even if they were true. Another suspicious aspect surrounding Fulford are his claims that he is personally negotiating with the Illuminati on behalf of the Chinese secret society. Why would he need to be involved in such negotiations and why would he want to place himself in such a dangerous position? He openly admits (or rather claims) that he provided the Green and Red society with the names and addresses of 10,000 Illuminati members. Why would *he* need to do this? One would think that the Green and Red society would do their own research and wouldn't need Fulford to be so involved. Whatever the truth is surrounding Benjamin Fulford's claims, nobody knows. While such a threat is certainly possible from a secret society that is not affiliated with the Illuminati, Fulford's story contains seeds of doubts with regards to its authenticity and his motives for publicizing it.

Hal Turner

On October 4th 2008, a white supremacist hate monger named Hal Turner posted a video on his YouTube channel, titled "Hal Turner Shows New AMERO Currency," where he claimed to have in his possession an actual Amero coin, the planned currency for when the North American Union is completed and the United States, Canada, and Mexico have a common currency. He also claimed that America sent 800 billion dollars of the new coins to China in preparation for the collapse of the U.S. Dollar. The video quickly received over 400,000 views, and reached the number one spot on Google Video's top 100 list.

Not only was Turner wrong about having an actual Amero coin, but he was purposefully lying about it in an attempt to create the idea that a regional currency, likely to be called the Amero, is a hoax and something American's don't need to worry about or look into.

Anyone can purchase a "novelty replica" Amero from www.AmeroCurrency.com or www.DC-Coin.com. In his video where he claims to have an actual Amero, the camera zooms in on the front and back of the coin to show the designs as he attempts to "prove" its authenticity, and the coin he is holding is EXACTLY like the replicas sold on the web.

One might be led to believe that Turner is simply mistaken, and that he actually thinks he has a real Amero coin, because the Council on Foreign Relations and other New World Order organizations have been planning such a thing for years. One might think that he just didn't do his research, and believes that someone had sent him an actual coin. This is simply not true.

A year earlier Turner had posted pictures on his website of what he claimed to be "real" Amero coins that he had obtained. He plastered his website name, HalTurner-Show.com on the pictures, knowing that people would spread them all over the web and give him free advertising by spreading his name. News of his "discovery" spread all over the Internet (falsely) reporting that Amero coins were being produced.

A quick Google search shows anyone that the pictures of the coins were taken from the various websites that create novelty coins and replicas. Countless people must have emailed him to point this out to him, as did the comments on his blog post. Then, one year later, Turner obtains a replica, and then posts a video claiming to have an actual coin!

Posting comments on the video on his YouTube channel had been disabled by him. He obviously saw that people were posting comments about replica coins being made and sold on the Internet. So this leads to the question of why. Why would he make such claims knowing he was lying when he claims to be a concerned citizen trying to expose the New World Order?

Turner has a history of urging and hoping for violence against others, including judges, and has posted their home addresses on his website and written blogs celebrating their murders. The Southern Poverty Law center and others report that Turner is an FBI informant, and many suspect he is a paid provocateur and a COINTELPRO asset, (an acronym for Counter Intelligence Program).

At the end of July 2008 Turner was forced to quit his Internet radio show and abandon his website due to constant attacks from the hacking group known as Anonymous. These are the same hackers that have targeted Scientology for its corrupt and litigious nature. The hackers kept causing Turner to have outrageous bandwidth costs, which ultimately forced him to shut down and give up his radio show.

One can see how a large percentage of the viewers of his video claiming to show an Amero will believe him at first that the Ameros are already being coined, only to later dismiss the idea of the U.S. Dollar collapsing and being replaced by a new currency because it turns out the video was a hoax. It's a classic case of disinformation by mixing facts with fiction, in an attempt to prevent the public from focusing on the impact of such issues that we will ultimately face in the near future.

It turns out that Hal Turner was not finished making claims that he obtained real Amero currency. On December 3rd 2008 he posted photos of "Amero paper currency" and wrote, "To the chagrin of the government, I have obtained new "AMERO" paper currency notes! You know, the "AMERO" . . . . the new currency that is going to replace the US Dollar, The Canadian Dollar and the Mexican Peso? Yea, the new currency that all three governments claim doesn't exist. . . I have it."[139]

---

[139] http://www halturnershow blogspot com/2008/12/urgent-new-amero-paper-currency-exposed html

His new article goes on to say how over a year ago he "first broke" the story about Amero coins being secretly created at the Denver Mint. He also explained that YouTube had notified him that the video he had posted showing his alleged Amero coin had been deleted and his account "permanently closed at the request of the United States Treasury Department." Turner wrote, "The Treasury department told YouTube/Google that my video was destabilizing the U.S. Dollar and was thus a threat to national security."[140]

While his articles allow readers to post comments, the user is notified that the administrator (Turner) must approve all comments first, and if and when this happens, it will show up on the website. So obviously, all comments posted informing him and the readers that the photos and his claims are fraudulent, are simply not approved, and never find their way on the website. It is incredible the number of gullible people that continue to believe Tuner. By reading the comments that he had approved, it becomes clear the inability of Turner's readers to distinguish fact from fiction. What's worse is that Turner's articles are often copied and pasted into emails and sent around to others by people who believe his writing and aren't aware of his continuous lies and his possible role as a paid government disinformationist.

Anthony J. Hilder

In today's modern world with the Internet, mp3s and YouTube, it can be somewhat simple to open the floodgates of information regarding the Illuminati and secret societies. Since 2006 and the creation of YouTube and Google Video, countless video clips and documentaries about such issues are literally a click away. But as we know, books on the

---

[140] Ibid

Illuminati have been around since at least the late 1700s as in the case of John Robison's *Proofs of a Conspiracy* and Abbe Barruel's *Memoirs Illustrating the History of Jacobinism*. There seems to be a tremendous gap in history from the time these books were published, until other authors and researchers continued the work such as Nesta Webster and Edith Miller in the 1920s and 30s, and later Gary Allen with his 1972 book *None Dare Call It Conspiracy*.

Another one of those researchers is Anthony J. Hilder, who in 1967 was producing vinyl records about the Illuminati with Myron Fagan, and after the 9/11 attacks in 2001 he was still watching the New World Order unfold and put out a film uncovering the hidden agenda and motives behind the attacks. In 1982, Hilder managed Gary Richard Arnold's campaign for Congress in California. Arnold made front page headlines around the country after he publicly confronted then President Ronald Reagan about lying to the American people about lowering taxes. The confrontation occurred in the east room of the White House and caused Reagan to angrily tell him to "shut up."[141]

I had the honor of meeting Anthony in 2006 and have spoken with him on numerous occasions since, including an interview I conducted when I hosted *Resistance Radio* on the Genesis Communications Network.

Transcript from August 12, 2007 Interview:

[Mark Dice]

We were just talking about how now we're using mp3s and streaming video and YouTube, Google Video, and back in the '60s you were getting this information out to people on vinyl records. How did you find out about the Illuminati back in the '60s?

---

[141] The Washington Times *GOP Candidate's remarks rile Reagan* October 7, 1982

[Anthony Hilder]
   Well, I actually learned about it before, I just didn't have a name. In the 1964 presidential election with Barry Goldwater, I was in San Francisco and putting out stars for Barry. We had individuals like John Wayne and Efrem Zimbalist Jr., and Roy Rogers...a number of people across the Hollywood landscape, coming out for what I considered to be the most honorable and courageous presidential candidate that I had ever seen in my lifetime, Barry Goldwater.
   And I learned then that there was a problem, a major problem. And that came about by having people believe the propaganda that was being fed, not by the left wing in this country, but coming out on stations like Gene Autry's. And I started to get the message that we had to have a major revelation in this country. We had to have an awakening of just who was behind the scenes. I found out that we had the one party system.
   I was getting that idea earlier than that, but by '64 I was convinced and during the next two years I had discovered a writer named Myron Fagan who was the most prolific playwright in our history. He had about nine plays running concurrently in New York, and he thought that Communism was part of the problem, but he discovered, and I discovered through him, that Communism is not a creation of the masses to overthrow the banking establishment; it's a creation of the banking establishment to overthrow and enslave the masses. It was never operated from Beijing, Moscow, or Havana. It was *always* controlled from New York, Washington, and London. That's where it's coming from.
   It is not my intention, nor has it ever been my intention since that period of time to deal with the people at the bottom of the pyramid, but rather to deal with the Luciferian head.

[Mark]

Anthony, I gotta tell you, that when I had first seen your film *The Greatest Lie Ever Sold*, I was becoming awakened to 9/11, and I could follow the information, I could swallow it, I could understand it, but then you had a clip in there of Ralph Epperson saying that President Bush worships Lucifer, knowingly and willingly and that he wouldn't be president if he didn't. And I gotta tell you, at that time, I thought that you just lost all credibility with me, and I was still early in my studies, and I have to tell you man, I've come to realize how right you were.

[Anthony]

Well, you don't lay nude in a coffin and are born again into a satanic order and have your grandfather support Adolf Hitler and your father named Magog and he laid nude in the same coffin, when Magog means the one who fights God in the last days of the earth.

This is a satanic Luciferian New World Order. This whole ein volk, ein right, ein furor, one world, one race one ruler scenario has carried over from Nazi Germany to the United States of America through the neocons. These are neoconazis and they are not Christians, they are not conservative and I don't want to put the blame on Israel or the Israeli's, but in the Bible it says beware of those who call themselves Jews but are not. So I said, well who are they? Who are these guys that are ruling this country? They're Luciferians. Certainly George Walker Bush, you take a look at him and say, well he's a Christian. He's no Christian and he's no conservative. He's anything but.

[Mark]

Tell us about some of the major steps that brought you the large pieces of the puzzle. How did you put this together? Now anyone who wants to know can just go to Infowars.com or go do some research on their own, but how did you put all these pieces together, some 40 years ago?

[Anthony]

I started at the age of twelve. I was a supporter of this government and certainly my father who fought in the Second World War out in Bermuda. I discovered that we were not being told the truth from a conversation that I overheard. I overheard a conversation between my uncle and his friend who was in the FBI and all that they went through to cover up the Pearl Harbor attack. In other words, the US government and Roosevelt knew about the Pearl Harbor attack before it occurred, allowed it to occur, provoked the Japanese, and I knew then that everything I was told by the then present administration was a lie.

I was prepped for the information that I got through Myron Fagan and I was prepped again in 1963 and 1964, so I came to the conclusion that we have a one party system and these Hegelian politics that are used by the controlling group which is like the puppet master in the center, keeps us against each other.

The legitimate left and the legitimate right are now joining together. We have an alliance and we must have a free world alliance. We must have a free world which is a federation of nation states: tribal, linguistic, racial, religious nation states, which allows everybody to do their own thing in their own time in their own way. And without this, with this division we're going to be screwed. Not only for tomorrow, but forever.

[Mark]

Were there any books, I mean you can go now to Barnes and Noble and pick up any one of numerous books on the Illuminati, you can order Fritz Springmeier's *Bloodlines of the Illuminati*, not that they carry it, but they will order it in. Some bookstores have had *Codex Magica* from Texe Marrs on the shelf. Were there any books available? I know John

Robison's *Proofs of a Conspiracy against all religions and governments* was...

[Anthony]

That's certainly one of them. But there was a book that was written as a take off from my *Illuminati CFR* recordings, and that was a book called *None Dare Call It Conspiracy*. Gary Allen, myself, and John Steinbacher were at Copper Kettle at Gower and Sunset in Hollywood, and he was climbing all over me saying he was going to expose me and this whole thing about the Illuminati was a bunch of crap and he went on and on. And eventually he said I'm going to prove that this is all wrong. So he went out to disprove the material that was laid out by Myron Fagan and in his discovery of what was going on, he concluded that it was in fact the truth.

And then he did an article called the *Establishment CFR*, and I said listen, now that you have the message, can I record this? "Certainly," he said. I had a friend of mine, John Carradine, an actor, John narrated it and we came out with the *Illuminati CFR* sequel which was the *Establishment CFR,* then he did this book called *None Dare Call It Conspiracy*. He printed about five and half million of them.

[Is the Illuminati a religious or satanic cult?]

[Anthony]

Well, the Illuminati are the elite. And if you go back to *Morals and Dogma* which is the bible of the Masonic religion, Pike says that Lucifer is god and they should follow the Luciferian doctrine.

If you go up to the Bohemian Grove, my friend Alex Jones went over there with a camera and got in and saw these guys dressed in black robes making a sacrifice at the feet of Moloch. In days gone by those were real children they sacrificed.

[How does Bible prophecy fit in with the Illuminati?]

[Anthony]

I believe the Bible is prophecy of what the Illuminati would do. Our major problem in this country today is that the support system for the Bush administration is coming from the Christian conservative community. They've been snookered. They've been had. We have to knock out the props of support that the Bush administration has. I support Dennis Kucinich in his move to impeach Vice President Cheney. We have to have impeachment. If you like what Adolf Hitler did, then you'll certainly love what George Bush is doing.

[Mark]

Do you think that the Illuminati believe that the Antichrist will rule earth as a god for an eternity? Or do you think that they know he's going to lose, and in their mind they think that he's going to sacrifice himself for them in a parallel to Christianity, or that they don't believe in an after life? What's your take on that?

[Anthony]

I believe that they believe that Lucifer is going to reign. What is it that Milton said? It's far better to reign in Hell than serve in Heaven. It's in Blavatsky's writing. If you look at madam Blavatsky and the religion that Hitler followed, he was a Blavatskyite.

And if you take a look at the overlapping of the Masonic religion, and with the Blavatskyites and the Theosophists, we are gradually moving towards a one world government.

[Mark]

Are they just too drunk with power to think that the Antichrist is going to lose, just like Hitler thought he would become an Antichrist god-like figure, and he died a cowardly suicide, or do they not think of these things, or do they think they're actually going to win?

[Anthony]

These people when they profess to be atheist are putting on a false face. They're not atheist. They believe in a god. I think our mistake is that we think of them as atheistic. There is a political agenda here and it is satanic. We have to, not only in *The Resistance* put forth, but we have to get this message out to people who do not share our opinion. We have to get right and left and black and white, and rich and poor and all come together and incite this revelation.

People are taking their lives and their fortunes and investing them in exposing and inciting a revelation. We need to do that which has never been done before. And if you're sitting there thinking what can I do, you can do plenty. You can reach one hundred people by getting on the phone. And there are more of us than there are of them. We've got to understand this is ours to lose. We can do this if we simply bring about this alliance.

Myron Fagan

Myron Fagan was one of the youngest successful playwrights in history who would later turn his focus to the Illuminati in the late 1960s. While working on Broadway, he directed plays for the top producers at the time, including Charles Frohman and David Belasco.

In the mid 1940s Fagan became vigorously involved in exposing communist agents in Hollywood which lead to the 1947 congressional hearings where hundreds of famous actors, writers, and directors were investigated for being communist agents or sympathizers. These hearings resulted in the imprisonment of various individuals who worked in Hollywood who would become blacklisted and known as the Hollywood Ten.

Fagan went on to write several plays depicting communist plots. *Red Rainbow* and *Thieves Paradise* were two plays which faced opposition from left wing groups. *Thieves Paradise* portrayed a communist group plotting to create the United Nations as a front for a global government. Even during his early research Fagan realized that there was actually a power behind communism that was even more powerful and largely unknown to the public. This same power was also manipulating American politics from behind the scenes. This power was the Illuminati.

Fagan began focusing deeper on the operations of the Illuminati and did not produce any more screenplays for the remainder of his life. In 1967 he recorded a vinyl record titled *The Illuminati CFR* which discussed the Illuminati's plans for a New World Order. He soon made other recordings as well. Anthony J. Hilder produced the records and was mentored by Fagan and went on to produce numerous films about the Illuminati, the New World Order, and 9/11. Anthony approached Fagan in 1966 and urged him to record the records so the information Fagan knew wouldn't be lost after he passed away, since he was nearly 80 years old at the time. Fagan's LPs were dubbed to cassette tapes and decades later copied into mp3s and YouTube videos and can still be heard today. Fagan died on May 12th 1972 in Los Angeles, California at the age of 85.

On the *Illuminati CFR* record Fagan explained, "The question of how and why the United Nations is the crux of a great conspiracy to destroy the sovereignty of the United States and the enslavement of the U.S. people within a UN one world dictatorship is a complete and unknown mystery to the vast majority of the American people. The reason for this unawareness and the frightening danger to our country and to the entire free world is simple. The masterminds behind this great conspiracy have absolute control of all our mass communication media, especially television, the radio, the press, and Hollywood." Fagan would go on to explain how the Illuminati set up the Council on Foreign Relations as a front and a mechanism to create the New World Order.

Without the work of Myron Fagan, Anthony J. Hilder and others, it is unclear how informed the world would be regarding the Illuminati. Aside being friends with, and mentored by Myron Fagan, Anthony J. Hilder was friends with Antony Sutton, who would later write the first book published exposing the Skull and Bones society at Yale University, and Gary Allen who published *None Dare Call It Conspiracy* in 1972. This small group of friends; Myron Fagan, Anthony J. Hilder, Gary Allen, and Antony Sutton were absolutely instrumental in exposing the Illuminati, and without their hard work and fearless dedication in the 1960s, it is likely that most of the people who now know about the sinister activities of the Illuminati would still be searching for answers as to who was secretly pulling the strings from behind the scenes and why.

Aliens and Reptilians

Since mystery and speculation surrounds the topic of aliens and UFOs, it is not surprising that the subject matter is sometimes included in discussions about the Illuminati. If government agencies are actually hiding the existence of a crashed spacecraft from another planet, or the beings who supposedly used such a device, then one would assume that the Illuminati is involved in that cover-up.

Discussion or speculation about UFOs and aliens often angers serious and credible researchers who investigate the Illuminati and government corruption because almost all information on extraterrestrials is limited to fuzzy video, supposed eye witnesses, or documents which the authenticity cannot be verified. While a large amount of documentation and irrefutable evidence exists proving large portions of the claims made surrounding the Illuminati's existence, satanic rituals, and secret agendas being carried out in politics, the area of aliens and UFOs is lacking such material.

Some people speculate that crashed alien spacecraft have been dismantled and reverse engineered and sparked scientific advancements in aeronautics, chemistry, and other fields. Others believe that aliens are actually working with the Illuminati and live beneath the earth in underground bases and tunnels. Such bases and tunnels do exist, although their purpose remains the topic of debate. One of the more bizarre ideas involving the Illuminati sounds like science fiction, but authors and proponents of the idea claim and believe that they are presenting facts. While a fringe idea in regards to the Illuminati, the theory maintains that members of the organization are actually aliens from another dimension, or a hybrid blend of alien DNA and human DNA. Such an idea has been popularized by author and lecturer David Icke.

David Icke

David Icke is a British author and former football player (known as soccer in America) and the author of several books on the Illuminati, including *The Biggest Secret*, and *David Icke's Guide to the Global Conspiracy*. Most of what Icke writes and talks about is fairly documentable and realistic. It is his "shape-shifting reptilian" bloodline theory that understandably draws the most criticism and dramatically damages his credibility.

This criticism comes not only from skeptics and average people, but from others who research the Illuminati as well. Many see David Icke's talk of hybrid shape shifters as destructive to more documentable and legitimate information about the Illuminati. Some see David Icke as an opportunist who is mixing fact with science fiction in order to get attention with the hopes of selling more books and separate himself from other Illuminati and New World Order researchers by publicizing such wild theories. Others think Icke actually believes what he is talking about, and some see him as a paid disinformation agent who is actually working for the Illuminati and purposefully putting out false and misleading information in an attempt to discredit other legitimate researchers.

Icke and other proponents of the "reptilian shape-shifting" theory point to the statements of people who claim to have seen individuals in positions of power morph from a human into a reptile type of creature, and then morph back into a human again. Icke insists that high level Illuminati members are hybrid reptilians who must regularly drink human blood in order to keep their human form.

He also points to a passage in the Book of Genesis as his evidence. Genesis 6:1-6 reads, "And it came to pass, when men began to multiply on the face of the earth, and daughters were born unto them, 2That the sons of God saw the daughters of men that they were fair; and they took them wives of all which they chose. 3And the LORD said, My spirit shall not always strive with man, for that he also is flesh: yet his days shall be an hundred and twenty years. 4There were giants in the earth in those days; and also after that, when the sons of God came in unto the daughters of men, and they bare children to them, the same became mighty men which were of old, men of renown."

Some Christians, and even Biblical scholars believe that the Sons of God which came and took the daughters of men and had children with them, were an alien race called the Anunaki. Some versions of the Bible use the word Anunaki instead of Sons of God, and the contemporary English translation uses the words "supernatural beings," and clearly refers to some kind of alien creatures who came down and mated with human females.

In the passages in the Bible following these statements is the story about Noah's Ark and the great flood, which is said that God used to destroy everyone on the earth except for Noah, his sons and their wives who were aboard the ark and later repopulated the earth. While it is an interesting idea, and one could understand how someone would interpret these passages in the Bible as being the creation of a hybrid alien-human race of supermen, there is absolutely no evidence of such creatures existing today. Icke places a tremendous value on the alleged testimony of anonymous eye witnesses who supposedly have seen people "shape shift." On the Internet, one can find various photographs of what look like enormous human skeletons that are said to be the remains of the Anunaki, but all such photos have been proven hoaxes, and no such remains have ever been produced. Icke also makes other radical and unverifiable claims.

In one of his video lectures, titled *Ruled by the Gods*, Icke claims that he met an individual who worked for the CIA as a researcher, and that the man showed him a device the CIA had implanted in his chest where he needs to inject a certain kind of drug every few days, and if he doesn't, the man will die. Icke says the CIA implanted this device in the man's chest as a way to control him and prevent him from quitting his research after he found it unethical. Icke took no photographs of the alleged device, and other inconsistencies lead one to believe that Icke has made up this entire story in an attempt to have an "exclusive" story about the Illuminati that no other researcher had discovered.

First of all, if such a device was real, why didn't Icke take any pictures of it, or if he didn't have a camera at the time, why didn't he ask the man to later email him some, or anonymously send them to him through the mail? Obviously, even if Icke had possession of such photos, they could easily be faked by having someone simply place a piece of plastic on their chest.

Secondly, if the CIA had implanted this man with such a device, what would happen if he were to go to the doctor or be taken to the hospital from a car accident, and the medical staff were to find this bizarre device stuck to his chest with no medial history of it in the man's medial records and no clues as to what such a device was used for?

Despite these dubious claims, David Icke has a loyal following, and has been involved in the conspiracy theory genre for almost twenty years. His work has a lot of New Age themes, and at times he seems to attack Christianity. In late 2006 he was the focus of a British documentary titled, *David Icke: Was He Right?* The film consists of news clips of Icke from the early 1990s when he appeared on talk shows around Britain claiming he was the son of God and delivering a warning to mankind about dark times ahead.

One such appearance was on the *Wogan Show* in 1991 which made him a laughing stock in Britain after the show had aired. The host, Terry Wogan started, "Let me get this story right. The press claim that you claim to be the son of God. Is that true?" to which David replied "Yes. Well, you see the thing is….(Audience laughs at him.) It's quite funny really. You know 2000 years ago had a guy called Jesus sat here and said these same things, you would still be laughing. It's really funny that we have not moved on that much."

Wogan then replies asking, "Was it a great shock for you to discover this at thirty-eight? (audience erupts in laughter again) David then went on to predict cataclysmic events that humanity would soon be facing. "When may we expect tidal waves, eruptions, and earthquakes? When is the first thing going to happen?" asked Wogan.

"It will certainly happen this year. The first sequence will begin this year," replied Icke.

"What will happen if they don't happen? What will happen to you?" Wogan pressed.

"They will happen, because if they don't happen, then there will be no earth," said Icke as he nervously picked at his fingernails.

It's surprising Icke was able to recover from such foolishness. Despite David Icke's valid points about society being influenced by mainstream media and the history and activities of the Illuminati, there are gaping holes in his credibility and it is advised that people use other sources of information other than Icke in order to ensure the quality of the information they are getting.

William Cooper

Milton William Cooper, known as William or Bill Cooper was an author and radio host who discussed the Illuminati, the New World Order, and UFOs. He claimed that he had a Top Secret, Q security clearance, Sensitive Compartmentalized Information with access authorized on a strict need-to-know basis.[142] While supposedly working for Naval Intelligence, he claimed to have seen classified

---

[142] Cooper, William – *Behold a Pale Horse* page 26

documents regarding the JFK assassination, UFOs, and the New World Order. Cooper was shot and killed on November 5, 2001 by a sheriff who was serving an arrest warrant at his Arizona home after Cooper allegedly tried to resist arrest and shot an officer in the head. He was 58 years old. Police and neighbors say Cooper had threatened a man with a gun for trespassing on his property, and a warrant was issued for his arrest. The circumstances surrounding his death remain the topic of debate and will be discussed at the end of this section. Many of Cooper's fans believe he was assassinated to stop him from continuing to discuss the information he claimed to have learned while in the Navy.

William Cooper is best known for this 1991 book *Behold a Pale Horse*, which discusses various aspects of the New World Order and contains his many claims to have seen classified government documents while in the Navy. The title is from the Bible's *Book of Revelation* chapter 6 verse 8, "And I looked, and behold a pale horse: and his name that sat on him was Death, and Hell followed with him."

In the forward to *Behold a Pale Horse*, Cooper recounts his time in the Navy and begins by explaining that he and his fellow ship mates had seen several UFOs rise up from the ocean and disappear into the clouds. He insists that the Navy's sonar had also detected these objects.[143] He explains that a superior officer then made him sign an agreement that he was not to discuss the event with anyone, including the other witnesses. Throughout his book are included various photos of Cooper while in uniform and on a patrol boat to show that he was actually in the Navy. He even includes his service record in the back of his book, in an attempt to give credibility to his claims, although these documents make no reference to him having any Top Secret security clearance.

Cooper explains that when he was registering for the

---

[143] Cooper, William – *Behold a Pale Horse* page 19-20

Navy a questionnaire asked if the applicant had been a member of any fraternal organizations, and that he circled the DeMolay society, since he said he was a member as a child.[144] The DeMolay society is basically a branch of Freemasonry for children of Masons. He says that this selection made him a viable candidate to become promoted into the inner circle of Naval Intelligence, since all people in that division were involved with Freemasonry.

At this point he claims to have been given another security clearance in the crypto category and served as the designated SPECAT operator. It was then that he writes he learned the Office of Naval Intelligence had participated in the assassination of President John F. Kennedy and that the Secret Service agent driving the limo had shot Kennedy in the head.[145] This odd theory isn't even considered credible by the least objective JFK assassination conspiracy theorists, and such an idea ignores the fact that nobody reported hearing a gunshot from the limo (or seeing the driver with a gun), which was just a few feet away from the crowd.

Throughout his book he continues to make repeated references to "the Top Secret documents" he saw when working in the Navy and how they pertain to the New World Order.

I will continue to list his far-fetched claims in a minute, but it first must be said that it is extremely suspicious that Cooper casually mentions "Top Secret documents he had seen" as if they were just laying out on someone's desk and he happened to spot them and had a chance to actually read through them. There are millions and millions of pages of classified material which fill countless filing cabinets which are extremely difficult to access, yet Cooper claims he simply "came across" various documents which discuss

---

[144] Cooper, William – *Behold a Pale Horse* page 26
[145] Cooper, William – *Behold a Pale Horse* page 27

material referencing the Council on Foreign Relations, the Bilderberg group, and the New World Order.

In his book, he published a text allegedly from a document titled "Silent Weapons for Quiet Wars" which he says was a Top Secret document that was discovered on July 7, 1986 in a photo copier that had been purchased at a military surplus sale, suggesting someone in the military had accidentally left the original in the machine after making photo copies.

The "document" contains information supposedly on how the government can control the world's resources, finances, and information, in order to further their goals of constructing the New World Order. It reads like a poorly written hoax. In the text of this supposed Top Secret document obtained by Cooper, it continuously refers to "the elite" and their diabolical plans. It also mentions the Bilderberg group and Rothschild's control of the banking system. The whole thing reads like a pathetic regurgitation of the *Protocols of the Elders of Zion.* (See Protocols of Elders of Zion page 146)

Cooper also reported that to mark the year 2000, the Illuminati would use the Galileo space craft to detonate 49.7 pounds of plutonium as it reached the planet Jupiter, which would cause a nuclear reaction turning the planet into another sun. He said that this new star would be called Lucifer and would be cited as a miracle or a sign that the Antichrist was a god and the messiah had appeared. This, all according to Top Secret documents he claimed to have read in the Navy concerning Project Galileo.[146] Cooper's book was published in 1991, giving him a full nine years to make such claims and collect the profits from his sales. He added that the Spear of Destiny, which is said to be the spear that was used to pierce the side of Jesus as he hung on the cross,

---

[146] Cooper, William – *Behold a Pale Horse* page 72

and other ancient relics believed to be lost to history would be united and give the world leader supernatural powers.[147]

When describing the various secret societies that are involved in creating the New World Order, Cooper included the Skull and Bones society at Yale University, and the Scroll and Key society, but incorrectly stated that Scroll and Key was a secret society at Harvard,[148] when in reality it is also at Yale in Connecticut, the same residence of Skull and Bones.

Eight years before Cooper had published *Behold a Pale Horse*, Antony Sutton had released *American's Secret Establishment*, which had exposed for the first time, the activities of the Skull and Bones society. (See America's Secret Establishment page 85) Cooper was well aware of the book, and included it in his references page, so any idea that he learned of Skull and Bones while working in Naval Intelligence can be easily dismissed.

Cooper states, "Top Secret documents that I read while with Naval Intelligence stated that President Eisenhower had commissioned the JASON Society to examine all evidence, facts, likes, and deception and find the truth of the alien question."[149] While not often mentioned in regards to the New World Order, the Jasons, or the Jason Society is a secret group of scientists and scholars who consult with the Department of Defense. Their existence was exposed to the public during the Vietnam War and was well known to all anti-war activists.[150] So Cooper didn't need to find a "Top Secret" document to learn about the group, and only needed to read the newspapers in the late 1960s and early 1970s when their activities were being discussed in the press.

[147] Cooper, William – *Behold a Pale Horse* page 75
[148] Cooper, William – *Behold a Pale Horse* page 81
[149] Cooper, William – *Behold a Pale Horse* page 83
[150] Finkbeiner, Ann – *The Jasons: The Secret History of Science's Postwar Elite* page 100

Cooper also writes about the alleged Majestic Twelve (also called Majesty Twelve), a group some believe is a scientific branch within the military which deals with aliens. Again, Cooper claims this information was discovered from secret documents that he just happened to find. He wrote, "I read Top Secret documents while with Naval Intelligence that stated President Eisenhower had appointed six of the Executive Committee members of the CFR [Council on Foreign Relations] to sit on the panel called Majesty Twelve also known as Majority Twelve for security reasons. Majesty Twelve is the secret group that is supposed to control extraterrestrial information and projects."[151]

Ideas surrounding Majestic Twelve had been circulating in UFO circles since 1984, and was not a new "discovery" by Cooper from "Top Secret" documents. Most in the UFO community did not take Cooper seriously, and he found the majority of his support from patriots and those against the New World Order.

Perhaps the most laughable and far fetched claim that can be added to the list is when he writes, "I read while in Naval Intelligence that at least once a year, maybe more, two nuclear submarines meet beneath the polar icecap and mate together at an airlock. Representatives of the Soviet Union meet with the Policy Committee of the Bilderberg Group," where "The Russians are given the script for their next performance...This method of meeting is the only way that is safe from detection and/or bugging."[152]

So, according to Cooper, there is no secure room in the Pentagon that is safe from being bugged or anywhere else on the planet, so the Bilderberg group must meet in a submarine beneath the polar ice cap.

Aside from numerous fabrications and obvious false

[151] Cooper, William – *Behold a Pale Horse* page 85
[152] Cooper, William – *Behold a Pale Horse* page 94

claims in his writings, you will find the occasional paranoid ranting including one where he writes using all capitol letters, "PATRIOTS MUST NOT BE AT HOME ON ANY NATIONAL HOLIDAY DURING THE DAY OR NIGHT EVER AGAIN UNTIL THE DANGER IS PAST. DISREGARD THIS WARNING AND YOU WILL FIND YOURELF IN A CONCENTRATION CAMP."[153]

Cooper claimed that he possessed photographs of a secret base located on the moon in the crater Copernicus.[154] Also in *Behold a Pale Horse* he included pictures of what he said were UFOs and diagrams and photos of what he called alien reproduction vehicles.

When looking for a motive for his outlandish claims, one needs only to look at the words of Mr. Cooper himself. In the forward to his book he describes that after he was discharged from the Navy that "we were broke and homeless at that point."[155] He had tried to make money by selling audio tapes of his lectures, which apparently wasn't making him any money, so he would later write and publish *Behold a Pale Horse* in 1991.

Also by Cooper's own admission he had fabricated documents and information concerning UFOs and the New World Order and posted them on a BBS network called ParaNet (Paranormal Network). Bulletin Board Systems (BBS) were a precursor to the Internet and allowed people to access another person's hard drive directly by using a modem. He fully admits that he fabricated information and posted it, but he claimed the only reason he did it was to throw the government off his trail by making them think that he was "a kook who didn't really know anything."[156]

---

[153] Cooper, William – *Behold a Pale Horse* page 178
[154] Cooper, William – *Behold a Pale Horse* page 94
[155] Cooper, William – *Behold a Pale Horse* page 33
[156] Cooper, William – *Behold a Pale Horse* page 28

Cooper was exposed and the information he had posted was proven to be false, and so it makes sense that he mentioned this in his book as a way to try to explain why it was that it had been shown he had spread fraudulent information in the past and been caught. The Sysop (system operator) for ParaNet, Michael Corbin, had this to say about Cooper: "First, I don't want to get into any protracted discussions about Bill Cooper. All I can say is that we, ParaNet, had a great deal of experience with Bill Cooper, up to and including ejecting him from the net for causing a variety of disruptions, not to mention strong attacks on other members of the net that were counter-productive to intelligent discussion. Our organization has investigated Cooper to the max and can find no truth in anything he says except that he was in the Navy, but not in the capacity that he claims. The bottom line is that Bill Cooper just doesn't hold water, so anything he says should be taken with a large block of salt and tongue planted firmly in cheek."[157]

Cooper had exposed nothing new in his book or in his lectures, and the information he claims to have read from Top Secret documents was nothing but a retelling of publicly known information that had been talked about in the anti-New World Order movement for decades. Actually, there is one exception in regards to no new information being published by Cooper, and that is the "Silent Weapons for Quiet Wars" document he claimed to obtain from an old photo copier. The "document" is rarely cited as evidence by people researching the New World Order, and its authenticity is doubted by many. He says it was given to him by a man named Tom Young and that Cooper himself had "read Top Secret documents which explained that "Silent Weapons for Quiet Wars" is the doctrine adopted by the Policy Committee of the Bilderberg Group during its first

---

[157] http://pdharris.com/cooper/fraud_hoax_fight.htm

known meeting in 1954."[158]

While no researcher is going to be 100% accurate with the information they compile, or the conclusions they draw from it, the repeated inconsistencies in Cooper's book and his claims to have "seen Top Secret documents" about various issues which were already public knowledge, combined with his own admission that he had written and published fraudulent information in the past, clearly prove that Cooper is an unreliable source, and a financially troubled hoaxer who was cashing in by mixing fact with fiction and presenting himself as a first hand witness.

There are a number of people who continue to believe that William Cooper is a heroic man who exposed the New World Order and was murdered to silence him. Many of these people perhaps have only read parts of Cooper's book and haven't seen the extent of the ridiculousness of his claims. Others who are aware of his wild tales and actually believe them prove their inability to discern facts from fiction.

The actual events surrounding Cooper's death remain the topic of debate and speculation amongst his fans. On November 5th 2001, sheriff deputies lured Cooper from his home in rural Eager, Arizona at approximately 11pm by posing as ordinary citizens playing loud music in their vehicle on or near his property, causing him to come out and investigate. A warrant had been issued for his arrest for allegedly threatening a man named Dr. Scott Hamblin with a gun for either trespassing or loitering on or near his land. Police claim that when they tried to apprehend Cooper, he pulled out a hand gun and shot one deputy, resulting in another officer shooting and killing Cooper. People who knew Cooper personally have said that anyone who attempted to approach his home would be confronted at

---

[158] Cooper, William – *Behold a Pale Horse* page 36

gunpoint and that over the last few years of his life he was growing increasingly paranoid and unstable. They also said that Cooper himself had said that he would never be taken alive after he failed to appear in court for charges that he refused to pay income taxes. Cooper's neighbor and friend Glenn Jacobs was the editor of a small local paper called *The Round Valley Paper*, and wrote, "local police with a warrant for a couple of aggravated-assault warrants (Bill was certainly guilty) went up in force to Bill Cooper's house, letting on to be teenagers drinking and partying, with the radio turned up loud. Bill came out of his house and drove over to them, demanding that they get off of his mountain. Two officers jumped Bill in his car. Bill backed it up, shoved one officer out and shot the other one twice in the head with his forty-five, but did not inflict any life-threatening wounds. Bill ran toward his house, whereupon the entire contingent gave Bill what he had been asking for— his martyrdom. This was not a federal ninja action, nor a rogue-cop riot. Bill had gone over to Dr. Scott Hamblin's house and wagged a gun in his face, and seems to have done the same to another person as well. The officers wisely went prepared, as Bill had broadcast hundreds of times that he would not surrender and would kill anyone who came after him."

Despite Glenn Jacobs and others in the Eager, Arizona community who were friends with Cooper and against the New World Order saying that Cooper had lost it and opened fire on the police first, many of Cooper's fans believe he was purposefully murdered because he talked about 9/11 and the New World Order.

The *Associated Press* published an article the day after his death labeling Cooper a "national leader of the militia movement" and tried to tie him to Timothy McVeigh saying "McVeigh, who was executed in May for the bombing of the federal building in Oklahoma City, listened to Cooper's broadcasts for inspiration, according to testimony by James

Nichols, brother of Oklahoma bombing co-defendant Terry Nichols during a 1996 pretrial hearing."[159] While Cooper's death is a tragedy and it's slanderous to tie him to Timothy McVeigh, and many of the issues he discussed on his radio show and in his book are true, it is inexcusable that he fabricated tales of seeing Top Secret documents in an attempt to add credibility to his story and sell more books.

His numerous claims to have personally seen Top Secret documents on a variety of issues and present himself as a whistleblower casts a dark cloud of doubt over his memory and his body of work since it leads people unfamiliar with such material to believe that some fictions are fact.

Criticizing Cooper is a sensitive issue since he is viewed as a martyr by many of his fans who are offended by anyone voicing doubts about his claims or credentials, and continue to believe that he was assassinated despite all the evidence to the contrary.

Phil Schneider

Phil Schneider is a man who not only claimed to have information about UFOs and aliens, but he also claimed to have gotten into a shootout with them in an underground military base. Schneider appeared on the UFO scene in 1995, and traveled around giving a series of lectures which he claimed were accounts of his experiences working on government projects and ultimately battling aliens in an underground tunnel. He claimed to have worked for seventeen years as a geologist and aerospace and structural engineer and to have had a level 1 security clearance while working on black budget government projects. Schneider

[159] Associated Press/The Arizona Republic *Militia Leader Killed, Deputy Wounded During Attempted Arrest* November 06, 2001

was found dead in his apartment on January 17, 1996 and apparently the body had been there for a week before anyone had reported him missing. The cause of death was officially from a stroke, but as will be discussed later, some speculate he was murdered to keep him from talking.

Schneider's statements are interesting in that it appears to be the first time someone has come forward and not only claimed to have been a part of an alien cover-up, but that the aliens are living and working in a series of tunnels below the earth's surface. Schneider maintained that some of these aliens are hostile, but others are friendly and work with the U.S. government.

At a speech given at the 1995 Preparedness Expo which can be seen on YouTube and Google Video, Schneider claims that the Army cavalry had a unit in 1909 stationed in the American south west who followed some "bandits" into a cave where they found "flying disks" and "little gray guys" and that the incident had been in secret archives ever since.

During his talk in 1995 he said that there were 131 active underground bases in the U.S. and 1477 world wide, with each costing 17 to 19 billion dollars, and that each base was connected by underground tunnels with magneto-leviton trains that run between them.

Schneider claims there are eleven distinct races of aliens and that two of these races are friendly and work in cooperation with the U.S. government. The other races of aliens, he says, are a danger to civilization. During his lecture at the 1995 Preparedness Expo he held up a photograph of a group of men who had worked on the USS Eldridge and said that one of the men was an alien that looked human named Val Valiant Thor and had worked for the Pentagon for 58 years and had not aged. Schneider says he met this alien, and that he had six fingers and six toes on each limb, and that he had copper oxide for blood.

As it is typical with most "researchers" or "whistle blowers" who make extremely far fetched claims, even for those who believe in so-called "conspiracy theories," Schneider is believed by most to be a fraudulent opportunist who was seeking to make money off of the UFO and anti New World Order subculture, or a disinformation agent who was muddying the water for serious researchers. Others, of course, believe his account was accurate and is more evidence that the government or the Illuminati, or a combination of the two, are in collusion with alien beings from other planets or dimensions.

From his May 8th 1995 lecture given in Post Falls Idaho:

"It is because of the rather horrendous designs and mechanizations of our federal government structure that I feel directly imperiled not to tell anybody about [these issues] so that's why I'm here telling you. In doing so I am breaking my security oaths, I am also guilty of breaking major federal law. How long I will be able to do this is anybody's guess. However, I would like to mention that this talk is going to be broken up into four main topics. Each of these topics will have some bearing on what you people are involved in, you patriot people, or even some of you people who aren't patriots but who may be leaning that way or considering it..."

"I want you to know that these United States are a beautiful place. I've traveled in over 70 countries, and I cannot remember any country that has the beauty, as well as the magnificence of its people, like these United States."

"To give you an overview of basically what I am, I started off and went through engineering school, which half of my schooling was in that field. I built up a reputation for being a geological engineer, as well as a structural engineer with both military and aerospace applications. I have helped build two main bases within the United States that have some significance as far as what is called the New World Order. Number one is Dulce, New Mexico. I was involved in 1979 in a horrendous fire fight with alien humanoids, and I was one of the survivors. I'm probably the only talking survivor you will ever hear. Two other survivors are under close guard somewhere in the United States. One is not in very good shape, he's been living in Canada. So I'm about the only one around that knows of the fire fight, and that knows all the detailed files of the entire operation. Sixty-six Secret Service agents, FBI, and the like, Black Berets, died in that fight. I was there."

"Number one: part of what I am going to tell you is going to be very shocking. Part of what I am going to tell you is probably going to be very unbelievable, though, instead of putting your glasses on, I'm going to ask you to put your 'skepticals' on rather than your spectacles. But please, feel free to do your own homework. I know the Freedom of Information Act isn't much to go on, but unfortunately it's basically the best we've got. The local law library in your nearest law university is a good place to look for Congressional Records. So, if one continues to do their homework, then one can be standing vigilant in regards to their country."

Alleged Firefight at Dulce Base

"Back in 1954, under the Eisenhower administration, the federal government decided to circumvent the Constitution of the United States and form a treaty with [alien] entities from outside of the United States and it was supposed to be secret. It was called the Greata 1954 Treaty, which basically said that the aliens could take a few cows and test their implanting techniques on a few human beings, but that they had to give detailed lists of the people involved. Slowly, but surely, the outer space aliens altered the bargain until they decided they wouldn't go by it at all. Back in 1979, this was the reality and the fire-fight occurred quite by accident."

"I was involved in building an addition to the deep

underground military base at Dulce, New Mexico which by the way is probably the United States deepest base. It goes down seven levels and over 2.5 miles deep. At that particular time, we had drilled four distinct holes in the desert ground, and we were going to link them together and blow out large sections at a time. My job at that time was to go down in these holes and gather rock samples, check them for their particularity, for particle count, give a detailed account of what kind of chemical explosive, or plastic explosive to use and we would go from there. As I was headed down there, to my total surprise we found ourselves amidst a large cavern that was already full of outer-space aliens, otherwise known as large Greys. I was petrified, as most people might be. The only thing I could think of doing at the time was shooting at them. I killed two of them, but by the time I could reload, and re fire, at that time I had a Walther PPK pistol, I was an engineer so I didn't feel I had to carry a gun around, and I always carried this particular one around, it was nice and small and quite effective. But anyway, I killed a couple of these things and at that time there were several other groups of people down there. About 40 more came down after this started, and all of them got killed. Basically what had occurred was that we had surprised a whole underground base of existing aliens. Later on I was to find out that we are not the highest ones on the food chain. These aliens have probably been living on our planet for, different groups of aliens anyway, the short and the tall Greys at least for a million years. This could explain a lot of the theory behind ancient astronauts, these other kinds of things, and it might also explain the blood thirstiness of different kinds of native populaces like the Aztecs..."

"Anyway, I got shot basically here [in the chest]. Their kind of weapon wasn't really a gun like thing, it was kind of like a box that they had on their body that they could manipulate. And it burned a hole in me and split my ribs apart, kind of gory and all that kind of stuff, but anyway it also gave me a high dose of rather nasty cobalt radiation. I have cancer to this day that's probably a result of that, although I can't prove that."

END OF TRANSCRIPT

Schneider's tales are pretty far fetched to say the least. I am not saying that aliens do not exist. I have an open enough mind to understand that their existence is certainly possible. Nor do I deny that they have visited the earth. It is an interesting topic, and while many, if not most supposed UFO sightings are fully explainable and the result of top secret aircraft, unknown atmospheric conditions, and even that of pranksters, hoaxers and mentally insane people, there does remain the very real possibility that intelligent life exists outside of planet earth and has perhaps traveled here. It is not my intention to completely discount the possibility of real aliens from other planets existing or visiting the earth or even working with the Illuminati. We need more evidence, and most of the so-called evidence that has come forth has been fraudulent and created for the purpose of getting the media's attention, and selling books.

In his lectures, Schneider mentions that he had actual metal from the UFO crash in Roswell, New Mexico that was given to him when he was fourteen years old. He shows metal samples at his speeches and says that the materials to build the Stealth Fighters and some submarines came from alien technology. The samples he shows which he claims were from alien technology are so hard they can scratch diamonds, he said. No one was allowed to test his claims, or handle the samples themselves.

As if his allegations of having a shootout with aliens weren't outrageous enough, they get worse. During his talks Schneider said that aliens use human blood and secretions as food, and that they "get high" off of the adrenochrome from the adrenal gland. He said it was like cocaine for them. It is actually rumored that Satanists participate in this practice for the same reason, which is most likely the inspiration for Schneider to include this strange practice in his stories about the aliens. (See Fear and Loathing in Las Vegas page 318) Schneider also claimed 100,000 children are unaccounted for and have recently gone missing and that he believed the children and other missing persons are victims of the aliens who take them and eat them.

By the year 2029, he said the aliens would reduce the world's population by seven-eights and then would rule the earth. Aside from giving a lecture on underground bases and tunnels and his alleged alien encounter, he would occasionally rant about the corrupt government, the loss of Civil Liberties, and the New World Order.

So in summation, he claims that in August of 1979 he shot and killed two aliens with his Walther PPK pistol and that before he was able to kill one of the aliens, it shot a blue beam out of its chest which hit him cutting him open and burning several of his fingers off. Schneider was missing the index and middle finger and part of his thumb on his left hand, which some say is "proof" of his story. At various points during his speeches, this injury can clearly be seen. He could have very well lost them in a work related accident and incorporated it into his stories about the aliens. The question of why he was carrying a gun to begin with is also perplexing. If he was a civilian engineer, why would he be carrying a gun? If he was working on a secure military installation, then why would he need a gun? Or would he even be permitted to carry one? Probably not.

Schneider also claims to have held a level 1 security clearance, which sounds impressive and appears to be the highest level available since it is labeled "level 1" but in reality a level 1 security clearance is only an entry level clearance. Level 1 is categorized as "confidential" with level 2 being "secret" and level 3 being "top secret." Schneider probably didn't know the structure of the hierarchy, and incorrectly believed a level 1 clearance would be the highest level.

There is also the question of how Schneider would know about how many races of aliens there were, and how he would come to know that they were eating people for the adrenochrome in their body, if in fact they were. If there are aliens living in the underground bases and tunnels, and Schneider did actually see them, or have a conflict with them, then he would have been debriefed and sworn to secrecy never to talk about it. Those who knew the whole story, certainly would not tell Schneider or others about the details of the aliens, or what they were doing living in those bases.

While Schneider didn't have any books or DVDs to sell after his lectures, word was that he had nearly completed, or was working on a book when he had died. Some who believe Schneider's stories use this as evidence that the government assassinated him to prevent him from getting his information out. Or perhaps people just assumed that he was working on a book, because nearly everyone who comes forward with tales of supposedly witnessing government programs or having been members of the Illuminati write books.

Underground bases and tunnels do exist. There are advanced tunnel boring machines (TBMs) that are making them, and video of such machines can be readily found on the Internet and they have been featured in shows produced by the History Channel. You can easily find the websites for the Robbins Company and others which build them. This author has a detailed chapter on these underground bases and tunnels in my book, *The Resistance Manifesto*. It is certainly likely that top secret tunnels span the country, if not the world and connect various military bases. Schneider may have actually worked on such projects, and used this knowledge and experience to concoct his entire "alien fire fight" story. Perhaps he was upset that enormous amounts of money were being spent on the projects and he thought that by blowing the whistle on them and mixing in fictional tales of aliens living in them, it would give him more attention and cause people to look into the tremendous waste of money that is being put into such projects.

Or perhaps Schneider was a retired engineer who was bored and thought that people who believed in aliens were kooks, and decided he would entertain himself by making up a bunch of stories about how he had a shoot-out with aliens when he was working in the tunnels and loved the attention he got as a result and he and his friends would laugh about how gullible the UFO crowd was as they drank a few beers. Of course it is also possible that Schneider was a paid government disinfo agent who had the job of publicizing ridiculous tales involving the underground bases and tunnels to make people think that any talk of the tunnels existing were conspiracy theories involving aliens.

Upon word of Phil Schneider's death in January 1996, rumors circulated on the Internet that he was murdered, as is common when people in the conspiracy theory genre die. While his death was ruled a natural cause by a stroke, a letter began circulating on the Internet, supposedly written by his ex wife, Cynthia Drayer. The authenticity of this letter has not been verified, and when one reads its contents, it becomes obvious that it is a hoax, or a joke, meant to stir up even more controversy surrounding Phil Schneider.

The letter explains that Schneider's wife suspected foul play, and another autopsy was performed "at the Multnomah County Medical Examiner's office (in Portland, Oregon) by Dr. Gunson, and she determined that Philip had committed suicide by wrapping a rubber catheter hose three times around his neck, and half-knotting it in front." Whoever actually wrote this letter, and whatever Schneider's motives for fabricating his fanciful stories, we may never know.

Mentions in Mainstream Media

The subject of the Illuminati and its subsidiary organizations such as the Bilderberg group, Skull and Bones, and the Bohemian Grove are rarely mentioned in the mainstream news, largely because they own most news outlets and have editorial policies in place to prevent such stories from being published or produced.

Even many so-called more independent forms of media such as talk radio will not cover such organizations. Most local hosts simply have no idea such organizations exist, and have probably not even heard of the Illuminati.[160] Other national hosts such as Rush Limbaugh, who is under a $400 million dollar contract, knows exactly what these organizations are, who is involved with them, and what they are doing. By the way, that is not a typo, in July of 2008 Limbaugh signed a $400 *million* dollar deal with Clear Channel to stay on the air through at least 2016.[161] Hosts like Rush Limbaugh, Sean Hannity, Bill O'Reilly, Alan Colmes and others know who is pulling the strings in global affairs, and that those same institutions are the ones who sign their paychecks as well.

Even with such safeguards in place as Operation Mockingbird, which uses editors and producers who are in the know as gate-keepers to prevent hard news about the Illuminati from making it out to the public, they can not keep *every* story from being killed. (See Mainstream Media page 33) What is even less under their control is what certain

---

[160] At the time of this writing in April 2009, many have not heard of the Illuminati. *Angels & Demons* the movie and other fictionalizations of the Illuminati may bring the subject matter into the mainstream, but in a tainted and fictionalized way.
[161] Washington Post *Rush Limbaugh Signs $400 Million Radio Deal* by Paul Farhi July 3, 2008; Page C01

guests may say when they are being interviewed live on the air. Of course, any guests who are prone to mentioning such things would only be booked in an attempt to attack them and discredit them, but all measures are taken to thoroughly screen guests to make sure they subscribe to the paradigm the network is attempting to maintain.

CNBC
October 24, 2008

After the entire U.S. economy began to melt down in the third quarter of 2008, many people were looking for answers as to how this could happen. A short but interesting answer was given on CNBC on Friday October 24, 2008 by Jeffrey Saut of Sentinel Asset Management, who said, "I think you're in a liquidation phase, I think Kirstin (another guest on the show) had it right, I think there is a bunch of wrong footed moves made by Hank Paulson (Treasury Secretary at the time) and the Illuminati of the country if you will, and I think we're paying for it right now."

Gerald Celente
December 8, 2008

CEO of The Trends Research Institute, Gerald Celente, is an extremely well respected trend forecaster who is noted for predicting the 1987 stock market crash, as well as the fall of the Soviet Union. In 2008 Celente made news reporting that by 2012 America would be in a depression worse than the Great Depression which occurred in the 1930s. He forecasted massive unemployment, food shortages, riots, and mass vacancies in retail spaces.

On the December 18th 2008 broadcast of the Alex Jones show on the Genesis Communications Network, Celente mentioned the Illuminati as the root cause of the economic collapse that began at the end of 2008. When asked for his analysis on what was happening, he said, "It's definitely a financial coup. Wall Street has hijacked Washington in broad daylight. Now as we know, of course, the U.S. Treasury Secretary Henry Paulson is a Goldman Sachs man, former CEO. They're bringing in now Obama, "backtrack Obama" we call him...the man of "change," and of course there's no change. They're bringing in Timothy Geithner, the Federal Reserve Bank president of the New York Federal Reserve. They're just bringing in this whole crew of Wall Street people running Washington. So it's being done in broad daylight as well as these bailouts. The Illuminati so to speak may have their agenda laid out."

Fox News Business

On December 12, 2008 a writer for Fox News Business made an interesting post concerning the economic crisis stemming from home foreclosures and failing banks and industries. Cody Willard posted an article titled, *Illuminating the Illuminati: Charles Schumer and Barney Frank are Owned by the Big Banks* where he wrote that the Illuminati controlled the banks and the politicians who were at the root cause of the financial collapse.

His post continued, "Here's a definition of Illuminati: individuals who are part of a secretive, historical organization that is comprised of mostly influential members with political and/or financial clout."[162]

It's amazing Willard wasn't soon fired or laid-off. Two months later in February 2009 Willard hosted a news segment on the Fox Business Channel titled *Illuminati Alert* which began with a graphic of an all-seeing eye on top of a

---

[162] http://cody.blogs foxbusiness.com/2008/12/15/Illuminating-the-Illuminati-charles-schumer-and-barney-frank-are-owned-by-the-big-banks

pyramid flying across the screen. Willard denounced the banker bailout in the segment and began by saying, "Here's how they were trying to hold you and me down today."

The Colbert Report

Satirist and comedian Stephen Colbert, host of *The Colbert Report* on Comedy Central, included a joke about the Illuminati on his July 24, 2007 broadcast where he explained that Benjamin Fulford, who used to write for *Forbes* magazine, was accusing the Illuminati of planning to depopulate the earth. (See Benjamin Fulford page 195)

Colbert explains, "Normally I would ignore this kind of raving from an obscure hack, but there is one reason I want to talk about it. The possibility that the Illuminati might let me join. Masters of the temple, please let me in. I tried every crazy handshake I could think of when I met president Bush... And I've got some great ideas about depopulating the earth. There has never been a better time to put me in charge of the destiny of mankind."

"I will await your answer every night for the next month in the exact center of the Brooklyn Bridge, whose cables by the way, are in the same geomantic ratio as the sides of the pyramid of Giza."

Several months later, on December 10th 2008, Stephen Colbert had Richard Haas, president of the Council on Foreign Relations, as a guest. Colbert started the interview by saying, "you're like the Illuminati, or the Masons, you control everything don't you? That's the rap on you guys."

What is strange is that Haas didn't have a new book to promote or any real reason to be on the show. It appears that one of the writers or producers of the show is familiar with the Illuminati and the New World Order and has worked these ideas into the show.

On January 29th 2009, this author (Mark Dice) received an email from a producer of *The Colbert Report* asking if I would be interested in being interviewed about the Georgia Guidestones monument. When I spoke with the producer on the phone she informed me that they were working on a series of segments about mysteries, and the punch line would be that Stephen solves them all. She also informed me that Colbert had not been familiar with the Guidestones and when one of the writers brought up the idea for a segment he doubted they even existed because he had never heard of them before.

So from the repeated references to the Illuminati on the show, and the request I received from the producer about the Guidestones, it becomes clear that someone working on the show is fairly familiar with such things, and has been able to work them into the show on several occasions. Their motive for doing so remains to be seen.

Fox News Channel
June 19, 2004
Guest: Kris Milligan

Kris Milligan, the editor of *Fleshing Out Skull and Bones*, one of the best books written on the Skull and Bones society was a guest on Fox News briefly to discuss the issue of both John Kerry and George W. Bush being members of the club and facing off against each other in the 2004 presidential election. The producers probably thought it would be an interesting segment and would present Skull and Bones as nothing more than a college fraternity for the elite, but as soon as Milligan mentioned the club's involvement in narcotics trafficking, he was cut off and the segment ended.

[Host]
What is the point of this club?

[Kris Milligan]
Well, some say the point of the club is bonding. I look at it

through the eyes of a social historian. And when you look at the grouping of people and the jobs that they have, you find that a very large amount of the membership have been involved in intelligence. One of the most disturbing things is that the family groups have been involved in drug running since the early 1800s.

[Host]
Drug running?

[Kris Milligan]
Yes, see the founder of Skull and Bones was William Huntington Russell, and his family business was Russell and Company, which was America's largest opium smuggler, the third largest in the world...

[Host]
Wow. Kris Milligan, unfortunately we're out of time, we're going to have to leave it at that. Fascinating subject.

60 Minutes
June 16, 2004

CBS's newsmagazine *60 Minutes* aired a segment prior to the 2004 presidential election talking about the Skull and Bones society which included an interview with Alexandra Robbins, author of *Secrets of the Tomb*, who was herself a Yale graduate and a member of the Scroll and Key secret society. The segment was like every other one which miraculously made the mainstream news that year and basically portrayed the organization as nothing more than a fraternity for rich guys.

NBC's Meet the Press

In 2004, NBC's Tim Russert on *Meet The Press* briefly

addressed the subject of George W. Bush and John Kerry being members of Skull and Bones, and asked them about it in a joking manner. Both Bush and Kerry laughed off his questions and moved right along with the interview. President Bush appeared on *Meet the Press* on February 8, 2004. At the very end of the show Russert asked him about Skull and Bones. Russert must have been aware to some extent of the power the organization holds, and his brief question and his joking manner suggest this was a tactic used to minimize the issue in the election and laugh it off like it's just another college fraternity. Russert himself was a member of the Council on Foreign Relations. A transcript from that broadcast follows.

MR. RUSSERT: You were both in Skull and Bones, the secret society.

PRESIDENT BUSH: It's so secret we can't talk about it.

MR. RUSSERT: What does that mean for America? The conspiracy theorists are going to go wild.

PRESIDENT BUSH: I'm sure they are. I don't know. I haven't seen Web pages yet. (Laughs)

MR. RUSSERT: Number 322.

PRESIDENT BUSH: First of all, he's not the nominee, and — but look, I look forward —

MR. RUSSERT: Are you prepared to lose?

PRESIDENT BUSH: No, I'm not going to lose.

A few months before, on August 31, 2003, John Kerry appeared on the show and was asked the same question in the same manner. The topic was the last to be discussed and after Russert and Kerry laughed off the questions, the show ended and the credits rolled. Here is the transcript.

MR. RUSSERT: You both were members of Skull and Bones, a secret society at Yale. What does that tell us?

SEN. KERRY: Not much, because it's a secret.

MR. RUSSERT: Is there a secret handshake? Is there a secret code?

SEN. KERRY: I wish there were something secret I could manifest there.

MR. RUSSERT: Three twenty-two, a secret number?

SEN. KERRY: There are all kinds of secrets, Tim. But one thing is not a secret. I disagree with this president's direction that he's taking the country. We can do a better job. And I intend to do it.

MR. RUSSERT: And we'll be watching. Be safe on the campaign trail. John Kerry, thanks for joining us.

SEN. KERRY: Thank you, sir.

MR. RUSSERT: And we'll be right back. (Announcements)

MR. RUSSERT: That's all for today. We'll be back next week. If it's Sunday, it is MEET THE PRESS.

Geronimo's Skull Controversy

The Skull and Bones society is said to have three real human skulls which are kept in their windowless headquarters, the "Tomb" in New Haven, Connecticut. For decades it has been rumored that one of the skulls was that of the Apache Indian chief Geronimo, which was stolen by grave robbers in 1918 from his resting place at Fort Sill, Oklahoma. One of the men identified as the thief was Prescott Bush, who was a Skull and Bones member and is the grandfather of George W. Bush and was stationed at Fort Sill at the time Geronimo's remains went missing.

Of course, Skull and Bones members deny the story is true, but a letter discovered that was dated 1918 that was written by a Bonesman explained that they had taken the skull. The letter was written on June 7, 1918 by Winter Mead '19 to F. Trubee Davison '18 and reads, "The skull of the worthy Geronimo the Terrible, exhumed from its tomb at Fort Sill by your club & the K — t [Knight] Haffner, is now safe inside the T — [Tomb] together with his well worn femurs[,] bit & saddle horn."

Harlyn Geronimo, the great-grandson of the Indian chief is suing Yale University and the Skull and Bones society to try to recover the remains. "I think what would be important is that the remains of Geronimo be with his ancestors," he said.

Alexandra Robbins, the author of *Secrets of the Tomb*, told CNN, "I spoke with several Bonesmen who told me that inside the Tomb there is a glass display case containing a skull and the Bonesmen have always called it Geronimo."[163]

The CNN story explained that they had attempted to contact Skull and Bones, but no one returned their calls. The

---

[163] CNN *Descendant sues Skull and Bones over Geronimo's bones* February 26, 2009

controversy began in 2006, when the letter was first found tucked inside a book in the Yale library. Some believe that the skull in question is not that of Geronimo's because they say his grave was unmarked and overgrown until a few years later. David H. Miller, a history professor at Cameron University in Lawton, Oklahoma said, "My assumption is that they did dig up somebody at Fort Sill. It could have been an Indian, but it probably wasn't Geronimo."

Geronimo's great-grandson Harlyn has said he is willing to submit a DNA sample if the skull is recovered to determine if it is Geronimo's. In his 32-page lawsuit, he has also listed President Barack Obama, Defense Secretary Robert Gates and Secretary of the Army Pete Geren as defendants.

Inside Edition

The tabloid news show *Inside Edition* ran a brief segment during the 2004 presidential campaign about the Skull and Bones society, lasting just over two and a half minutes, which started with the narrator saying, "You may think that George W. Bush and John Kerry have little in common, but both men count themselves as members of Skull and Bones, Yale University's oldest, and some say, elite secret society."

The segment included several sound bites from an interview with author Alexandra Robbins, where she stated, "the only purpose of Skull and Bones, is to get its members into positions of power, and then to hire other members."

A brief sound bite from George W. Bush's fellow bonesman, Don Etra, who is a Los Angeles criminal attorney showed he wouldn't comment on the organization. Harvey Bundy, a portfolio manager in Chicago who was senator John Kerry's roommate at Yale, but not a member of Skull and Bones, arrogantly laughed after he states, "They pick people who are leaders on campus, and people who they believe will be future leaders, and they pick pretty well."

The subject of new members laying in a coffin nude and recounting their entire sexual history was mentioned, and footage of members wearing black robes was briefly shown and said to have been taken by the *Inside Edition* video crew with night vision cameras.

The segment ended with Alexandra Robbins saying, "Skull and Bones has told me that they don't really care who wins, Bush or Kerry, for the 2004 presidency, for Skull and Bones it's a win-win situation."

CNN
December 4th 2008
Guest: Peter Schiff

Financial analyst and president of the brokerage firm Euro Pacific Capital, Peter Schiff, made an appearance on CNN to discuss the unfolding economic crisis in December 2008 and when he started mentioning the cause was the Federal Reserve, the network had "technical difficulties" and the segment abruptly ended while Schiff was mid-sentence. While some see the dropped feed as accidental technical difficulties, others wonder if an editor at CNN decided Schiff was giving away too much information and that he had to be silenced.

[Peter Schiff]
Capitalism is not about propping up failed companies, we need to let them fail. Now of course behind it all is the Federal Reserve, if the Federal Reserve had not intervened...had they not poured all this alcohol then Wall Street wouldn't have got drunk, but they did. I am convinced that everything the government is doing to fight this off is gonna make... [Feed dropped]

Schiff had precisely predicted the 2008 mortgage meltdown and the following economic crisis. By watching video clips of his earlier appearances on TV in 2007 and 2008, you can see other guests on the shows laugh out loud as he warned the audience of exactly what was coming.

CNN in London
May 2005
Guest: John Ronson

While to date, the Bilderberg group has never been mentioned on CNN in America, a brief segment on CNN in London mentioned the group when they were meeting in Germany in 2005.

The segment mentions that *The Financial Times* of London had mentioned the meeting was occurring and guests included Nokia CEO Jorma Ollila, Daimler Chrystler's Juergen Schrempp, and outgoing World Bank president James Wolfensohn.

It featured an interview with Jon Ronson, who explained, "Bilderberg is a meeting of powerful centrists, industriousts, and politicians. They always meet in secret once a year in a five star hotel with golfing facilities, and they've taken on the image for conspiracy theorists of the fabled shadowy cabal that secretly rules the world."

When asked by the host what the purpose of their meeting is, Ronson answers, "They see themselves as head hunters. They'll get an up and coming politician who they think may be president or prime minister one day and as globalists industrials leaders who believe that politics shouldn't be in the hands of the politicians, they try and influence them with wise words in the corridors outside of sessions."

Jon Ronson doesn't really think the Bilderberg group is a big deal. That's probably the reason he was chosen for the segment, because he downplays their power and influence.

He says, "Bilderberg's secrecy I think goes back specifically to Henry Kissinger, who in kind of a silly way, I think, loves the idea of being this shadowy secret figure and it was Kissinger as a founding member of Bilderberg who had this idea to be this kind of secret organization, in quite, you know, quite a silly way really."

Ronson is the author of a book called *Them: Adventures with Extremists*, and hosted a four part television series called *Secret Rulers of the World* where he covered several issues involving "the New World Order conspiracy theory." (See Secret Rulers of the World page 271)

While Ronson admits the existence of such organizations as the Bilderberg group and the Bohemian Grove, he downplays their influence on society, and insists that only "conspiracy theorists" are worried about what these organizations are doing.

PBS News Hour with Jim Laher

Alan Greenspan, who worked as the Chairman of the Federal Reserve for over eighteen years, did an interview with Jim Laher on the *PBS News Hour* promoting his book, *The Age of Turbulence*, when he made a startling admission that the privately owned Federal Reserve Bank can enact any monetary policy it wants to, and the U.S. government can't do anything about it.

[Jim Lahr]
What is the proper relationship, what should be the proper relationship, between the chairman of the Fed and a president of the United States?

[Alan Greenspan]
Well, first of all, the Federal Reserve is an independent agency, and that means basically that there is no other agency of government which can overrule actions that we

take. So long as that is in place, and there is no evidence that the administration or the Congress or anybody else is requesting that we do things differently than what we think is the appropriate thing, then what the relationships are don't frankly matter.

C-Span
February 2002
Dick Cheney's CFR speech

In a video widely available on YouTube, Vice President Dick Cheney can be seen addressing the Council on Foreign Relations and everyone erupts in laughter as an inside joke reveals the elitist attitude of the organization.

Cheney says, "Well, Les, Pete, I want to thank you all for the warm welcome today. I see a lot of old friends in the room. And it's good to be back at the Council on Foreign Relations. As Pete mentioned, I've been a member for a long time, and was actually a director for some period of time. I never mentioned that when I was campaigning for reelection back home in Wyoming—(laughter)—but it stood me in good stead. I value very much my experience, exposure to the tremendous people involved and the involvement and the ideas and the debates on the great policy issues of the day."

Notice how Cheney admitted being a member for a long time and a director, but never mentioned it when he was campaigning for reelection to the U.S. House of Representatives in Wyoming and then the audience laughed. Obviously Cheney was trying to keep his affiliation with the Council on Foreign Relations quiet and knows that the organization has a bad reputation with those Americans who see it for what it is. Everyone in attendance for Cheney's speech knew this, of course, which is why they all laughed when he said he never mentioned his affiliation with the CFR.

Lou Dobbs Tonight
Aired June 9, 2005

One of the only mainstream hosts to even mention the Council on Foreign Relations' plan for a North American Union is CNN's Lou Dobbs. Starting back in 2005 Dobbs was doing segments about the elite's plans to merge Canada, Mexico, and the United States into a North American Union modeled after the European Union, and eliminate the countries borders. The plan for the NAU had been hatched in secret, and was carried out in stealth until it was discovered.

One segment Dobbs aired on the subject showed Robert Pastor, the Chairman of the CFR say, "The best way to secure the United States today is not at our two borders with Mexico and Canada, but at the borders of North America as a whole."

The segment goes on to report on the CFR's report titled, *Building a North American Community* and how it envisioned a common border around the U.S., Mexico and Canada in the near future.

The North American Union had been called a conspiracy theory when the Security and Prosperity Partnership's website, SPP.gov had first appeared and the CFR's plan for a North American Union was first released to the public.

Dobb's report sited Mexico's problems with drug trafficking, and Dobbs blasted Robert Pastor's idea that the only way to secure America was to eliminate the border with Mexico and Canada.

Such a plan is an obvious push for a New World Order and a regional currency. Once there are several large regional unions, each with their own currency, it will be one small step to then merge all currencies into one global currency, and then to an electronic currency, which is ultimately the Illuminati's plan.

THE ILLUMINATI: FACTS & FICTION

While Lou Dobbs was obviously stunned at the secretive moves to create a North American Union, he failed to see the big picture of why such actions were being taken. Dobbs concluded the segment saying, "Americans must think that our political and academic elites have gone utterly mad at a time when three-and-a-half years, approaching four years after September 11, we still don't have border security. And this group of elites is talking about not defending our borders, finally, but rather creating new ones. It's astonishing."

A year and a half later, Dobbs seemed to have put more of the puzzle together. A segment that aired on January 14th, 2007 was titled "George W. Bush fulfilling his fathers dream of a New World Order" and began with correspondent Bill Tucker saying, "It's not a new idea. President Bush talked about it back in 1991" and then cut to the infamous video clip of Bush 41 giving his state of the union speech were he said, "It is a big idea, a New World Order where diverse nations are drawn together in common cause."

Tucker goes on to explain that the former United States Trade Ambassador Robert Zoellick is talking about a New World Order with business at the helm of trade and economic policy and advocating what he calls the Association of American Free Trade Agreements, which is a non government entity which would include North, Central and South America.

Tucker called it a stealth trade agenda that, "goes hand in hand with the United States, Mexico and Canada working quietly and behind the scenes to promote a common market with common deregulation for the benefit of multinational corporations."

The segment warned that such agreements were being set up by a small group of the corporate elite that was not accountable to anyone but themselves and said they were, effectively surrendering the sovereignty of the United States.

Dobbs concluded the segment saying that the corporate

and political elite in America were more concerned with profits than with the United States or democracy.

C-Span's Washington Journal

Brian Lamb, the director of C-Span dedicated a segment of the show *Washington Journal* to the Bohemian Grove and slanted the coverage in an attempt to remove any suspicions surrounding the club. Professor Michael Barkun was the guest for the segment, who is the author of a book titled *A Culture of Conspiracy*.

Lamb stated, "A lot of things people feel are organized behind the scenes with the Bilderbergers, Trilateral Commission, Council on Foreign Relations, the Masons, you can keep going down the list...the Illuminati, one world government, New World Order, Skull and Bones."

Lamb then admits he was listening to *Coast to Coast AM* one night when Alex Jones was a guest, and said, "he was talking about the Bohemian Grove club as if that's where it all happens. That's where all the decisions are made. There are thousands of people who go there, and there is some kind of ceremony and an owl and all that, have you followed this?"

Barkun replies, "Yes I have, even though the show is on past my bedtime, but, Alex Jones has been talking about this for quite a while. The Bohemian Grove, of course, is a privately owned redwood grove, up in Sonoma country, north of San Francisco where every summer there is a get together of the wealthy and well placed, all male, who get together for general cavorting, socializing, lecture, symposium and so on, in an atmosphere that is completely removed from public scrutiny. Alex Jones and some others have suggested for a long time that there are all sorts of nefarious rituals that go on, and a matter of fact, and I talk about this incident actually in my book, someone who had listened to the Alex Jones show about this was arrested within the Bohemian Grove, very heavily armed, because he said he was trying to bring attention to what he thought were human sacrifices that were being committed by the elite who attend these gatherings."

The topic was then changed to Skull and Bones. Regarding the man arrested in the grove, Barkun is referring to a man named Richard McCaslin who broke into the club in January of 2002 with hopes of exposing the Cremation of Care ritual which he believed involved an actual human sacrifice. During their discussion both Lamb and Barkun avoid any reference to the Cremation of Care ritual, and the fact that a ritual involving burning a human effigy is done each year as a sacrifice to Moloch. Instead they end their discussion and leave the viewer thinking that the intruder was completely insane for thinking such things were occurring there. (See Dark Secrets: Inside Bohemian Grove page 269) (See Chris Jones page 192)

National Geographic

In 2004, *National Geographic* published a photo of a 1915 Cremation of Care ritual taken by Gabriel Moulin and included a caption below the photo explaining the picture. "To purge himself of worldly concerns, a member of the elite Bohemian Club participated in a 1915 Cremation of Care ceremony—complete with candles and a robed and hooded comrade to guide him. This private club of influential men still meets annually north of San Francisco and uses this symbolic ritual to kick off its summer retreat. But today the ceremony involves burning a mummy-like effigy named Care at the foot of the group's mascot: a 40-foot-tall (12-meter-tall) concrete owl."[164]

---

[164] http://magma.nationalgeographic.com/ngm/bestvintage/photogallery_02.html

ABC News Report on Bohemian Grove

On July 23, 1981 ABC News aired a segment about the Bohemian Grove which someone had obtained from their archives and posted on YouTube in 2006. This segment would mark possibly the only attention given to the Bohemian Grove by a mainstream news source. The fact that no other television news stations have since devoted *any* attention to the subject speaks volumes as to the control the organization has over the media.

The anchor at the time was Frank Reynolds, who begins the segment asking, "What have Herbert Hoover, Art Linkletter, Jack London and Richard Nixon all had in common? Well, they've all been members of the exclusive all male, Bohemian Club in California, where every year at this time the elite from around the country get together for two and half weeks of, um, fun and games."

Steve Shepard went on to report that more than 2000 members spend two weeks encamped in the 2700 acre privately owned redwood forest. He named Gerald Ford, Henry Kissinger, George H.W. Bush, Ronald Reagan, and Richard Nixon as members, as well as high ranking executives at Standard Oil and Bank of America. Shepard went on to say "Privacy is one of the grove's most cherished virtues. Members may not photograph, record, speak or write about activities at the retreat. While many public officials are grove members, the press is a distinctly unwelcome guest."

The segment even showed a photograph from the Cremation of Care, and interviewed sociologist William Domhoff who explained, "with the ceremony called the Cremation of Care that begins the two week encampment where the body of dull care, symbolizing woes and concerns is burned on an alter in front of a big owl statue, when that ceremony ends, they all start to cheer and yell, and hand each other a beer."

The segment also explained that no women were allowed in the club, not even as employees, and admitted that aside from a summer getaway, the club hosts private talks from insiders, citing the development of the nuclear bomb.

Since this rare occurrence, as of the date of this writing, literally no national broadcast has ever discussed the Bohemian Grove, not even the tabloid news shows which focus less on hard news, and instead on scandals and celebrities.

Pitching the Bohemian Grove to Producers

There was a period of time when this author (Mark Dice) would call producers for different television shows and try to get them to do a story about the Bohemian Grove, but it never happened. I got a call back once from a producer for *20/20*, a show on ABC known for its investigative reporting. I told them I had authentic video footage, and I told them about the rare mainstream news articles, and that I would put them in contact with eye witnesses who had seen the ritual with their own eyes, but no segment was ever produced.

I personally pitched the idea to Geraldo Rivera at Fox News over the telephone, yet nothing happened. I told him that unlike his segment twenty years ago when he opened Al Capone's vault for the first time live on television and found nothing, his audience would be shocked when they were given a glimpse inside the Bohemian Grove and it would be the most sensational story he had ever done. I even left voicemails at the Howard Stern Show thinking they would be interested, at least for the bizarreness of the story, but I never got a call back.

One of the most interesting outcomes was with a producer at MSNBC named Greg Cockwell who produces *Countdown with Keith Olbermann*. I had spoken with him on the phone and told him all about it, and offered to email him photos and links to videos and an article in *National Geographic* magazine about the club. I never heard back from anyone, so after some time I called him again. I proceeded to make the case to him about the existence of the Bohemian Grove and the video footage of the Cremation of Care ritual, when he cut me off saying, "I know, I know." I proceeded to tell him that I wasn't joking, and this wasn't a hoax when he told me that he knew I was telling him the truth, and said "you opened up a whole new world to me." I then asked if he would run a segment about it, and he responded "It would never make it to air."

"The network wouldn't let you do it?" I asked.

"It will never happen," he responded.

I figured if anyone in mainstream television would cover the story it would be Keith Olbermann. After all, he hated President Bush so much, why wouldn't he do a story exposing his friends at the Grove? Olbermann and his producer probably feared the repercussions from airing such a segment, or weren't allowed by the higher-ups.

The Mancow Show

In mid 2008, this author was a guest on *The Mancow Show* hosted by Eric "Mancow" Mueller, and I was able to bring the Bohemian Grove up in the conversation, and to my surprise, he was familiar with it. "Let's talk about the Bohemian Grove, do you know anything about it?" I asked him live on the air.

"I do, I know they get naked and dance around a big owl out in the middle of nowhere. I've been invited to go there and I refused."

He asked me some questions about the club and I explained the Cremation of Care ritual to him and the audience and he ended the segment saying, "I know as crazy as this sounds, a bunch of politicians dancing out in the woods around a giant owl...I always thought it was some conspiracy thing, some lie. And then, I got invited to join and then footage came out that somebody smuggled out. Sure enough. It exists. I don't know if its satanic...I don't know who's involved, but fascinating stuff. Thank you Mark Dice. *The Resistance* is his group. Don't laugh at him. Let him have his say. This is the Free Speech Radio Network. This is *The Mancow Show*."

Walter Cronkite

A video posted on YouTube showing Walter Cronkite accepting the Norman Cousins Global Governance Award in 1999 at the United Nations includes a disturbing joke about Satan running the New World Order and countries giving up their sovereignty. Cronkite was the anchor for the CBS evening news from 1962 to 1981.

During this event Cronkite said, "What Alexander Hamilton wrote about the need for law among the thirteen states applies today to the approximately two hundred sovereignties in our global village, all of which are going to have to be convinced to give up some of that sovereignty to the better greater union, and its not going to be easy."

He then referenced Pat Robertson's 1991 book, *The New World Order* and that Robertson said the construction of the global government is the work of the Devil, at which point Cronkite added, "Well, join me, I'm glad to sit here at the right hand of Satan."

This video is widely available on YouTube. Cronkite is believed to be the voice for Moloch played over the loudspeakers in the Bohemian Grove during the Cremation of Care human effigy sacrifice done each summer. (See Pat Robertson's The New World Order page 83)

Henry Kissinger

Anyone who mentions the fact that we are moving into a

New World Order is often labeled a conspiracy theorist, and for decades mainstream publications and political leaders had denied that such a plan was being implemented. Henry Kissinger has had his hands in just about every New World Order front group in the 20th and 21st century. He was originally named the Chairman of the 9/11 Commission by President Bush, but he stepped down after widows of 9/11 victims discovered his business ties with the Bin Laden family.[165]

In an interview on CNBC in February 2009, Kissinger was asked about the problems the new Obama administration was facing regarding the ongoing "War on Terror" and the economic meltdown, and Kissinger responded that Obama, "can give new impetus to American foreign policy partly because the reception of him is so extraordinary around the world. His task will be to develop an overall strategy for America in this period when, really, a new world order can be created. It's a great opportunity, it isn't just a crisis."

President Bush at the United Nations

The Bush administration was aware of criticisms immediately following the September 11, 2001 attacks citing "security failures" and prior knowledge, and with a small number of people suspecting that 9/11 was a false flag operation, President George W. Bush made an unusual statement as he spoke to the United Nations shortly after the attacks. He said "Let us never tolerate outrageous conspiracy theories concerning the attacks of September the 11th; malicious lies that attempt to shift the blame away from the terrorists themselves, away from the guilty."[166]

---

[165] CNN *Kissinger resigns as head of 9/11 commission* December 13, 2002
[166] President Bush Speaks to United Nations 11/10/2001 Press Release

Since a growing segment of the population was aware of governments attacking their own people and then blaming it on another country, the Bush administration had a lot of explaining to do, and the propagandists were already trying to label anyone asking serious questions a "conspiracy theorist."

Maxim Magazine
March 2006 Issue

A thorough analysis of the 9/11 attacks can be found in *The Resistance Manifesto*, and is not this author's intention to do so in these pages, but I thought I would acknowledge one of the first articles in a mainstream publication to discuss the 9/11 Truth Movement as it began to grow exponentially in 2006. Until 2006 it had largely remained underground and hadn't received any mainstream media attention. While in the months and years to come it would be acknowledged and attacked by everyone from Sean Hannity to Bill O'Reilly, I thought I would pay homage to *Maxim Magazine* for publishing an article in their March 2006 issue.

The article was titled *What Really Brought Down the Towers?* and began reading, "As major questions surrounding the official version of the truth emerge, "What really happened on 9/11" is becoming the "Who shot JFK?" of a new generation. How crazy are the new conspiracy theories? Depends how far down the rabbit hole you're willing to go."

The article mentions a 2004 CNN.com poll where 89% of the respondents voted that they believe there was a cover-up surrounding 9/11. It also briefly covered the controlled demolition hypothesis, and speculation that a jet liner wasn't what really crashed into the Pentagon. It also mentioned the possibility that Al Qaeda had planned the attack, but that the American government stood down and allowed it to happen on purpose.

The article concluded by saying, "Many of these theories stretch the patience of the most credulous. But dismissing an entire tree for one rotten apple may be rash. For those who simply can't wrap their minds around such an epic deception many are eager to frame things in a more pragmatic perspective."

Charlie Sheen's 9/11 Comments

In March of 2006, actor Charlie Sheen was a guest on Alex Jones' radio show and discussed his thoughts about the 9/11 attacks and how the government's official account didn't seem accurate to him. "We're not the conspiracy theorists on this particular issue," said Sheen.

"It seems to me like 19 amateurs with box cutters taking over four commercial airliners and hitting 75% of their targets, that feels like a conspiracy theory. It raises a lot of questions."

Within days, *The New York Post* published a story with the headline, *Sheen: What 9/11 Hijackers,* and said, "Charlie Sheen has joined the 9/11 gone-bonkers brigade."

Sheen's comments created a media firestorm and he was viciously attacked. Sheen was the first celebrity to publicly say such things, and not long afterwards other celebrities or well known actors came forward and made similar statements, and in some cases, far more inflammatory ones. Christine Ebersole, Daniel Sunjata, Willy Nelson, Ed Asner, Rosie O'Donnell, Jesse Ventura and others soon followed in Sheen's footsteps.

Jesse Ventura on Hannity & Colmes

Former governor of Minnesota, Jesse Ventura, released a book in 2008 titled *Don't Start the Revolution Without Me,* and did the usual publicity tour on major media outlets. When he appeared in the studio on *Hannity and Colmes* on the Fox News Channel, Sean Hannity was discussing Ventura's various stances found in the book, and then said, "The one thing that I read in the book that I totally found just alien to me, is this idea that you believe in 9/11 conspiracies."

Ventura replied, "Let me tell it to you this way. Why is it that when you ask any question about 9/11, you're immediately attacked...my problem is, I look at it and I go, how can two planes knock down three buildings? ...First of all, jet fuel is four fifths, I don't want to stay on this, I'd rather talk about other things, but jet fuel is four fifths kerosene, it doesn't burn hot, so using the analogy that it could melt the metal...then propane burns hotter, so if you turn on your camp stove for three hours shouldn't it melt the grates? But it doesn't, does it?"

Hannity replied, "He's going Rosie O'Donnell on me here."

Venture answered, "How could they fall at the rate of gravity? They fell at the rate of gravity. They blew into powder."

Hannity stops him and says "But if it were true, a lot of engineers would have come out," and then he changes the subject and moves on. The truth is that a lot of engineers have risked their careers by going public and challenging the official story. Richard Gage founded Architects and Engineers for 9/11 Truth and has over 500 members, all of which have concluded that explosives or cutting charges were used to demolish the Twin Towers and Building 7 that morning.

The View

On March 6th, 2007 actress Christine Ebersole was a guest on the popular woman's talk show *The View* when she brought up the topic of this author's YouTube videos which consist of me visiting various college campuses in southern

California and educating the students about 9/11. Rosie O'Donnell jumps in to explain, "He goes around the country with a bullhorn, like to UCLA or wherever he wants, and he says, "9/11 was an inside job! 9/11 was an inside job!" and within five or ten minutes, the police show up and his friends videotape him getting arrested, and boy does it annoy people, I can tell you that much."

Elisabeth Hasselbeck responds, "That would probably annoy just a handful of people in the United States."

And Rosie concludes, "Well, you've got to look and make your own decision, you know."

Actor James Brolin would later plug a 9/11 truth website when he was a guest on the show, and Rosie O'Donnell would become a lightening rod for controversy after she made some very bold statements about the issues.

Durring one broadcast O'Donnell asked her fellow hosts, "historically, have governments ever faked incidents, or incited incidences to get them into war?"

When pressed on the issue by conservative Elizabeth Hasselbeck, Rosie explained, "I do believe that it is the first time in history that fire has ever melted steel. I do believe that it defies physics for the World Trade Center Tower Seven, Building 7, which collapsed in on itself, it is impossible for a building to fall the way it fell without explosives being involved. World Trade Center 1 and 2 got hit by planes, [Building] 7 miraculously, the first time in history, steel was melted by fire."

Elizabeth Hasselbeck, fired away, "and who do you think is responsible for that?" and Rosie answered, "I have no idea...look at the films, get a physics expert here, from Yale, from Harvard, pick the school, it defies reason."

Later, a video was posted on YouTube that was possibly shot by a cell phone camera by someone in the audience of *The View* which showed Rosie addressing the audience before the show went to air about the inconsistencies about the World Trade Center attack and telling the story of 9/11 hero William Rodriguez.

She said, "He was the last guy pulled out, he was on sublevel two, and he heard a bomb. And the guy who was filling the soda machine came to him and his skin was falling off. And he said, what happened, what happened? Did the generator blow up? He said a bomb. He then took him up, carried him outside, and saw the plane hit." The audience gasps. She continues, "And he was omitted from the 9/11 report. Why? It was omitted. Building 7, omitted. Never in the history of the world has a building fallen from a fire into its own footprint, eliminating the core. Twenty five steel beams. Really, it's impossible. Physics wise. It's impossible."

Information was then posted on Rosie's blog, Rosie.com, about how she had become friends with William Rodriguez, a janitor at the World Trade Center responsible for helping fire fighters access different parts of the building to help people evacuate after the buildings were attacked. Rodriguez was known as the Keymaster because he had a key that opened most doors in the building. Shortly after the tragedy, Rodriguez would travel around the world giving speeches about the 9/11 attacks being an inside job.

Operation Inform the Soldiers

On June 10th 2008, this author made an appearance on the Fox News Channel's show *America's Newsroom*, to discuss a campaign that I had started called Operation Inform the Soldiers, which involved mailing DVDs to troops stationed in Iraq to help educate them about the lies surrounding 9/11 and the war.

There is no doubt that Fox News had invited me on the show simply to attack me, but I held my own and made several points during the brief time I had on air. Host Megyn Kelly started, "Imagine you are a soldier stationed in Iraq. Mail call comes around and you got a letter from back home. But it is not from your family or your friends, it is a letter telling you that you are a pawn in the service of the New World Order and that you are risking your life for a government that helped carry out the 9/11 attacks. This is not a joke. This is actually happening. The letters are the work of Mark Dice, the founder of a group called *The Resistance*. Mark joins us live now."

This segment would spark talk show host Michael Reagan to tell his audience that I should be found and killed for treason and then he would pay for the bullets. Michael is the adopted son of President Ronald Reagan and hosts a syndicated radio show.

Reagan said, "Excuse me folks, I'm going to say this. We ought to find the people who are doing this, take them out and shoot them. Really. You take them out, they are traitors to this country, and shoot them. You have a problem with that? Deal with it. You shoot them. You call them traitors, that's what they are, and you shoot them dead. I'll pay for the bullets."

He continued, "How about you take Mark Dice out and put him in the middle of a firing range. Tie him to a post, don't blindfold him, let it rip and have some fun with Mark Dice."

The statements were made June 10th 2008 and came to my attention a few days later after someone who heard Reagan's show emailed me to inform me. I immediately filed a report with the FBI and the FCC. I personally called Radio America, his show's syndicator, and demanded that he be fired immediately. About an hour later Michael Reagan himself called me and apologized. I don't think he was actually sorry, he just understood the repercussions from saying such things, and feared for his job and getting sued. He invited me to come on his radio show as a guest the following Monday and when on the air I told him, and mainly his audience, as much evidence about the 9/11 attacks being an inside job as I could. Reagan was a bumbling idiot on air.

When I first received an email informing me about Reagan's comments, I downloaded the show's podcast to hear it for myself, and posted a brief clip on YouTube so others could hear it. Reagan's entire show was available on mp3 for free on his website, Reagan.com. The short clip I had posted quickly received over 75,000 views and he promptly filed a copyright infringement claim against me to have the audio removed. As a result, my entire YouTube channel, along with nearly 100 videos I had posted were deleted. He then removed the June 10th 2008 podcast from his website in an attempt to stop others from obtaining the audio, but it was too late. Dozens of other YouTube users had posted his death threats and if one searched for "Michael Reagan" on YouTube, page after page of videos appeared which contained the audio clip. I filed a counterclaim with YouTube citing the fact that posting the audio fell under the fair use laws, and was able to get my videos restored.

Six months later people would still email me asking why I didn't sue him, and how he could keep his job. Apparently the FCC did nothing, despite hundreds, possibly thousands of complaints that were filed about his comments. The District Attorney had looked into the case after I filed a report with the FBI, but decided not to charge Reagan since none of his listeners had acted on his wishes, and he retracted them on his next broadcast. I had contacted several law firms who specialized in civil cases, and none of them would take the case. I didn't have any money to pay a lawyer to sue Reagan anyway, but I thought if I could at least get them to see what kind of a case I had, and that it was against a national talk show host and Ronald Reagan's son, that they would want to take the case for the publicity, and I could convince them to do it on the basis that if we won a settlement, then I would pay them a percentage. All the law firms I spoke with didn't think we would win the case since he retracted his comments and called me to apologize and none of his listeners had promptly taken his advice to harm me.

Aside from suing him for threatening my life, I wanted to sue Reagan for compensatory damages because my girlfriend at the time would leave me two weeks later citing one of the reasons that her mother feared if we would get married as we had planned, that the Illuminati would one day murder me for exposing them and my girlfriend would be left a widow, or if we had children, she would be a single mother. Before this had happened, my girlfriend's mother had spoke several times that she feared for my life and thought I would be killed for writing and speaking about such topics. Reagan's threats were confirmation of her fears.

One of the lawyers I talked with was interested in what exactly I did to anger Reagan so much. I proceeded to tell him about how the 9/11 attacks were an inside job and about the documentary films that were being sent to soldiers stationed in Iraq to educate them about this fact. Instead of telling me I was crazy, he basically agreed, and started asking me for advice on how he could get a book published that he had written about how elements within the Drug Enforcement Agency are actually working hand in hand with the Mexican drug cartels to import narcotics into the U.S. He had the manuscript finished for several years and wanted to get it published.

Kevin Barrett's Comments

In the fall of 2006, a man named Kevin Barrett taught a class at the University of Wisconsin, Madison called "Islam: Religion and Culture," which was an undergraduate course. The course included the topic of the September 11th attacks and the War on Terrorism.

This portion of Barrett's course focused on current issues surrounding Islam's connection with 9/11 and the War on Terror, and discussed various readings representing a

variety of viewpoints. One of those viewpoints, some had
feared, was that Barrett believed the 9/11 attacks were not
the work of Muslim terrorists, but rather an inside job by
intelligence agencies, or that the United States had allowed
the attacks to occur as a false flag operation.

On July 11, 2006, Bill O'Reilly host of *The O'Reilly
Factor* on Fox News said Barrett, "would have been gone at
Boston University, my alma mater, in a heartbeat. The
Chancellor there, John Silber, would have—would have—
this guy'd be in the Charles River floating down, you know,
toward the harbor."

O'Reilly basically said Barrett should be killed and his
body dumped in the river. Other media outlets would attack
Barrett, including the usual attack dogs Hannity and Colmes.
After the semester, Barrett's contract was not renewed at
UWM.

Coast to Coast AM

The largest syndicated radio show in America that deals
with secret societies and conspiracies is *Coast to Coast AM*,
which airs seven days a week from 10pm to 2am Pacific
time. The show was created by UFO buff Art Bell, who has
since retired. George Noory is currently the primary host.

The show deals with some extremely fringe topics, and
is not considered a serious or credible show by most
standards. Discussions surrounding the paranormal, UFOs,
and alternative history are the usual topics. Guests often
include authors and researches in these fields.

Despite the fringe material discussed on the show, it
shouldn't be considered completely fraudulent with regards
to its format. Some fairly well respected guests often appear
on the show to discuss issues that are too far out for
mainstream news. Some frequent guests are Jim Marrs and
Alex Jones, who are very well respected researchers in what
the mainstream media would call conspiracies. Host George

Noory simply keeps an open mind, and provides a platform for esoteric issues to be discussed no matter how outrageous they may seem.

Documentary Films

Since an extremely effective way to present evidence or a point of view is to produce a documentary film, such works have been created by numerous independent film makers which cover a variety of issues surrounding secret societies, government corruption, terrorism, and the banking system. Some films, such as *Loose Change: Final Cut* or Alex Jones' work are extremely accurate and meticulously researched and sourced and have only the intention of exposing government corruption or the activities of the Illuminati. Others such as *Zeitgeist the Movie*, and its sequel, *Zeitgeist: Addendum*, have other motives, which are covertly aiding the Illuminati and the New World Order.

Very few of these films will ever be shown on national television, but are instead sold on DVD and often available to watch for free on YouTube and Google Video. While most mainstream films cannot be viewed for free on such services due to copyright issues, often the independent producers of these films will allow their work to be freely available and even encourage people to make copies of their DVDs to give away to friends and family to educate them about such topics.

Dark Secrets: Inside Bohemian Grove

The film *Dark Secrets: Inside Bohemian Grove* (2000) by Alex Jones clearly shows the Cremation of Care ritual, and other aspects of the ultra elite Bohemian Club. In July 2000, Alex Jones and Mike Hanson, author of *Bohemian Grove: Cult of Conspiracy*, successfully infiltrated the club and captured video of just a fraction of the activities which occur inside. This was the first video footage ever to have been taken inside the club and released to the public.

During the Cremation of Care, a group of men who are

wearing black hooded robes stand at the base of a 40 foot tall statue of an ancient Canaanite god named Moloch, and perform a human sacrifice ritual using a life-size paper mache effigy of a person. At the feet of Moloch stands an alter which the effigy is laid on, and the man with the role of the "high priest" uses his torch to light the effigy. An elaborate sound system and fireworks display is used during the ritual, and as the "body" is burning, human screams are played over the loudspeakers and fireworks are set off. Across the Russian river, an audience of 1000 men watch the ceremony, which is where Jones was seated when he captured the footage.

In 2005 Jones released *The Order of Death*, which is a 45 minute addition to *Dark Secrets*, and is included on the same DVD. *The Order of Death* includes new footage and photos that were secretly taken by a worker at the Bohemian Grove. (See Chris Jones page 192)

This author (Mark Dice) must admit that when I had first seen clips of Jones' film, I thought it was a hoax, or if such a ceremony was real, that he was mistaken thinking presidents, politicians, and high level business executives were in attendance. It was only after my own investigation, including interviews with local residents who lived near the club, finding rare news reports about the place, and meeting Chris Jones (a worker at the club), that I became convinced Alex Jones was right.

When David Gergen, who was a presidential advisor to Presidents Ford, Nixon, Regan and Clinton, was asked if he had ever attended the ritual at the Bohemian Grove, he answered, "Frankly I don't think that's something I need to talk to you about." When he was pressed again as to whether he had seen the ritual, he angrily replied, "That's none of your damn business!" and walked away.

The brief interview took place on the streets of New York during the 2004 Republican National Convention and can be viewed on YouTube or in *The Order of Death*.

270

Gergen didn't ask "what ritual?" and he obviously knew what was being asked and clearly did not want to acknowledge that such a ritual takes place. Gergen snapped, "I don't know anything about you and I don't know anything about your film, but if you go in there with an understanding, then you violated that understanding by releasing that film."

The Cremation of Care human sacrifice ritual is performed to kick off a two week party for the club, and aside from showing clear footage of the ritual, Jones' film also covers other issues surrounding the club. During this two week "encampment" as it is called, are numerous Lakeside Talks which involve political and industry insiders giving lectures on what policies, technology, or major world changing events will be occurring in the near future. From these talks, club members are given advanced knowledge about what the Bilderberg group and the Illuminati have planned for the rest of the world.

Secret Rulers of the World

British journalist Jon Ronson produced a series of four television programs titled *The Secret Rulers of the World* which included one episode about the Bohemian Grove, and another about the Bilderberg group where he investigated the claims of what he called "conspiracy theorists" surrounding such groups. Ronson takes a very skeptical approach to the subject matter, and seems as if his purpose is to prove the allegations wrong and "debunk" the claims surrounding these organizations.

In the episode titled *Shadowy Satanic Elite?*, Ronson chronicles Alex Jones and Mike Hanson's attempt to sneak in the Bohemian Grove and secretly film the rumored human sacrifice ritual, the Cremation of Care. Near the end of the program, after Alex and Mike got the footage and returned from the Grove, Jon Ronson admitted, "As incredible as it sounds, some kind of bizarre secret ritual witnessed by world leaders really does take place in the forests of northern California."

Back at the hotel they all sat down and watched the footage that they had obtained. Although to Ronson's surprise, the rumored ritual was indeed a fact, he didn't seem to think it really mattered all that much, and began siding with the Bohemian Grove, insisting it was no big deal.

[Ronson] Do you think this was unholy?

[Hanson] It's very strange to me. These people are supposed to be running the world and they're out there doing this.

[Ronson] You seem freaked out.

[Hanson] I am.

[Jones] These people point their fingers all day and call people extremists or cult members or whatever for their religious beliefs, this was a pagan ceremony and engaging in human sacrifice, a mock human sacrifice...

[Ronson] Aren't they just saying that for two weeks they don't need to worry about anything?

[Jones] But they're burning someone in effigy and as it's burning they "ahh ohhh nooo!"

[Ronson] But they're not killing a person.

[Jones] We understand they're not literally killing a person...

[Ronson] They're killing something that is symbolic...

[Jones] Wait a minute. You saw it. You've got Death on this black boat bringing a pallet with the paper mache person obviously, its got the feet and the head and they take it over and burn it.

[Ronson] But wasn't it just a metaphor?

[Hanson] To me it doesn't matter. I think they're sacrificing in the real world too.

[Ronson] Was this the New World Order?

[Hanson] Yes definitely. I looked the New World Order in the face out there.

Nazis: The Occult Conspiracy

If one doubts that elite politicians would be involved in occult philosophies and rituals, then they need to look no further than the Nazis and Hitler's inner circle of henchmen. While everyone knows that the architects of the Holocaust were evil and heartless human beings, many still do not have a clue that the SS was more than a military order, and that at its heart were occult philosophies and goals.

In the History Channel's two-hour program titled *Nazis: The Occult Conspiracy*, these bizarre beliefs are explained in somewhat detail, and give the viewer a glimpse into the root cause of the Nazi's path of destruction. The show features interviews with Dr. Nicholas Goodrick-Clark, who is a historian at Oxford University, as well as Wolf Rudiger Hess, the son of Rudolf Hess, who was one of Hitler's closest allies.

It includes actual footage from Nazi expeditions to Tibet as they searched for evidence of descendents from the lost city of Atlantis and clearly shows that Hitler, Rudolph Hess, Alfred Rosenberg, Joseph Goebbels, and Heinrich Himmler believed in some extremely bizarre mystical ideas surrounding the occult and the city of Atlantis.

In the show, it is also presented that the Nazis wanted to eliminate all Jews, and probably all non-whites, to create a New World Order comprised only of Aryans so that the purified race could then reawaken the mystical powers that they had lost since the destruction of the city of Atlantis. The Nazis believed that the white race is descended from a civilization that lived in the mythical lost city of Atlantis. They believed Atlantis was a real city, and not just a myth, and that its inhabitants were god-like supermen.

Historian Peter Padfield explains, "It's difficult for us afterwards to equate this man who certainly believed in a god and to link him up with a man who was a master of the killing machine in Germany, but actually the two things of course are linked because what he was trying to do was to root out the forces which he believed had corrupted Germany and get back to their pure blooded forefathers."

Most people think that Hitler and the Nazis were simply inhumane racists who used the Jews as a scapegoat for Germany's economic problems, but do not understand that there were occult religious beliefs behind these actions.

Terrorstorm

In the summer of 2006 Alex Jones released *Terrorstorm: A History of Government Sponsored Terrorism* which details numerous declassified and proven cases of corrupt elements within governments staging terrorist attacks while blaming those very attacks on a rival or political enemy so the event can be used as a catalyst for military action. Several of the events covered are the Gulf of Tonkin incident which sparked America's involvement in the Vietnam War, as well as the Reichstag fire, Operation Ajax, and Operation Northwoods.

While Jones shies away from labeling such incidences the work of the Illuminati, it is clear that a pattern of such events has occurred throughout history, and that secret agreements have been made at the highest levels of governments to green light such actions.

The Gulf of Tonkin incident occurred in 1964 when President Johnson conspired with his secretary of Defense Robert McNamara to tell the media and the public that the North Vietnamese had attacked an American ship patrolling the Gulf of Tonkin. No such attack had occurred, and the story was fabricated to escalate America's involvement in the conflict in Vietnam and would ultimately lead to the U.S. becoming fully committed to war. The Johnson administration had wanted this to happened, but needed to be able to justify their actions to the American people, so the Gulf of Tonkin incident was concocted.[167]

Also covered in *Terrorstorm* is the Reichstag fire in Germany in 1933. The Reichstag is the German Parliament building, similar to America's Congress. The Reichstag was set on fire in 1933, and it was quickly blamed on the Communist Party which was opposing the National Socialist Party, or the Nazis. Hitler used the event to remove civil liberties, and rise to the level of a dictator. It turns out the Nazis themselves had set the fire to then use it as a pretext to expand their power while blaming their political enemies for the event.

One of the most chilling examples of false flag terrorism covered in the film is Operation Northwoods which is a declassified document written in 1962 which outlined various terrorist attacks that the United States would perpetrate against targets in Washington D.C. and Miami, Florida and then blame on Cuba as an excuse to invade them. The document is chilling and would later be used as a

---

[167] Audio tapes of President Johnson's private phone conversations have been released and are available for download at the National Archives website. Below is the exact url.
http://www.gwu.edu/~nsarchiv/NSAEBB/NSAEBB132/tapes.htm

blueprint of what would happen years later on September 11th 2001 when the Twin Towers were attacked and ignited the "War on Terror" and the invasion of Iraq.

Loose Change: Final Cut

Online video sharing services such as Google Video and YouTube became an instant success in 2006, providing a way for individuals and independent film producers to make their work available for the entire world to view with the click of a mouse.

One film which became one of the most downloaded films in history was *Loose Change 2nd Edition*, which is a documentary about the 9/11 terrorist attacks. In May of 2006 the film had been viewed over 10 million times and became the most popular 9/11 documentary available. It was written by Dylan Avery, and produced with the help of his two friends, Jason Bermas and Korey Rowe. Due to its popularity, the film was featured in mainstream news articles such as *USA Today*[168], *Vanity Fair*[169], and *Time Magazine*[170], helping to break through the wall attempting to keep the 9/11 "conspiracy theories" from going mainstream.

In November 2007, *Loose Change: Final Cut* was released on DVD which was a completely new film from the previous versions, and featured mainstream news casts and interviews with intelligence experts and firefighters, showing *dramatic* inconsistencies between the *9/11 Commission Report*, and what actually happened regarding the attacks.

The film, like many others that focus on 9/11, doesn't

---

[168] USA TODAY *Conspiracy film rewrites Sept. 11* 4/29/2006 By William M. Welch

[169] Vanity Fair *Click Here For Conspiracy* August 1, 2006 by Nancy Jo Sales

[170] Time Magazine *Why the 9/11 Conspiracy Theories Won't Go Away* by Lev Grossman Sunday, Sep. 03, 2006

mention the word "Illuminati" or "secret societies" but instead focuses on specific individuals and government operations that were involved in the attacks. Many film makers shy away from referring to the perpetrators as "the Illuminati" since it is often more effective to focus on specific government procedures, declassified documents, and specific investigations that were thwarted.

Fabled Enemies

In 2008 Jason Bermas, a producer for *Loose Change,* released a film which detailed the various intelligence agencies knowledge of, and aid in the attacks of 9/11. While not mentioning anything about a controlled demolition or the controversy surrounding the attack on the Pentagon, the film sticks to documented information about Al Qaeda's ties to intelligence agencies such as the CIA, Pakistan's ISI, and Israel's Mossad. *Fabled Enemies* paints a very damaging picture of how elements within these agencies had full knowledge of the hijackers and their goals.

The 9/11 Chronicles: Truth Rising

In July of 2008, filmmaker Alex Jones released a DVD titled *The 9/11 Chronicles Volume 1: Truth Rising* which largely consists of amateur footage shot by 9/11 Truth activists as they confront various suspects and political figures who are aiding or abetting those who are building the New World Order.

The film is extremely exciting to watch as numerous activists get face to face and confront countless officials including Rudy Giuliani, Governor Arnold Schwarzenegger, New York Mayor Michael Bloomberg, Alan Greenspan, Senator John McCain, Vice President Joe Biden, and others in what sometimes turn into rather heated situations with security intervening. The film is truly incredible and gives the viewer a first person perspective of what it's like when an ordinary citizen speaks truth to power.

Endgame: Blueprint for Global Enslavement

Alex Jones' 2007 film *Endgame* covers the secret plans that are being implemented to forge the New World Order, and includes for the first time ever, clear video footage of high profile Bilderberg members getting out of their armored cars and entering the hotel where the conference was taking place. The footage was taken outside the Brookstreet Hotel in Ottawa, Canada in 2006. Many of the members' faces are clearly visible and it's indisputable what is occurring.

Donald E. Graham CEO of the *Washington Post*, Indra Nooyi CEO of PepsiCo, Illuminati kingpin David Rockefeller along side his body guard James Ford, George Pataki governor of New York, James Wolfensohn former chairman of the World Bank, Ahmed Chalabi former Iraqi oil minister who has been under investigation for numerous crimes, and others were captured on video and are clearly identified in the film.

Endgame also covers plans for a North American Union by eliminating the borders of the United States, Canada, and Mexico, and streamlining everything from the transportation systems to the currency. A history of Eugenics is also presented.

Zeitgeist the Movie

One of the most popular films on the Internet is *Zeitgeist the Movie*, and *Zeitgeist: Addendum* which is its sequel. The first movie was released on Google Video in 2007, and became extremely popular among the 9/11 Truth Movement particularly those who are anti-Christian. The film is broken up into three parts, the first part is an attack on Christianity and presents the "Jesus never existed" theory as part of its assault on religion, saying it is a method of control used by the elite to keep us mentally enslaved. The second part is a compilation of clips from the most popular 9/11 documentaries, and the third part is about the private Federal Reserve banking system. The film was produced by a man using the name "Peter Joseph" which is possibly a pseudonym.

The entire first third of the film proposed the idea that Jesus never even existed, and that the writers of the Bible had made up the entire story as a continuation of the tradition of the solar deities, or gods that are personifications of the sun. Even the most radical scholars admit that a man named Jesus of Nazareth existed around the time the Bible says he did, and that he upset the social order of Jerusalem with his teachings, although the debate about whether he was God in the flesh or just a spiritual teacher continues. But "Peter Joseph" presents the widely debunked theory that the entire story of his life and teachings are a fabrication by the Catholic Church. Such ideas are not seriously considered in scholarly circles, but many young viewers of *Zeitgeist* believe the film is true.

In October of 2008 a sequel was released titled *Zeitgeist: Addendum*, which ended with an extremely unsettling solution for the issues society is facing. The film begins with an explanation of how the Federal Reserve banking system works and is fairly accurate in its presentation, but then the film takes a disturbing turn.

A large part of *Addendum* pushes the idea that society would not need money anymore if we would design and build robots and mechanical systems to operate the world, which would rid mankind of the need to work. "Peter Joseph," and the proponents of what is called the Venus Project, envision a world in which the machines will do work for us, and everything will be in such an abundance that humans will not need to work and instead can spend their time enjoying themselves.

What's even more shocking is the support that the film and these ideas have gained. A measurable number of illogical, naive dreamers not only believe such a thing is possible, but ruthlessly attack anyone who is critical of the film and its premise. Who wouldn't like a world where you wouldn't have to work? Unfortunately the supporters of this film cannot grasp the reality of a medium of exchange, nor the value of rare artifacts or the need for human labor, and that even if sophisticated machines or robots are able to replace a fair amount of human labor, there will always be countless jobs that they will not be able to do, from teaching children to various service oriented jobs or research and development. Such a techno-utopia has been the dreams of many who envisioned microwave ovens, cell phones, and laptop computers as the tools which would free mankind from the burdens of work, but such inventions have only complicated the issue.

As if this techno-utopia idea wasn't bad enough, the unsettling conclusion of the film conveys one of the central goals of the Illuminati, in that all religions should either be eradicated or unified in preparation for the Antichrist to then claim to be the long awaited messiah. The end of *Zeitgeist: Addendum* shows an elaborate scene using actors and CGI graphics which depicts a Christian, a Muslim, and a Jew standing on the street and the Christian takes off their cross necklace and throws it on the ground as the Jew removes his yarmulke and does the same, and the Muslim takes off his hat, and all during this bizarre sequence the film cuts to a close-up of a human eye with colors swirling around inside, and after each person has symbolically shed their religion, the frame zooms out to show the entire planet earth from space which then has rays of light shooting out from all the continents, and is transformed into a ball of light.

In a radio interview with Alex Jones on the Genesis Communication Network, "Peter Joseph" stated that nobody would need guns in the utopia he envisioned, but danced around and avoided stating that they should be outright banned. When asked what if someone didn't want to go along and participate in his supposed utopian New World Order, he basically said the person would need to be taken to a re-education center. It's extremely disturbing that many of the views "Peter Joseph" espouses are synonymous with the Illuminati's blueprint for the New World Order. His continued attack on Christianity and religion while pushing the idea of a communist techno-utopia should be seen as nothing more than Illuminati propaganda, with "Peter Joseph" himself a pawn in their game.

The Clinton Chronicles

The Clinton Chronicles: An Investigation into the Alleged Criminal Activities of Bill Clinton is a 1994 documentary film created by Patrick Matrisciana that explores the "Clinton Body Count" which consists of all the close friends and associates of President Bill Clinton who have ended up murdered or supposedly committed suicide.

Many of these deaths are a result of the criminal enterprises Clinton has been involved in. Some of these include the death of Vince Foster and the murders of witnesses of the Mena Arkansas cocaine smuggling ring involving the CIA in the 1980s. Some of the names on the Clinton Body Count such as Kevin Ives and Don Henry are also the focus of a separate documentary titled *Obstruction of Justice: The Mena Connection* which can also be viewed online.

The number of names on the Clinton Body Count is staggering and when the strange circumstances of many of these deaths are analyzed, one can't explain them away as mere coincidences. Several of the names on the Clinton Body Count list have been disputed by Clinton supporters, and since they claim to have "proved" that several deaths had not directly been connected to Clinton, or are actual coincidences, Clinton supporters claim the entire Clinton Body Count is a "hoax." These defenders ignore the numerous conclusive cases of murder that are directly connected to Clinton and his involvement with the Illuminati.

Years after *The Clinton Chronicles* was produced, during the campaign season preceding the 2008 election, *Hillary the Movie* was released which details some of the crimes and misdeeds of Hillary and Bill, but barely scratched the surface of how deeply involved in the Illuminati the Clintons are. Perhaps the producers didn't want the film to be labeled a bunch of "conspiracy theories" and focused on issues that would be received by the audience as more mainstream and easier to believe. *Hillary the Movie* is still an extremely disturbing and damaging film.

Monopoly Men

A little known documentary series hosted and narrated by Dean Stockwell called *Phenomenon: The Lost Archives* focused on topics found in declassified government documents. The series featured a powerful episode on the Federal Reserve which originally aired on March 1, 2000 and was titled *Monopoly Men*.

The episode starts with Stockwell asking, "Is there a secret history of the United States intentionally hidden by the mainstream media? Could there be a secret society of fat money businessmen whose agenda has been the cause of every major war and economic depression? Is there a shadowy elite gently pulling the strings of our world to bring about their own self-serving political program? The answers may surprise you."

The show then details the creation of the Federal Reserve Bank, and the secrecy and manipulation on the part of the rich and powerful men who did so.

The Money Masters

Possibly the most in-depth film on the Federal Reserve banking system is *The Money Masters*, which was produced in 1996 by Bill Still. This three hour long film covers the history of money, banking, and the Federal Reserve. It contains the most powerful quotes from historical figures, past presidents, and even powerful men who worked in the banking industry, which clearly show that the corrupt Federal Reserve system has been, and will continue to be the downfall of America's economy.

The film is available for viewing for free on Google Video. Several of the most powerful historical quotes about the banking system referenced in the film are as follows.

"If the American people ever allow private banks to control the issue of their currency, first by inflation, then by deflation, the banks...will deprive the people of all property until their children wake-up homeless on the continent their fathers conquered.... The issuing power should be taken from the banks and restored to the people, to whom it properly belongs. ... The modern theory of the perpetuation of debt has drenched the earth with blood, and crushed its inhabitants under burdens ever accumulating." *–Thomas Jefferson*

"History records that the money changers have used every form of abuse, intrigue, deceit, and violent means possible to maintain their control over governments by controlling money and its issuance." *–James Madison*

President Woodrow Wilson signed the 1913 Federal Reserve Act into law, and several years later wrote, "I am a most unhappy man. I have unwittingly ruined my country. A great industrial nation is controlled by its system of credit. Our system of credit is concentrated. The growth of the nation, therefore, and all our activities are in the hands of a few men. We have come to be one of the worst ruled, one of the most completely controlled and dominated Governments in the civilized world no longer a Government by free opinion, no longer a Government by conviction and the vote of the majority, but a Government by the opinion and duress of a small group of dominant men." *–Woodrow Wilson*

Money as Debt

An entirely animated film about the banking system is *Money As Debt*, which on the surface seems like an educational film for a classroom, but actually contains some very important information regarding the creation of money and the collection of interest for loaning it out. The film was created by Paul Grignon in 2006 and is one of the most informative films on the subject of the creation on money and fiat currency. At the time of this writing, the film is available to view on Google Video, although it is unclear whether this will remain. Many films are posted by individuals and are later removed by the request of the copyright holder.

The film explains how in the past, goldsmiths would hold peoples' gold coins in their vault for safe keeping, and issue the people paper receipts which they could redeem when they wanted their gold back. People began trading the actual paper receipts in the marketplace as a form of what today we would call cash, since it was easier to carry and they didn't have to travel to visit the goldsmith to get their gold out every time they wanted to buy something. The goldsmith realized that he could write up his own receipts and spend them in the market and nobody would notice. By doing this he was essentially creating his own money for free. As long as everyone who held a paper receipt in their possession didn't come all at once to redeem it for their gold, nobody would know what he was doing.

The film brilliantly, yet simply lays out this concept and

explains how such ideas evolved into modern banking and are still used today. It then goes on to detail how banks actually loan out money they don't have. When one is new to the concepts of money, this can be a startling revelation, but *Money As Debt* lays it out in a very understandable format and should be watched by everyone who would like to understand the heart of the banking system.

Riddles in Stone

An incredible film that features interviews with Dr. Stanley Monteith, Ed Decker, and S. Brent Morris PhD the Masonic historian who is also featured on the History Channel, is *Riddles in Stone: The Secret Architecture of Washington D.C.* which was produced by Cutting Edge Ministries in 2007 and directed by Christian J. Pinto. The information in the film is presented in an unbiased fashion and the budget must have been enormous, because instead of simply using old stock footage and historical paintings and photographs as B-roll, much of the film contains scenes with actors dressed up in clothes from the time periods being discussed. Such a practice is common on the History Channel or Discovery Channel with their large budgets, but for a small independent film maker to have produced such a high quality film is astonishing.

The film is almost three hours long and explores the influence of Freemasonry on the design and construction of the street layout of Washington D.C. The infamous pentagram that is built into the layout with the bottom point leading to the White House is shown from a satellite view, along with other symbols and conflicting explanations are given from the individuals who were interviewed in the film.

Since much of *Riddles in Stone* contains stunning videography of various monuments, buildings, and sculptures, words cannot do the film justice, and it must be seen to appreciate its quality and information. One notable scene includes footage of *The Awakening*, a giant statue buried in the earth, originally located in Washington D.C. for nearly 28 years and later sold and relocated to Prince George's County, Maryland in February 2008. This strange statue holds a hidden meaning for occultists, which is explained in the film.

It shouldn't be a surprise to anyone familiar with secret societies that the Freemasons had their hand in the founding of America, but what some viewers may not know is how the Masons incorporated various symbols and designs into the architecture of Washington D.C., including the street layout and numerous sculptures and murals. What's even more fascinating is how such designs stand right out in the open with few even taking notice.

The History Channel: Secret Societies

A surprisingly balanced piece was produced by the History Channel on secret societies in 2001 and covered some of the allegations involving Skull and Bones, the Freemasons, and the Bilderberg group. It featured interviews with David Icke and Jim Marrs as supporters of the "conspiracy theories" and Daniel Pipes as the skeptic and attempted debunker. Due to his blood drinking reptilian shape shifting theory, David Icke is far from a credible commentator, but the show did give a fair and balanced viewpoint between Icke, Marrs, and Pipes.

Daniel Pipes is the author of *Conspiracy : How the Paranoid Style Flourishes and Where It Comes From*, which tries to make the case that people who believe in "conspiracy theories" have over-active imaginations. Jim Marrs is the author of several respectable books including *Rule by Secrecy*, *The Terror Conspiracy* and *The Rise of the Fourth Reich*. His 1989 book, *Crossfire: The Plot That Killed Kennedy* made the New York Times Best Seller List and Marrs worked as a script consultant on Oliver Stone's film *JFK*.

THE ILLUMINATI: FACTS & FICTION

Conspiracy of Silence

A disturbing film that is only circulated on the Internet, and has never aired on television is *Conspiracy of Silence* which details allegations of a child prostitution ring operating in Washington D.C. catering to high-level U.S. politicians. This film and the allegations of child abuse are the most disturbing issues found surrounding the Illuminati. While *Conspiracy of Silence* doesn't mention the Illuminati by name, it is none the less exposing individuals and activities which have long been associated with the group.

The film follows what has been called the Franklin Cover-Up which involves the Franklin Credit Union in Omaha, Nebraska and an orphanage called Boys Town and the investigations of a lawyer and former senator of Nebraska, John DeCamp. The film begins with a scrolling text message reading that the production had originally been scheduled to air on the Discovery Channel on Tuesday May 3rd 1994 and that the April 30th to May 6th *TV Guide* listing and newspaper supplements had the program listed to air, but at the last minute some individuals had arrived at the production studio and purchased the rights to the film for a quarter of a million dollars and then removed all known copies. It goes on to read that the copy the viewer is watching was sent anonymously to John DeCamp who later distributed it on VHS and has since found its way onto the Internet.

In 1988 it was discovered that thirty-eight million dollars was embezzled from the Franklin County Credit Union in Omaha, Nebraska. As the investigation into the embezzlement continued, evidence of a child prostitution ring began to surface. As the missing money was followed, it lead to dark places nobody could imagine. On June 29, 1989, the *Washington Times* ran a front page story with the headline "Homosexual Prostitution Inquiry ensnares VIPs with Reagan, Bush." Paul M. Rodriguez and George

Archibald wrote the article and alleged that individuals close to Ronald Reagan and George H.W. Bush were connected to an underage homosexual prostitution ring. The article also mentioned that one of the children (Paul Bonacci) was taken on a midnight tour of the White House by one of the perpetrators.

On January 10, 1990, a special committee was assigned to look into the allegations. The credit union's manager, Lawrence E. King would later be convicted of embezzling thirty-eight million dollars from the organization, but he was also named as a key player in an underage homosexual prostitution ring that he allegedly funded with the embezzled money. King was a prominent man within the Republican party, and at the 1984 and 1988 Republican National Conventions he was the person who sang the national anthem.

Nebraska's State Senator Ernie Chambers said that Lawrence King was "just the tip of an iceberg, and he's not in it by himself."[171]

The New York Times reported Chambers claimed to have heard credible reports of "boys and girls, some of them from foster homes who had been transported around the country by airplane to provide sexual favors, for which they were rewarded."[172]

Paul A. Bonacci won a default judgment of $800,000 in compensatory damages and $200,000 in punitive damages in a civil action against Lawrence E. King in which the petition alleged kidnapping, mind control, satanic ritual abuse, and sexual abuse, and alleged various personal injuries, both physical and psychological.

A private detective named Gary Caradori, who was

---

[171] Robbins, William – *A Lurid, Mysterious Scandal Begins Taking Shape in Omaha.* The New York Times. December 18, 1988
[172] Ibid

hired by a special Nebraska state legislative committee to investigate the allegations, was killed when his plane crashed in Illinois on July 11th 1990. Senator Loran Schmit, chairman of the legislative committee, told the *Omaha World-Herald* that "[Caradori] believed that something was going to come out of this investigation. He believed that the evidence was there to be developed and that things couldn't stay under cover forever."[173]

Some say on that very airplane Gary Caradori had the evidence needed to prove his case. Strangely, within 24 hours of his death the FBI impounded all his files. His widow and brother both appear in *Conspiracy of Silence* and believe Gary was murdered and said that his car had been tampered with in the recent past. Investigators would later say that they could not determine what had caused his plane to break up in the air and crash. Gary Caradori's brother Dick Caradori says in the film that Gary told him he would be murdered if the perpetrators knew of the evidence that he had recently discovered. His wife sites that his briefcase was missing from the wreckage. Some say Caradori had actual photos that were given to him by Rusty Nelson which showed prominent politicians engaged in improper acts with children. It's not a radical assumption to think that Caradori would have been placed under surveillance by the Illuminati, and his phone calls were monitored by them to determine what evidence he had obtained and what kind of a threat he posed to the perpetrators. If he had obtained such evidence as the photos from Rusty Nelson, they would have done anything to cover it up. Even if he had not obtained such damning evidence, it was in the Illuminati's best interest to kill him, and they probably did.

The information found in this section is only the

---

[173] *Caradori's Airplane Broke up in Flight*, Omaha World-Herald. Omaha, NE: July 12, 1990. Page 01

beginning of the story of what happened surrounding the Franklin County Credit Union. For a more detailed explanation see The Franklin Cover-Up page 120. *Conspiracy of Silence* is basically the film version of John DeCamp's book *The Franklin Cover-Up*, although the book covers more details about Satanism, snuff films, and the Bohemian Grove. *Conspiracy of Silence* contains interviews with several children who were allegedly victims, including Paul Bonacci, Alicia Owen, Troy Boner and others. Be warned that this film is extremely disturbing and may leave the viewer feeling physically ill.

Decoding the Past: The Templar Code

Another well done History Channel production is the two hour *Decoding the Past* episode titled *The Templar Code*. The program covers some interesting history surrounding the formation of the Knights Templar, and their ultimate demise. The show begins with the narrator saying they were "a society so secret that its true purpose is debated even to this day."

The Templar Code begins by telling how the first crusade left Europe in 1096 and Christians all over Europe were encouraged to travel to Jerusalem and fight the Muslims in order to take back the Holy Land.

In 1099 Christians had succeeded in capturing Jerusalem, and pilgrims then began traveling to the Holy Land. Around 1119 the first Knights Templar came forward. A man named Hugues de Payens from France recruited nine members of his family and offered to protect people traveling from the coast of the Mediterranean to the Holy Land. They said they would patrol the roads and offer security, but these knights were middle aged and not young and strong like a knight should be.

It becomes clear that these knights didn't go there to protect the travelers, but to start excavating for treasure.

They made their headquarters the Dome on the Rock, which was on the same site as the original Solomon's Temple which was destroyed by the Babylonians in 586 BC. This is where the Knights Templar got their name. They were called the Knights of the Temple of Solomon, or the Knights Templar. In 1128 they returned to Europe and became very rich and powerful immediately afterward.

In 1867 British archeologists excavated under the Temple Mount and found a span of tunnels. Templar artifacts were discovered in these tunnels, showing that they had been the ones who dug them. Rumors spread that they found the Ark of the Covenant or the Holy Grail, which some believe is a cup that held the blood of Christ, or a set of documents recording a bloodline of Jesus and Mary Magdalene.

It is also believed that the Knights Templar recovered massive amounts of treasure that was hidden under the temple stemming from the 66 AD Jewish revolt against the Roman Empire. In 1952 one of the Dead Sea scrolls that had been discovered, the copper scroll, itemizes 200 tons of gold and silver which has not been found.

Around 1150 the knights had devised a system to give travelers receipts for their gold and jewelry. The receipt was coded to protect the person and allowed them to travel without the burden and fear of carrying large amounts of heavy gold and silver. The Templars had a reputation for codes and secrecy and their methods became the model for today's banking system.

They ultimately became bankers and issued loans to people and governments. The Church wouldn't allow people to charge interest, which they called usury, but the Templars did it anyway and the Church would look the other way. Some suspect that the Catholic Church was paying them off to keep silent about the information they had found in scrolls under Solomon's Temple.

They began building churches and castles and an

elaborate hierarchy was set up. The grand master was elected for life and was the head of the international organization. As time passes, the Templars became less involved in fighting, and more involved in business.

In 1244 the Turks recaptured Jerusalem and in 1291 the seaport of Acre had fallen, which was the last Christian stronghold in the region. After this, the reason for the Templar's existence was in question. After 200 years the Crusades were over.

Friday the 13th is considered unlucky because on Friday the 13th of October 1307, King Philip of France had the Templars rounded up and arrested for allegedly denying Christ, spitting on the cross, sodomy, and worshiping Satan. Templar headquarters in France were all raided and Jacques de Molay was arrested along with his leading knights. Some think the King of France made up the charges in order to claim the Templar's wealth, but others believe the accusations were authentic.

The majority of the Knights Templar escaped and vanished and their massive amounts of treasure vanished with them. Evidence suggests that the Knights Templar created Freemasonry and continued their occult practices and business ventures under this cloak. The order of DeMolay is a children's branch of Freemasonry for children of Masons and is named after the Knights Templar grandmaster Jacques de Molay who was burned at the stake for his satanic activities.

Mysteries of the Freemasons

Another interesting History Channel documentary is *Mysteries of the Freemasons* which was most likely the result of the popularity of films like *National Treasure*, which has a storyline largely to do with Freemasonry. The History Channel often capitalizes on topics that are found in forthcoming films or pop culture topics. *Mysteries of the*

Freemasons: The Beginning is the first hour of a two hour show which covers the history of Freemasonry including the secret handshakes and their mysterious rituals. It explains that geometry is seen as more than just mathematics, but a link to the Divine and that ancient stone mason guilds teachings of math and mysticism lives on in what became Freemasonry.

The program has some interesting history about the group, including that the oldest minutes of the Masons meeting as a labor union were in 1599, and that sometime between then and 1717, the first Grand Lodge in England was formed and the organization had evolved into a gentlemen's club. During the Enlightenment, in order to avoid persecution from the Church, many scientists and political thinkers joined the Freemasons and the fraternity had created symbols and stories aimed at developing moral character and improving society.

S. Brent Morris PhD, a Masonic historian admits, "There are many anti-Masonic conspiracy theories that we are the secret controllers of government and industry world wide. There is also a theory out there that the secret inner circle of Freemasonry worships Satan." He then tries to downplay these ideas by saying, "If we can't agree whether to serve ham sandwiches or tuna sandwiches after the meeting, how can we possibly agree to take over the world?"

Akram Elias, a 33rd degree Freemason also mocks the idea of a secret agenda in the program saying, "didn't you know that it was a Jewish Masonic imperialist conspiracy that killed Lady Di?"

When explaining what the term "on the level" means, S. Brent Morris, says "it doesn't matter how great you are, or how insignificant you are. Everyone is going to the same place. You're going to the grave." Such statements seem to reveal that Freemasons don't believe in an afterlife.

The show admits that each Freemason is resurrected from a symbolic death as they are initiated into the order, and that in 1738 the Catholic Church forbade any Catholics from joining the Freemasons. It is also admitted that Freemasons were at the heart of the American Revolution and the Boston Tea Party.

The connection to the Knights Templar is also explored, including their digging for Solomon's gold, the Holy Grail, or the papers of the Essenes which were said to contain information on how Man might communicate with God directly. It was also briefly mentioned how the Templars were the first multinational bankers and how rumors began to spread that they participated in strange rituals that certainly were not of Christian origin, including their alleged worship of Baphamet.

Christopher Night, co-author of *The Hiram Key,* who was interviewed for the show says that he believes the rituals were learned by the Templars from the ancient scrolls they had discovered while excavating under Solomon's Temple.

After the order was disbanded and many of its leaders arrested in 1307, Night points out the popular belief that the Knights Templars joined the stone mason guilds and that the secret knowledge was brought to Scotland's Rosslyn Chapel.

The first hour ends explaining that Masonic ideals were crucial in the creation of the United States, and then continues with a second hour which then covers the symbols found in the street layout of Washington D.C.

One of the Masons interviewed for the second hour fully admits that Washington D.C. is laid out to Masonic ideals, including the street layout and placement of certain buildings, but then Brent Morris PhD, Masonic historian and 33rd degree Mason mocks the idea saying, "I can also look at the streets of Washington and also find a piggy and a horsy. I don't think they're there."

Surprisingly, the William Morgan incident of 1826 was discussed, where Freemasons kidnapped and murdered a man just before he could publish a book exposing Freemasonry's secrets. It even briefly mentioned John

Robison's book, *Proofs of a Conspiracy* and how the Illuminati is said to have been behind the French Revolution and created an inner circle inside Freemasonry. But then the narrator goes on to say that the Illuminati conspiracy theory is unfounded and that "historical records show that the Illuminati existed as a group for less than ten years. They were abolished in 1785 with public trials and banishments. But the Freemasons would never completely escape from the shadow of the Illuminati."

While the show covers some fascinating history about the Freemasons, it shamelessly presents them in a favorable light and basically presents only the Freemasons view of the organization, while obviously attempting to dismiss any opposing information, particularly ideas about a secret society within the secret society, such as the Illuminati.

Hacking Democracy

In 2006 HBO aired a documentary film titled *Hacking Democracy* which showed just how easy it is for electronic voting machines to be rigged, and elections to be stolen. The film was nominated for an Emmy Award for Outstanding Investigative Journalism.

The documentary begins showing that on election night in 2000 in Volusia Country, Florida the electronic voting machines showed Al Gore had negative votes because the computers were automatically deducting the number of votes that were cast for him. The machine showed -16,022 votes. An investigation was launched into why this had occurred, and many suspected it was a simple computer malfunction, but only the presidential race totals were affected. All other categories for state and local officials and propositions were tallied correctly. It was determined that a second memory card was plugged into the machine which likely changed the vote totals.

The software for such machines is a trade secret held

closely by the companies which manufacture them. David Jefferson PhD, was the chief technical adviser to the California's Secretary of State and even he was not allowed to look at the software of the electronic voting machines.

The film continues to show how a Seattle woman named Bev Harris became worried after her county began using electronic voting machines and she was able to find files on the Internet from Diebold Election Systems which showed how the software for such machines worked and how easy it was to hack. Diebold Election Systems (now renamed Premier Election Solutions) are used to count over 40% of America's votes.

Harris took the information to a security specialist to analyze it and figure out how it worked and how secure it was. She later founded BlackBoxVoting.org as a way to inform the public about the issues and dangers involved in the vote counting process.

In 2003 it was discovered that Walden O'Dell, the CEO of Diebold Election Systems, had written a Republican fundraising letter in which he was "committed to helping Ohio deliver their electoral votes to the President next year." He was obviously referring to President Bush who was facing John Kerry in the 2004 election. When asked about this, Mark Radke, Diebold's marketing director answered, "that quotation that appeared in a letter is something that, uh…he regrets. It's a situation where his personal preference has come over into his business practice and he has committed to keeping a much lower profile when it comes to those kinds of activities."

Dr. Hugh Thompson, a security expert and director of Security Innovations Inc. was approached by Bev Harris at a hacking conference and asked to look at the software she was able to obtain from Diebold. "The thing that shocked me was how easy vote totals could be changed. So, imagine, you could go into a box and essentially rewrite history. And there is no record of you rewriting history. And the only record of history itself is the thing that you changed. And that's pretty scary to me," Thompson said.

Harris and Thompson had obtained a meeting with Governor Howard Dean to show him how easy the machines would be to hack and change the vote totals that were added from all voting machines nationwide.

The film then goes on to show that on election day in 2004, a voter helpline in Ohio received over 200,000 calls. Many of the callers left voicemails, some of which were played in the documentary. One caller left a voice mail complaining there was one voting booth for 3000 people. Another complained he had to wait seven and a half hours to vote. In the poorer areas that historically and statistically would vote Democrat, very few machines were put in place so that there would be less votes cast in those areas. Such a strategy was implemented in order to discourage people from waiting hours in line and to minimize the number of votes cast in those areas. This, of course, would minimize the number of votes for John Kerry.

On election night in 2004 when John Kerry faced off against President George W. Bush, exit polls were showing John Kerry had the lead in Ohio which was the key swing state. Kerry later lost the state, and thus the election and quickly conceded which stunned many of his staff and legal team.

Cliff Arnebeck, an election attorney from Ohio was on a conference call with Senator Kerry shortly after the election. Arnebeck said that Kerry knew there was fraud in Ohio but did nothing and didn't activate the massive legal team that he had prepared for such an event. The Illuminati had told Kerry that it wasn't his time and that the brotherhood had decided Bush would remain the President.

Perhaps the most unsettling aspect of *Hacking Democracy* was when it showed how easily an election could be stolen by only using a simple memory card that had been programmed to do so.

Ian Sancho, the Supervisor of Elections for Leon County Florida, asked BlackBoxVoting.org to look at his county's electronic voting machines. They brought along Finnish computer security expert Harri Hursti who claimed to discover how by using only a memory card purchased from the Internet, he could sway an election any direction he desired.

Before they had attempted the memory card hack, Mark Radke (Diebold's marketing director), as well as the head engineer for Diebold had denied that such a hack was possible at a public meeting. "It is my understanding that because there is no executable program on the memory card that the actual votes on the memory card cannot be altered," said Radke. Someone then asks, "Could you remind us, are you an engineer yourself?" Radke responds, "No I am not an engineer but I work with our engineering crew, in fact, Pat do you want to step up here for a second."

A man approaches the podium and takes the microphone. "Hi I'm Pat Green, I'm the director for research and development for Diebold."

Bev Harris then asks Green her question. "Can votes be changed using only a memory card?"

"No. I do not believe votes can be change using only a memory card." He went on to downplay a report that claims that it was possible, referring to a paper written by Hursti.

The film then shows Harri Hursti and others arriving in Leon County, Florida where Ian Sancho, the supervisor of elections, held a test election using actual machines and ballots, and the memory card that Hursti had provided. Hursti had not been given access to the ballots or the machine itself, only the memory card. To Sancho's and others astonishment, Hursti's altered memory card was able to rig the test election in a way that he had desired. This was a direct contradiction of Diebold's statements and showed how easily any election could be rigged by simply having access to the memory cards before the vote totals had even been stored on those cards.

The *Hursti Hack,* as it has been called, was undetectable and would also be undetectable in an actual election. Ion Sancho acknowledged this saying, "If I had not known what was behind this I would have certified this election as a true count of a vote."

Diebold had publicly denied that the Hursti Hack was legitimate and had pressured HBO in an attempt to have the documentary shelved before it had aired. Diebold claimed that Hursti's hack was a fraud. California's Secretary of State commissioned a special report by computer technicians at UC Berkeley to investigate the Hursti Hack, and they concluded, "Harri Hursti's attack does work: Mr. Hursti's attack on the AV-OS is definitely real. He was indeed able to change the election results by doing nothing more than modifying the contents of a memory card. He needed no passwords, no cryptographic keys, and no access to any other part of the voting system, including the GEMS election management server."[174]

Diebold Election Systems has since changed its name to Premier Election Solutions, most likely because the name Diebold has become synonymous with suspicion and allegations of election fraud. By using such methods, the Illuminati decides who becomes president of the United States, or who gets elected to Congress. As more and more states and counties implement electronic voting machines, it will practically guarantee the Illuminati will decide who "wins" elections.

---

[174] *Security Analysis of the Diebold AccuBasic Interpreter* (page 2) by David Wagner, David Jefferson, Matt Bishop, Voting Systems Technology Assessment Advisory Board (VSTAAB) with the assistance of: Chris Karlof Naveen Sastry, University of California, Berkeley, February 14, 2006

Other films

9/11 Revisited
9/11 Mysteries
9/11 Press for Truth
Illuminati: Our Secret Masters
Guerilla News Network: Mind Control
H.A.A.R.P. Holes in Heaven
DNA vs. The Book of Mormon
Waco: A New Revelation
Secrets of the CIA
The Vatican's Baker
Fiat Empire
U.S.S. Liberty: Dead in the Water
The Light Behind Masonry
They Sold Their Soul for Rock and Roll
The Coming Financial Collapse of America
America: From Freedom to Fascism
Satanism in the CIA
Aleister Crowley: The Wickedest Man in the World
Skull and Bones (a Dutch documentary)
The Power of Nightmares
Iraq for Sale: The War Profiteers
Zeitgeist Refuted
War Made Easy
Why We Fight
Secrets of the Freemasons — National Geographic
Echelon: Most Secret Spy System
Mind Control - America's Secret War
Big Brother, Big Business
Eye of the Phoenix: Secrets of Dollar Bill
The Obama Deception
Fall of the Republic
Invisible Empire

Snuff Films

The most disturbing aspect of the occult and the Illuminati are the allegations of child abuse, pedophilia, and snuff films. Just thinking about such things can make one physically ill, and it is much to the regret of this author that such issues must be included in this book. However, in our search for the truth we must boldly face the facts no matter what road they lead us down.

When one thinks of snuff films and the deliberate killing of someone for the purpose of enjoyment while the incident is being videotaped, the perpetrators and suspects are often thought of as lone nuts and sociopaths who act alone and without the knowledge or aid of others. After all, if someone were asked by a friend of theirs if they wanted to participate in such a thing, what are the odds that they would accept such a proposal instead of distancing themselves from that friend, or calling the police?

When one learns of the allegations and extent of snuff film production and distribution, and the depth of brutality involved, difficult questions arise as to motives for such crimes and how such sick and demented individuals could actually find others who were interested in such things. If one can grasp this reality, then yet more difficult questions arise when the cost of such films are discovered, and that people pay large sums of money for such things. One also wonders how individuals who desired such things could actually accumulate the large sums of money that are charged for snuff films. The fact that most snuff films are extremely expensive shows that the customers of such material are financially well off, and able to afford to spend thousands, or tens of thousands of dollars on the videos, and the demand for snuff films is greater than one could ever imagine.

In the year 2000, authorities launched the largest ever

international investigation into child snuff films and a 30-year-old Russian named Dmitri Vladimirovich Kuznetsov was arrested for distributing thousands of such videos and photos.

Kuznetsov was identified after British Customs and police traced the origin of several snuff films which were found in the UK. The previous week Italian police had seized 3,000 of Kuznetsov's videos which were being shipped to clients in Italy. This was not just child pornography, but videos of children being abused and murdered on video. Many of the films were produced in Russia.

Approximately a dozen British men were arrested in connection with the Russian tapes. "We have seen some very, very nasty stuff involving sadistic abuse of very young children, but actual deaths on film takes it a whole step further. That is very worrying," said one senior customs officer who was involved in the case.[175]

British pedophiles were not only buying such tapes, but were paying to access a website that featured pictures of such abuse.

One of Kuznetsov's partners, Dmitri Ivanov was sentenced to only eleven years for participating in the abuse that was being videotaped. Others were released under an amnesty aimed at clearing Russia's overcrowded prisons.[176]

When officers from the Moscow Criminal Investigation Department raided Kuznetsov's house they found two boys in a makeshift studio. They seized a huge number of films and other pornographic material as well as lists of clients in Italy, Germany, America, and Britain.

---

[175] London Observer – *British link to 'snuff' videos* October 1, 2000 by Jason Burke in London, Amelia Gentleman in Moscow, Philip Willan in Rome
[176] Ibid

Italian authorities arrested eight people and searched more than 600 homes, and gathered evidence against 500 people. Some of the suspects were businessmen and public employees. Hundreds of people were also under investigation in Germany.

The Russian videos, which had been ordered over the Internet, were intercepted when they were shipped into Italy and then delivered by undercover police officers.

Police in Russia and the UK believe that Kuznetsov and his associates had been producing such videos for over two years and that they had lured around 100 boys between nine and eleven to participate in the videos. Most of the children were orphans and were told they would be given something to eat by the men if they came with them.

This is just one of numerous cases of such horrific things. Most people assume that such disgusting things are extremely rare and only committed by a lone nut, but this case and others show that there are hundreds if not thousands of people around the world who want to view such material and pay large amounts of money to do so. High level Satanists and members of the Illuminati are believed to not only view such material but participate in such abuse at places like the Bohemian Grove.

Sex Magic

When looking for an explanation as to why the Illuminati would sexually abuse children, the answer is found in what is called sex magic. This kind of magic, (sometimes spelled sex magick) involves using sexual arousal to achieve altered states of consciousness and harnessing these states of consciousness to transcend physical reality or to metaphysically alter it.

Some believe that the highest guarded secret in the occult and the Illuminati is that by participating in such activities one's brain chemistry is altered and creates a permanent change in one's mental alertness, thus amplifying that person's senses and perceptions. It is said the mind is put in a state of hyper-alertivness, which dramatically increases a person's brain power.

The central belief of sex magic is that at the moment of orgasm a man's sexual energy is somehow channeled and used to manifest images he is holding in his mind, and metaphysically bring them into his physical reality. This philosophy of manifesting one's thoughts into physical reality is nothing new, and is a popular idea in New Age circles and self-help books. The vast majority of people who practice visualization and manifestation simply do so by meditation techniques, but it is believed that a highly guarded secret in the occult and the Illuminati is that this visualization and manifestation technique is dramatically amplified by involving some kind of sexual rituals. This sexual technique is then amplified by involving violence at the same time. By overloading the mind with adrenaline produced from viciously raping an innocent child, the Illuminati believe that this type of sexual ritual unlocks magical and metaphysical aspects of the human mind, allowing them to literally and physically alter their experience of reality.

The popular DVD called *The Secret* teaches what is called the "law of attraction" and promotes the idea that whatever images you visualize in your mind can be metaphysically manifested into your life. This is certainly not a new idea, and self-help gurus and spiritual teachers around the world have taught this technique for decades if not centuries. Practitioners of sex magic believe that these spiritual principles can be dramatically increased by using sexual energy in conjunction with the visualization techniques. There is nothing particularly evil with this belief or practice as long as one's sexual partner is a consenting adult. But it appears that a core group within the Illuminati have twisted these teachings and use children and violence in an attempt to increase the power of sex magic even further.

The founder of the Ordo Templi Orientis (the O.T.O.), Carl Kellner, would hint that the best kept secrets of the OTO were of a sexual nature. In 1912, an obscure German Masonic magazine called *Oriflamme* included an interesting admission, saying, "Our order possesses the key which opens up all Masonic and Hermetic secrets, namely, the teachings of sexual magic, and this teaching explains, without exception, all the secrets of Freemasonry and all systems of religion."[177]

There are rumors that scientific experiments using this kind of sexual magic were analyzed in what is called the Montauk Project which were allegedly conducted at the Montauk Air Force Station on Montauk, Long Island in New York in the early 1900s. This program is believed by some to have been involved in metaphysical research and experiments involving parallel universes and time travel. As strange as this sounds, the existence of multiple dimensions of reality that exceed the three that we perceive are essentially considered fact in physics and quantum

---

[177] King, Francis –*The Magical World of Aleister Crowley*, page 78

mechanics. Some physicists believe that there are unlimited parallel universes of reality and that each universe contains a reality similar to the one that we are experiencing. Each of these parallel universes is said to contain a slightly different reality, and that anything and everything that could possibly happen, is actually happening, but in other universes.

Following along these same lines of thought is the theory that there can be no reality without an observer. This means that you, or the person observing what is called reality, is actually reality's co-creator, and that your mind and your thoughts are actually shaping and creating the reality that you see and experience. Continuing with this line of thought, somehow an individual can change from one universe to another, thus changing their entire experience of reality. The adherents to this theory have somehow concluded that the only way to effectively shift from one universe to another is by using sex magic, and that by combining sexual arousal with mental visualization techniques, and then mixing in violence, the violence acts as a sort of steroid for the manifestation power of the metaphysical mind and reality.

Some people believe that they themselves are the only person who actually "exists" and that their entire experience of reality is a three-dimensional hologram that they can control with their mind. Following this line of thought, a practitioner of sex magic believes that in order to harness their mind's power to shape their three-dimensional experience in reality, they must use visualization techniques involving an orgasm. Sexual energy and a sexual climax is seen as the most powerful force in the world since it is used to create life. The dark sex magic practitioners somehow believe that by sacrificing (killing) an innocent child while simultaneously "channeling" their sexual energy by defiling the child, that it virtually unlimitedly amplifies their mind's metaphysical power.

Whatever their motives, sex magic involving raping

children have been proven to occur on a large scale as in the case of the Franklin Cover-Up. What would seem to be something too brutal and disgusting for a Hollywood horror writer to even think of, has been happening in reality. This proves beyond a doubt that the Satanists and Illuminati members who participate in these activities are not simply seeking enlightenment, but are committing the sickest kinds of perversions and violations of morality imaginable in their quest for power.

Whether or not such techniques actually work as some believe is unknown. It is possible that they do, but even if that is the case, it is inexcusable for anyone to even consider such a thing. Certainly it is possible to point a gun at someone and demand their money, and they will likely hand it over. Such a technique works, but even considering such an action is a violation of the code of conduct humanity should live by.

Fictional Books

Art imitates life as the cliché goes, and over the years various novelists have incorporated the Illuminati or their activities into various fictional books. Some of these books use the Illuminati by name and are fictionalized stories based on the historical Illuminati such as Dan Brown's *Angels & Demons*. Others clearly refer to Illuminati operations and plans in an attempt to seemingly warn the readers of what may come, as in the case of George Orwell's classic *Nineteen Eighty-Four*. Other books such as Hunter S. Thompson's *Fear and Loathing in Las Vegas* take a more disturbing turn, and refer to esoteric satanic practices in ways that make many suspect that Thompson himself had intimate knowledge of such things, or even participated in them himself and cloaked his experience in the form of a novel.

The Illuminatus! Trilogy

Robert Anton Wilson and Robert Shea were perhaps the first authors to incorporate the Illuminati into the plotline of a fictional story when they released the first book of *The Illuminatus! Trilogy* in 1975. The series includes various conspiracy theories, some historical, and some fictional, which involve the Illuminati. The three different volumes comprising the trilogy are titled *The Eye in the Pyramid*, *The Golden Apple,* and *Leviathan.*

Robert Anton Wilson died on January 11, 2007 at the age of 74. Throughout his life he had capitalized tremendously on the Illuminati, and after the *Illuminatus! Trilogy* was completed, he continued to write books which focused on the subject.

In 1980, Wilson published *The Illuminati Papers* which expands upon characters and themes from *The Illuminatus! Trilogy*. In 1981 he released *Masks of the Illuminati* which was about three men who "discovered that an ancient criminal order is preparing to take over the world." Between 1982 and 1991, Robert Anton Wilson wrote and released *The Historical Illuminatus Chronicles* which are an additional three novels written as a follow up to *The Illuminatus! Trilogy*. This new trilogy is composed of three books: *The Earth Will Shake* (1982), *The Widow's Son* (1985), and *Nature's God* (1991).

While Robert Shea was his coauthor for *The Illuminatus! Trilogy*, Wilson went on to write his additional works by himself. Wilson did not believe the Illuminati continued to exist after their discovery in the late 1700s. When asked why people believe in conspiracies, he said, "I think there are three factors: A, nobody likes to take the blame for their own problems so they look for somebody else to blame. And if you can find a big enough group, you've explained everything in your life that doesn't work. It's not your fault, it's the Jesuits, the Freemasons, the Jews, the Bilderbergers, the Council on Foreign Relations, you've got a wide choice to pick of who to blame, as long as you don't have to blame yourself."

"The world is changing so rapidly that most people are living in a world they can't understand, and when people can't understand something they tend to go for sinister explanations of it. Somebody is manipulating things in a way I don't like. That's the way people feel when things change too fast and they can't understand it."[178]

Aside from seeming to insult people who believe in the Illuminati or conspiracies, Wilson was personally interested in the occult and admired Aleister Crowley. He said, "Crowley was the first writer of so-called New Age, or mystical, or occult things that I ever took seriously...So I started studying him and found out he did have a lot of

---

[178] YouTube video "Robert Anton Wilson on Conspiracy Theories"

important things to say, and I value him highly. I think relativity is one of the most important ideas of the twentieth century. Einstein gave us physical relativity, [James] Joyce, gave us artistic relativity…and Crowley did the same thing for the mystical occult world with his law of Thelema. Do what thou wilt shall be the whole of the law. The Crowley system does not have any disciples, it doesn't tell you what to do, it tells you to decide for yourself what to do."[179]

In 1983 Wilson published his dissertation which was written to earn his PhD in psychology from Paideia University, an unaccredited University which has since closed. He titled it *Prometheus Rising* which he called an "Owner's manual for the human brain." The dissertation was based on a variety of philosophies and scientific views including Aleister Crowley, Timothy Leary's 8 circuit model of consciousness, and quantum mechanics.

Wilson demonstrated a tremendous amount of knowledge about the occult, but his writings about the Illuminati should be seen nothing more than a creative writer's attempt to capitalize on such ideas. Wilson said, "My goal is to try to get people into a state of generalized agnosticism, not agnosticism about God alone, but agnosticism about everything."[180]

The Illuminati by Larry Burkett

A Christian author named Larry Burkett also incorporated the Illuminati into a fictional tale in his 1991 book simply titled, *The Illuminati.*

The description of the book on the back cover reads,

[179] YouTube video "Robert Anton Wilson Talks about Aleister Crowley"
[180] Robert Anton Wilson Contemporary Authors Online, Gale, 2007. Reproduced in Biography Resource Center. Farmington Hills, Mich.: Thomson Gale. 2007

"From before the time of Christ, there have been rumors of a secret society called *The Illuminati*—a vicious tribe of Druids with mystical, supernatural powers. Many saw them as demons or gods. Those who opposed them simply disappeared...or met an even worse fate."

"As the centuries passed, this shadow-like group cloaked themselves in new identities, slowly infiltrating world organizations and financial institutions. The stealthy society had a singular goal—to bring the planet to its knees by controlling the world's economic system."

"Now fast-forward to the year 2015. The Illuminati has succeeded in placing one of their people in the office of the presidency of the United States. With the worldwide launch of a financial system known as Data-Net, they have gained seemingly unlimited power."

Burkett died on July 4, 2003 at the age of 64. He had written more than a dozen books and during his career had hosted several different radio shows on money and personal finance. It is clear from his writings that he believed the Illuminati existed, and his book was an attempt to address these issues in the form of a novel.

Angels & Demons

Published in the year 2000, Dan Brown's *Angels & Demons* is a fictional novel revolving around the Catholic Church and the Illuminati, and is a prequel to *The Da Vinci Code* which was later published in 2003. The common theme in *The Da Vinci Code*, as many know, is that the Catholic Church allegedly has been trying to cover up a family tree containing the bloodline of Jesus and Mary Magdalene which still exists today.

According to Brown and supporters of this widely discredited theory, numerous secret societies have been protecting this bloodline from the Catholic Church, who allegedly will do anything to keep this "secret" from getting out and ruining Christianity and the Vatican's grip on power.

In *Angels & Demons*, the Illuminati is set out to destroy Vatican City as retribution for suppressing them hundreds of years ago and forcing them deeper underground. The story is most likely a purposeful whitewash of the real Illuminati, or the result of a creative writer seizing on topics of interest in the underground and making them mainstream. Either way, Brown's writings and subsequent films which followed can only be seen as a deliberate attack on Christianity and muddying the water for real researchers of the Illuminati.

Thanks to Brown, the brainwashed masses of people think that when someone discusses the Illuminati and the very real effects the organization has on society and Bible prophecy, that one is too wrapped up in *Angels & Demons*. Many of those who have become victims of the Illuminati's agendas don't even believe such a thing exists. *Angels & Demons* was made into a motion picture starring Tom Hanks and released in May 2009. (See Angels & Demons the movie on page 335)

The main character, Robert Langdon, is a Harvard professor and expert on religious symbology. He becomes involved in trying to stop the Illuminati from destroying Vatican City in Rome by using an anti-matter bomb. Brown cleverly mixes historical facts into the plotline and blurs the line between fact and fiction by referencing actual quotes about the Illuminati from historical figures. Most of Brown's readers (and viewers of the film) have no idea that the Illuminati he is referring to is a real organization and some of the "historical facts" he writes in his book are actually true.

For example, he writes that the Illuminati infiltrated Freemasonry, saying "...in the 1700's, the Masons unknowingly became a front for the Illuminati. The Illuminati grew within their ranks, gradually taking over positions of power within the lodges. They quietly reestablished their scientific brotherhood deep within the

Masons—a kind of secret society within a secret society. The Illuminati used the worldwide connection of Masonic lodges to spread their influence."[181]

Brown even explains that the Illuminati are satanic, writing, "The church claimed Lucifer was a reference to the devil, but the brotherhood insisted Lucifer was intended in its literal Latin meaning—*bringer of light*. Or *Illuminator*."[182]

Dan Brown even cleverly refers to numerous websites which feature material about the Illuminati and the New World Order. At one point his book reads, "This morning" Kohler challenged, "when I typed the word 'Illuminati' into the computer, it returned thousands of current references. Apparently a lot of people think this group is still active."

"Conspiracy buffs," Langdon replied. He had always been annoyed by the plethora of conspiracy theories that circled in modern pop culture. The media craved apocalyptic headlines, and self-proclaimed "cult specialists" were still cashing in on millennium hype with fabricated stories that the Illuminati were alive and well and organizing their New World Order."[183]

Besides weaving in various historical facts about the Illuminati, Brown also includes some far-fetched ideas that have no basis in reality at all. He makes his readers think the Illuminati were a group of scientists that included Galileo, as well as famous artists such as Bernini, when both men had died a hundred years before the Illuminati had actually formed.[184] He also includes other ideas that have never been associated with the Illuminati, and are clearly fictions created by Brown. One such example is his claim that the

[181] Brown, Dan – *Angels & Demons* page 38
[182] Brown, Dan – *Angels & Demons* page 39
[183] Brown, Dan – *Angels & Demons* page 40-41
[184] Galileo died in 1642 and Bernini died in 1680

Vatican holds in its possession several "Illuminati brands" which consist of ambigrams in the names of earth, air, fire, and water, which he says the "scientific Illuminati" had designed to depict the four elements ancient scientists believed made up the physical universe. An ambigram is a design that spells out one or more words that can be read whether looked at right-side up or upside down. These "Illuminati brands" are heated up and used to burn the different symbols into the chests of various Cardinals who the Illuminati murder in the novel as revenge for the Catholic Church allegedly burning a brand of a cross in the chests of heretics in the past.

Brown even says that the Catholic Church murdered Nicolaus Copernicus for introducing heliocentrism, the idea that the earth revolves around the sun, and not vice versa as the church had claimed. I'm certainly not a supporter of the Catholic Church nor a defender of their past and present atrocities, but to say that they murdered Copernicus is simply a lie. He died at the age of seventy, which in the sixteenth century was quite an old age. There are numerous other lies and disinformation in Brown's book as he repeatedly paints the Illuminati as a group of innocent scientists and artists who the Church had set out to torture and kill. Brown is clearly well informed regarding conspiracy theory culture and at one point has Robert Langdon discuss the mysterious all-seeing eye on the back of the one dollar bill and explains that mysterious symbol is what got him interested in the Illuminati. At one point he also mentions that the Bilderberg group financed the Illuminati. (See Jim Tucker's Bilderberg Diary page 110)

Brown actually defends the Illuminati in his novel. His character Robert Langdon, who is an "expert" on the Illuminati, fails to see them as a sinister power hungry gang, but instead says, "The Illuminati may have believed in the abolition of Christianity, but they wielded their power through political and financial means, not through terrorists acts.   Furthermore, the Illuminati had a strict code of morality regarding who they saw as enemies."[185]

Regardless of how entertaining and captivating Brown's novel may be, it serves only to disarm an already ignorant and degenerate public, leading them to believe that the Illuminati is a fictional creation.   When told it is a historically verifiable secret society that continues to exist today, many are only reminded of the doubtful Robert Langdon from *Angels & Demons* and the sinister satanic cult which plotted to blow up the Vatican with an anti-matter bomb.

At the very end of *Angels & Demons*, in a very dramatic twist, Dan Brown writes that there is actually no such thing as the Illuminati, and that a demented Vatican official who holds the position of the Camerlengo had concocted the story and was actually behind the plot himself.   In the book, it turns out that the Illuminati really did go into extinction in the late 1700s and the Camerlengo played off of people's fears that they had secretly continued to exist.

The success of Dan Brown's books are not due to their exceptional quality, but rather that the Illuminati had used their influence to promote both *The Da Vinci Code* and *Angels & Demons* to spread their tainted message about Jesus and the Illuminati.   Dan Brown himself has some interesting ties to the real Illuminati, and it's possible that he was used for the purpose of muddying the waters surrounding Christianity, the Illuminati, and the New World Order.   Brown is a graduate of Philips Exeter Academy which is a private boarding school which was set up for the children of the elite.   The Illuminati has largely funded this school and used it to educate their children and prepare them for their duties later in life.

In 1930 Edward Harkness donated 5.8 million dollars to

---

[185] Brown, Dan – *Angels & Demons* page 41

the school with the conditions that their method of teaching students would change to what he called the Aristotelian method of antiquity. Harkness was the second largest share holder in Rockefeller's Standard Oil in the early 1900s and was in John D. Rockefeller's inner circle. The Rockefeller family has been one of the most powerful Illuminati families for generations. Aristotle was a student of Plato who believed that most people were too stupid to govern themselves, and that society should be structured in a way that "philosopher kings" would rule and decided what was best for the people.

Dan Brown's publisher for the first printing of *Angels & Demons* was Random House[186] which is owned by the Bertelsmann media group in Germany which was the largest producer and publisher of Nazi propaganda during World War II.[187] The Bertelsmann media group is a private company that has its primary owner listed as the Bertelsmann Foundation, the largest "non-profit" organization and think tank in Germany. *The Da Vinci Code* was also originally published by Random House through its subsidiary Doubleday. The reprint rights for *Angels & Demons* have since been sold to Simon and Shuster. The Illuminati thread leading through Dan Brown's education, publisher, and themes of his books, clearly raises strong questions about his novels' success and the messages they spread. It could very well be that Dan Brown is a willing participant in one of the biggest disinformation campaigns waged by the Illuminati in history.

---

[186] http://www.randomhouse.com/catalog/display.pperl?isbn=9780739326756
[187] The London Times *German media giant grew fat on Nazi propaganda* by Roger Boyes October 9, 2002

Fear and Loathing in Las Vegas

Hunter S. Thompson, the controversial "gonzo" journalist, published a book in 1971 under the guise of a novel based on autobiographical incidents in a roman à clef style, which is a literary style of a novel describing real life behind a facade of fiction. *Fear and Loathing in Las Vegas* would later be made into a Hollywood movie in 1998 starring Johnny Depp.

The book is about a journalist and his friend who go to Las Vegas to cover a motorcycle race for a writing assignment but instead go on a drug binge using LSD, cocaine, mescaline, and more. Thompson had experimented with drugs on a regular basis, and much of the book is considered to be a reflection of his real life experiences. Aside from being a story about a drug fueled adventure, a few things start to become noticeable, and extremely disturbing to some who have knowledge about the Illuminati.

In the book, and depicted in the movie, Thompson talks about buying adrenochrome from a Satanist, which is a powerful hallucinogen that is now synthesized in a lab, but originally believed to have been obtained from the human body immediately after a person was killed. The main characters ingest the adrenochrome and have uncontrollable hallucinations. Later in the film, a scene shows one character explaining how, "Satan worshippers kill six or eight people every day. All they want is the blood. They'll take people right off the street if they have to."

He goes on to say how he had witnessed some Satanists kidnap a sixteen year old girl and "cut all kinds of holes in her head and sucked the blood out," alluding to the Satanists harvesting the adrenochrome from the girl's body.

The question remains how Hunter S. Thompson would even know about adrenochrome, and why did he write about ingesting some in his book, which he says he received from a Satanist. Even more unsettling are allegations made by several individuals that Hunter S. Thompson was a videographer for snuff films allegedly made in the Bohemian Grove in the late 1980s. A snuff film, for anyone who doesn't know, is when someone is murdered on video for the sole purpose of selling that video or watching it and finding enjoyment from it.

Rusty Nelson, [Russell E. Nelson] the photographer of a known pedophile Larry (Lawrence E.) King from the Franklin Cover-Up scandal in Omaha, Nebraska alleges that Hunter S. Thompson offered him $100,000 in 1988 to produce a snuff film involving a child. Rusty said he turned the offer down.[188]

One of the victims of child pornography that was allegedly produced in the Bohemian Grove during this same timeframe was a boy named Paul Bonacci. Former Nebraska Senator John DeCamp was Bonacci's lawyer, and without doubt concludes that child pornography and snuff films were being produced in the Bohemian Grove during this timeframe. In his journal, Bonnaci described picking up a "Hunter Thompson" in Las Vegas who was the individual Bonacci described as the photographer for a child pornography video, which ultimately ended up being a snuff film when the other child was murdered.[189]

Hunter S. Thompson's former editorial assistant, Nickole Brown, wrote in an article titled *In Memory of Hunter S. Thompson: Postcard from Louisville, Kentucky* (posted 4-15-05) about some of the bizarre behavior she had witnessed while working for him. "For weeks he played a tape recording of a jack rabbit screaming in a trap," the article explained. She also wrote that one time, "he threw me out of the house for refusing to watch a snuff film."[190]

[188] *A Closer Look* with Michael Corbin April 12, 2005
[189] DeCamp, John – *The Franklin Cover-Up* page 105
[190] http://www.pw.org/mag/pc_thompson.htm

As she left, he allegedly called her a coward and was mad. Brown thought he was possibly joking, and didn't think much of it, citing his unique character.

During an interview on May 20, 2005 by this author (Mark Dice), Nickole Brown said despite rumors, he never threatened her, she never felt in danger while she worked for him as his editorial assistant, and she couldn't imagine him being involved in such things as the allegations from Bonacci, Nelson, and others. She and others believe Hunter was possibly investigating such claims, which they cite as the source of such allegations.

Adding, yet again, another twist to the story is the fact that Hunter S. Thompson wrote in his 2004 book titled *Hey Rube* in the first article titled *The New Dumb*, "The autumn months are never a calm time in America...There is always a rash of kidnapping and abductions of schoolchildren in the football months. Preteens of both sexes are traditionally seized and grabbed off the streets by gangs of organized perverts who traditionally give them as Christmas gifts to each other to be personal sex slaves and playthings."

This writing clearly shows Thompson knew something not many people know. That each year children are kidnapped by organized kidnapping rings and sold as sex slaves. Thompson was known for getting personally involved in his stories, as was the case when he lived with the Hells Angels for nearly two years in the 1960s, where he chronicled his activities in his book *Hells Angels: A Strange and Terrible Saga*.

With Paul Bonacci's testimony implicating Thompson, and Rusty Nelson's allegations of being propositioned to shoot a snuff film for him, some are led to believe he was involved in even more sinister activities than hanging out with a motorcycle gang.

Thompson named his estate "Owl Farm," some believe as a reference to Bohemian Grove, also adding to the suspicions. Thompson committed suicide by shooting himself in the head on February 20, 2005.

Nineteen Eighty-Four

The term "Big Brother" is commonly used to describe the increasing high-tech invasion of video cameras, biometric scanners, and the erosion of privacy. The term was coined by George Orwell in his popular novel *Nineteen Eighty-Four*.

The book was published in 1949 and has a storyline surrounding what was described as life in future in the year 1984. The book was made into a British film of the same title and released, ironically, in 1984. In the book (as well as the film) a man named Winston Smith grows to hate the fascist and repressive Big Brother system of government and starts seeing through the lies and propaganda that is spread and the lack of civil rights and education found in society.

The book paints a dark picture of society, and incorporates what at the time was science fiction, but as the years have passed since its original publication, have become a scary reality. The government consists of "the Party" which itself is made up of Inner members and Outer members. The Inner members have access to luxuries such as real food, wine, and live in spacious and furnished homes, while the Outer members are given small food rations and live and work in much worse conditions. A step below the Outer members on the socioeconomic scale are the proles (or proletariats) who live in deplorable conditions and are seen as immoral and out of control animals who are not given any of the "luxuries" of Party members.

Orwell explains, "Heavy physical work, the care of home and children, petty quarrels with neighbors, films, football, beer, and above all, gambling filled up the horizon of their minds. To keep them in control was not difficult...All that was required of them was a primitive patriotism which could be appealed to whenever it was necessary to make them accept longer working hours or shorter rations. And when they become discontented, as they sometimes did, their discontentment led nowhere, because being without general ideas, they could only focus it on petty specific grievances."[191]

Life wasn't always so boring and meaningless. After what is called the Revolution, the Party gained power and created a society where each individual is reduced to nothing more than a worker, working for the sake of the Party. A man named Big Brother is supposedly the head of the Party, and his picture is plastered on walls in every building and on every street. "Telescreens" as they are called, are mounted in every home and are used as televisions which continuously communicate Party propaganda to society. These telescreens are also used to watch and listen to every member of the Party, and nobody dares question their authority. Such an act would amount to ThoughtCrime and would cause one to be eliminated from society. The telescreens and microphones are continuously monitored and even facial expressions and body language can be understood by the Big Brother system. No one dares even whisper a word of disagreement or doubt about the Party or Big Brother.

An area in London called Oceania, the society in which *Nineteen Eighty-Four* takes place, is in a perpetual state of war with another superpower, Eastasia (and later with Eurasia but society doesn't realize the difference when the name of the "enemy" suddenly changes) and the ongoing war is used as an explanation for various food and supply shortages in society. The telescreen announcements of victories on the battlefield always bring the war "within measurable distance of its end" but it continues on and on and society continues to support it. People, and particularly

---

[191] Orwell, George – *Nineteen Eighty-Four* page 73-74

children, have all been turned into spies and are encouraged to report "ThoughtCrime" to the Party. Families are almost nonexistent, since each individual must give his or her full allegiance and love to Big Brother and the Party.

Winston finds a woman named Julia who feels the same way he does about the Party, and the two discuss finding the Brotherhood, an underground and secret Resistance that is plotting to overthrow the Party and restore freedom. As they discuss finding the Brotherhood (called *The Resistance* in the film version) they begin unraveling the extent of the lies of the Party. When discussing the ongoing war, Julia remarks, "The rocket bombs which fell daily on London were probably fired by the Government of Oceania itself, just to keep people frightened."[192]

In reality, there is no man named Big Brother, he is only used as an image to personify the Party. "Big Brother is the guise in which the Party chooses to exhibit itself to the world. His function is to act as a focusing point for love, fear, and reverence, emotions which are more easily felt toward an individual than toward an organization."[193]

A similar personification has been the use of Osama Bin Laden in the War on Terror. The American government has been blaming this one man for all of the problems in the world, even though the man had been dead shortly after the 9/11 attacks had occurred. The myth of a living Bin Laden has been perpetuated and an occasional video tape or audio message is "released" to the public, supposedly of the man, but such video taped messages are always old videos of typical "death to America" and "death to Israel" messages, and nothing new is ever discovered. The myth that Bin Laden remains alive and is directing his global terrorist organization, Al Qaeda, is a continuous lie that is spread to

---

[192] Orwell, George – *Nineteen Eighty-Four* page 156
[193] Orwell, George – *Nineteen Eighty-Four* page 213

the public to keep them in a state of fear, and is used as the reason for the War on Terror to continue.

The term Big Brother continues to be used today to describe the high-tech surveillance system that is invading society. The term "Orwellian" also came to use stemming from George Orwell's dark picture of the future. While in the novel, Winston Smith and others were continuously being monitored by microphones in the telescreens that could pickup everything they said, such a system has now become a reality. In 2006 it was reported that the search engine Google was planning on using the microphone that is built into all laptop computers to listen to the user and the surrounding areas and to then analyze the sound for keywords which would then be used to direct advertisements to that user which reflected the conversations he or she were having in earshot of the microphone. The system also planned to place advertisements which were chosen as a result of what television or radio shows were detected which happened to be playing in the same room.[194]

In the novel, Orwell also explains that the war Oceania is fighting isn't a real war, but that it is a fabrication that needs to continuously be fought in order to destroy the fruits of society's labor, thus ensuring a continuous shortage of goods and maintain the social structure that the ruling elite has constructed.

Nineteen Eighty-Four remains one of the greatest novels of all time, and serves as a warning that seems to have been ignored about the road society is on. "George Orwell" was actually a pseudonym used by Eric Blair, who is the author of many books, including *Animal Farm.*

---

[194] The Register *Google developing eavesdropping software: Audio 'fingerprint' for content-relevant ads* September 3, 2006

Games & Collector Cards

While some individuals have written fiction and non fiction books, documentary films, or Hollywood narratives incorporating the theme of the Illuminati, a small number of people have designed either card games or factual trading cards revolving around such topics. The makers intend the cards to be used and traded similar to baseball cards, and feature dozens of different cards consisting of a photo of Illuminati members or organizations on the front, and information about them on the back.

The Illuminati Card Game

A card game simply titled *Illuminati* was created in the early 1980s by a man named Steve Jackson who was inspired by Robert Anton Wilson's novels *The Illuminatus! Trilogy* The game consists of various secret societies competing for world domination through sinister means. It was designed as a tongue-in-cheek take on conspiracy theories.[195]

Jackson and his freelance designer had originally thought about designing the game around Robert Anton Wilson's *Illuminatus!* novels but decided against it due to the difficulties and expenses surrounding legal issues that would be involved, so they settled on making the game about the Illuminati.

Robert Shea, coauthor of The *Illuminatus! Trilogy* wrote an introduction to the rulebook for the *Illuminati Expansion Set 1* (1983), which read, "Maybe the Illuminati are behind *this game*. They must be—they are, by definition, behind

---

[195] Jackson, Steve. "Illuminati Designer Article" Steve Jackson Games http://www.sjgames.com/illuminati/designart html

everything."

Despite Shea's support for the game, his coauthor Robert Anton Wilson criticized Jackson for exploiting the *Illuminatus!* name without paying royalties.

Steve Jackson's game company would go on to produce several versions of card games focusing on the Illuminati. In 1990, the company released a game titled *The Illuminati— New World Order* which consisted of various playing cards depicting Illuminati plans. Years later, after the 9/11 terrorist attacks of 2001, the game would be seen by some as predicting the future, and by others as having the game itself designed by the Illuminati.

Several of the cards that Jackson had designed depicted terrorist attacks eerily similar to those of 9/11. For example one card shows what looks like the World Trade Center's Twin Towers being blown up which is a card a player could use to gain points for the organizations they control. Another card labeled "Pentagon" shows the building being blown up and reads, "Each corporate group controlled by the Pentagon lets you draw one extra Plot card each turn." Another card is titled "Population Reduction"

Some see such cards as showing that the designer Steve Jackson was fairly informed about the Illuminati and the ideas that are spread surrounding their goals and operations. Others believe that the Illuminati was involved in the game's creation, and that Jackson himself was aware of the planned attacks years later on September 11th.

The story surrounding Steve Jackson and his Illuminati card game would take another interesting turn when his office was raided by the Secret Service in 1990 and some of his equipment was seized. A message posted on his website reads, "On the morning of March 1, [1990] without warning, a force of armed Secret Service agents—accompanied by Austin police and at least one civilian 'expert' from the phone company - occupied the offices of Steve Jackson Games and began to search for computer equipment. The home of Loyd Blankenship, the writer of *GURPS Cyberpunk*, was also raided. A large amount of equipment was seized, including four computers, two laser printers, some loose hard disks and a great deal of assorted hardware. One of the computers was the one running the *Illuminati BBS*."

The message goes on to say, "The company, "S.J. Games" fought back in court and finally won, but nearly went under financially. The investigation zeroed in on "fraud" supposedly committed by the company regarding the hacker activity and the fact that the company promoted the hacker's newsletter, "Phrack." However, this is so flimsy that it makes no common sense; in fact, the affidavit made so little sense that a Judge threw the case out, awarding S.J. Games $50,000 plus $250,000 attorney's fees."[196]

Of course some believe that Steve Jackson had been targeted by the Illuminati for using them as the central figure in his games. In reality, the Illuminati is probably pleased that Jackson did such a thing, because it fictionalizes them and causes people to think the Illuminati is nothing more than the name of a group of bad guys in a game. Steve Jackson's card game is also referenced in Dan Brown's novel *Angels & Demons*. (See Angels & Demons page 312)

New World Order Trading Cards

In 2008 a website was set up at www. NWOTradingCards.com which was the first of its kind to create trading cards similar to baseball cards, only covering issues surrounding the New World Order.

The designer's website explains, "*NWO Trading Cards* have arrived to assist you in your efforts to awaken the public. Each card is overflowing with hard hitting facts that

---

[196] http://www.sjgames.com/SS/

will amaze truth seekers from all ranks. *NWO Trading Cards* are not playing cards; they are for trading, collecting and using as a tool to wake up the sleeping masses. *NWO Trading Cards* feature patriots, who fight for freedom against the New World Order, as well as those, who have chosen to align themselves with the globalists, pushing the New World Order ahead."

"*NWO Trading Cards* are perfect for any activist; you will hit the streets confident, armed with knowledge. And for those of us who are trying to wake up our friends and families, *NWO Trading Cards* are invaluable. Movies can be effective, but too many people refuse to watch, and even fewer will actually read an entire book. But *NWO Trading Cards* will expand your arsenal and rejuvenate your efforts."

"Inside of every pack are six *NWO Trading Cards* and one chance to win great prizes in our Big Chance Game. All cards are unique and some are rare, presenting a valuable collection. Our research team is dedicated to finding the truth and uncovering news blacked out by the Main Stream Media. Their work has been featured on *Infowars.com*, *Rense*, *Prison Planet*, *We Are Change*, *What Really Happened*, *TruthNews.us*, *Jones Report*, *Illuminati Conspiracy Archive*, *Opednews*, *DavidIcke.com* and many other great blogs and news sites. The team updates existing cards and adds new players regularly, keeping NWO Trading Cards current, and keeping you ahead of the game."

"Unlike mass produced trading cards, *NWO Trading Cards* is a quality product, hand crafted using only American made goods. Every pack is wrapped in the Constitution and sealed with red wax. All proceeds will be returned to the fight, send someone a wake up call, or start your own collection today."

The card's designer sent this author (Mark Dice) a box containing over a dozen packs of cards and I was very impressed with their quality and design. Topics range from suspected Illuminati members to secret societies and New

World Order organizations, as well as modern heroes who are working to expose them.

Conspiracy Cards

Another similar idea comes from the maker of *Conspiracy Cards*, although some of these cards cover topics that are considered on the fringe within some circles, including aliens and UFOs. The cards' designer had the intention of designing professional looking collector cards as a way to educate people about the Illuminati and the New World Order. These cards feature a photo of a person, organization, or issue on the front, and information about it on the back. The message on the website reads as follows:

Greetings and welcome to ConspiracyCards.com

These factual cards are specifically designed with the intention of informing you about very important issues of which you may not be aware.

This vital information should be mainstream as some of the issues are a matter of life and death. But don't expect to see these topics discussed or debated in traditional media such as TV or newspapers.

Most all media sources are owned by very powerful groups who have no intention of divulging the truth.

Why?

...well we hope to clarify their agenda and explain their motive with these factual cards...

...that may just save your life.

Fictional Films

Some people think that Illuminati symbolism or themes in movies is the result of the organization flaunting their power and influence on the audience, or an attempt at mind control or subliminal signals. While this may sometimes be the case, it is far more frequent that the writers and producers of the films are very aware of the workings of the Illuminati, and are using their art form to tell the viewers about the nefarious activities of the Illuminati by using a narrative.

Some films clearly have storylines or activities that are based on actual people or events, but use different names, and others actually use the name of the Illuminati as the evil organization that the antagonist character or characters are working for.

In the following pages you will find just a sample of some of the most well known films starring famous actors which have incorporated Illuminati activities into their plotlines. While some of the writers of such films have good intentions, fictional films incorporating the Illuminati or their activities are also used to fictionalize facts as a way of discrediting legitimate claims about the Illuminati and their activities.

By paralleling actual history or events, some films cause the public to believe that certain conspiracies or activities are the plot of a movie and when they are told about real events and agendas, they think the person trying to educate them has "seen too many movies."

V for Vendetta

One of the most chilling fictional films which clearly reflects reality is *V for Vendetta*. It's based on a comic book series written by Alan Moore and was released in theaters in 2006 after being produced by the Wachowski brothers, who also wrote the screenplay.

The plot revolves around a masked man simply known as "V" who is taking a stand against the fascist government of England which has fallen under the control of a dictator as a result of the War on Terror.

V begins his quest by taking over London's television station and broadcasts his own message to the people in an attempt to get them to take a look at what has become of their country as a result of the war.

That message, in part is, "The truth is, there is something terribly wrong in this country isn't there? Cruelty, and injustice, intolerance, and oppression…and where once you had the freedom to object…to think and speak as you saw fit, you now have sensors and systems of surveillance coercing your conformity and seducing your submission. I know you were afraid. Who wouldn't be? War, terror, disease, there were a myriad of problems which conspired to corrupt your reason and rob you of your common sense. Fear got the best of you."

He continues to say that he is going to blow up the Parliament building on November 5th to make a statement and deliver a symbolic blow against the government, and spark a revolution and an uprising of the people to take back their freedoms and eliminate the fascist dictatorship.

When the lead detective starts to uncover the truth about the war and what is motivating V, he says to another detective, "I see this chain of events…these coincidences…and I have to ask what if that isn't what happened? If our own government was responsible for the deaths of over 100,000 people, would you really want to know?"

It turns out that elements within the government had released a plague in the recent past in order to spread chaos so they could increase their power and make a fortune from selling a vaccine.

The film has too many important messages to convey

them in writing. It should be seen by everyone, and its principles absorbed by the viewer. However valid the film's points are about the government being involved in terrorism and using fear to justify fascism, some elements in the movie must be seen with caution. There appears to be a subtle anti-Christian message woven into the plot. The fascist government, whose symbol represents a Christian cross, has outlawed the Koran, yet a popular preacher is seen on television daily who is obviously representing a Christian. Also in the film, a sub plot shows that the Christian fascist government has put all gays in jail.

If one can overlook these references, and see the larger message *V for Vendetta* is trying to make, then the film proves to be an entertaining, yet educational piece of work.

The Matrix

The popular *Matrix* trilogy has become a part of pop culture for its philosophical metaphor regarding knowledge and reality. The Wachowski brothers who directed it demonstrate an extensive knowledge of esoteric mysticism which becomes apparent in the film.

The premise of the first film, as many people are aware, is that the world in which we are living in and think is "the real world" is actually a computer generated hologram to keep us blind to the truth. In "reality" according to the film, human physical bodies are kept in pods and are used as bio generators to power *The Matrix* three dimensional hologram, thus making us prisoners who are unaware of our own captivity. When one is "unplugged" from the Matrix, then they can see and experience the true reality.

Aside from presenting this interesting philosophic view of reality, the film also includes multiple references to Christian theology, as well as the Illuminati. First of all, the main character "Neo" who is played by Keanu Reeves, is "the one" who is chosen to save the world, so he is basically portrayed as a messiah figure. The name "Neo" means "new" and he is symbolically "born again" when he is unplugged from the Matrix and experiences reality. He is actually called "my personal Jesus" by a character after Neo gives him a black market computer program. His love interest is named "Trinity" clearly referring the Christian Trinity of the three different forms that God has manifested himself in, being Father, Son, and Holy Spirit. The city where the people staging a rebellion against the evil Matrix live in is called "Zion" a term that depicts the Land of Israel, or the Promised Land. The spaceship that the group uses is called the Nebakanezer, named after King Nebakanezer who ruled in Babylon and created the famous hanging gardens, which are considered one of the original seven wonders of the world.

In the sequel to *The Matrix*, titled *The Matrix Reloaded*, Neo and his crew are in search of "the Architect" of the Matrix, and hope to find out why it became a tool of deception and oppression. In their search they seek out the Keymaker who can help them gain access to parts of the Matrix. As it turns out, the Keymaker was being held captive by a man called Merovingian. In real life, this is the name of the supposed guardians of the Holy Grail, and the most powerful bloodline of the Illuminati. So it is interesting, to say the least, that the film depicts this man, Merovingian, as the corrupt keeper of the Keymaker, who can write computer programs that allow people to basically become gods in the Matrix. This is analogous to the Illuminati's possession of the Holy Grail, or their Luciferian doctrine, which allows them to be like gods on earth. Merovingian is also married to a woman named Persephone in the film. Persephone is the name of an ancient goddess said to be the Queen of the Underworld.

The Wachowski brothers demonstrate an extensive knowledge of esoteric symbolism, and are also the writers of the screenplay for *V for Vendetta*, which ties in false flag terrorism and fascism, so they clearly are informed as to what is really happening in the world.

Choosing such names as Merovingian, Persephone, Zion, and Trinity, are clearly not ordinary or random names, but were instead used to depict certain characteristics, many of which symbolically represent what the Illuminati does in real life.

Angels & Demons

In May 2009, the film version of Dan Brown's book *Angels & Demons* was released starring Tom Hanks. It is the prequel to *The Da Vinci Code* (2006), also a film adaptation of Brown's book of the same title. This is probably one of the works which has caused the greatest exposure of the Illuminati in modern history, but a closer look at the film's plot reveals damaging distortions and inaccuracies from the historical Illuminati.

A teaser trailer released in late 2008 showed an ambigram of the word "Illuminati" across the entire screen and cut to a frantic Tom Hanks who whispered, "It's the Illuminati." The plot of the film is that the ancient Illuminati has secretly survived since being exposed in the 18th century, and are now seeking revenge against the Vatican for suppressing them.

The film was directed by Ron Howard, produced by Brian Grazer, and the screenplay was written by Akiva Goldsman. For a more complete analysis of Dan Brown's take on the Illuminati, turn to page 312 in the Fictional Books section.

It must be made clear that this film, as well as *The Da Vinci Code*, and Brown's books of which these films are based off of, are not designed to educate the public about the Illuminati, or expose their nefarious activities. Their purpose is to introduce the public to a tainted and fictionalized version of the Illuminati which serves only to disarm the public by leading them to believe that the Illuminati is nothing more than a fictional group of bad guys, who have been invented by Hollywood.

The twist at the end of *Angels & Demons* the movie is that the Illuminati doesn't exist after all, and that the corrupt Camerlengo (Pope's assistant) was behind the threats to Vatican City to get people interested in religion again after he saves Vatican City from the very anti-matter bomb that he himself had placed on the property. This dramatic twist also reinforces the idea that the real Illuminati has been extinct for hundreds of years and conspiracy theorists' paranoid over-active imaginations lead them to believe that they still exist.

The Texas Chainsaw Massacre

The original *Texas Chainsaw Massacre* film, released in 1974, has spawned several sequels and prequels of a cannibalistic family in a remote region of Texas and is one of the most popular cult classic horror films.

In 1995 a version of the film was released titled *The Texas Chainsaw Massacre: The Next Generation*, which starred Renee Zellweger and Matthew McConaughey. On the surface, the film appears to be a typical slasher horror film about a group of four teenagers on prom night who end up getting in a car accident in the middle of nowhere. After being lured to a secluded old farmhouse, they are terrorized by Leatherface's family.

A few interesting things stick out if someone is familiar with the Illuminati and the kinds of things they are involved in. First of all, McConaughey's character, Vilmer, who is the bad guy in the film, drives a tow truck for a wrecking company, and in a brief shot, guess what the name of the towing company is that is printed on the truck's door? "Illuminati Wrecking."

Now this in and of itself wouldn't be that strange, but

what comes later in the film clearly shows that the writer knew about the Illuminati and their activities.

There is a part in the film where McConaughey's girlfriend shows some sympathy for Zellweger as she is being held captive and tells her that Vilmer is not really a bad guy and that "he's just doing his job." She goes on to say that he works for the people you hear rumors about who really run the world. The kind of people who killed JFK. She also says that these people put a device in her head that would explode if she did not go along with what they wanted.

Later, at the end of the film, a well dressed man arrives in a limo driven by a chauffer and enters the house. He chastises Vilmer and tells him he wants the captors to "know the meaning of horror." He had a strange symbol burned into his chest. A few minutes later Zellweger narrowly escapes the murderous family and gets in the back of the limo. The man is seated inside and speaks with a European accent and is reading *Le Figaro*, which is one of the most popular newspapers in France. He then starts talking about how "all this" was supposed to be a "spiritual experience" and that he was striving for a sense of harmony. He then takes Zellweger to a hospital and the film ends.

In the credits the man's name is revealed simply as Rothman. Now, for those who don't know, the Rothschild family has been one of the most powerful Illuminati families for hundreds of years and lives in Europe. This man "Rothman" was obviously written into the script to represent a high level Illuminati member.

The film ends without giving the viewer an explanation of who Mr. Rothman is, or why he has shown up at the house or what his bizarre talk of a "spiritual experience" meant. The only logical conclusion is that this was one of the men Vilmer's girlfriend was referring to as the ones who she and her murderous boyfriend worked for. But what kind of work were they doing? And why? Viewers not familiar with the

Illuminati were completely confused and had no idea what to make of this. Others who noticed the Illuminati references thought that perhaps the Leatherface family were producing snuff films for the Illuminati. (See Snuff Films page 301)

During the course of my research for this book, I was able to contact the film's writer and producer, Kim Henkel, and on January 6th 2009 had a 31 minute and 13 second phone conversation with him about the film and his reasons for including references to the Illuminati. Henkel was a bit hesitant at first to give his reasons, and wanted the audience to draw their own conclusions, but as our conversation progressed, he slowly revealed some interesting insights.

Henkel revealed that others working on the film had urged him not to include the references to the Illuminati, and that they feared repercussions from the organization for doing so. Henkel included the references anyway and said that if the Illuminati in any form actually exists, he did not think they would be concerned with them.

Henkel did not appear to be very familiar with the Illuminati or its activities, but said he chose the term for the film as a symbolic reference to any clandestine or wealthy and powerful group who participates in criminal activity, or that exploit others for personal or professional gain.

Emphasizing not to take any one interpretation of the reference or the activities of the psycho family literally, he suggested as one possible interpretation that Mr. Rothman was perhaps purchasing human flesh from Vilmer, and that Rothman was in turn selling it to others who enjoyed eating it and were addicted to it. He also suggested that the victims needed to be terrorized and put in an intense state of fear before they were killed so that the meat would contain high levels of adrenaline and other hormones, which the individuals who consumed it found appealing and addictive.

While denying that the name for Mr. Rothman was inspired by the Rothschilds, Henkel did admit that he was familiar with the Rothschilds, and that they were rumored to be involved with the Illuminati. Many artists, including song writers and film directors, do not like to give their interpretation of their art because it can then influence or shatter the interpretation that others had made. I have a strong feeling that this is the case with Henkel's "hypothetical interpretation" of his film. At the end of our conversation when I asked him if there was anything else he would like to say about the film, he regretfully told me he had already said too much.

Teddy Bears' Picnic

Harry Shearer, the voice of Mr. Burns in the animated cartoon, *The Simpsons*, directed a comedy that he also had written which was based on the Bohemian Grove, titled *Teddy Bears' Picnic*. Shearer's film was released in 2002, just two years after Alex Jones had infiltrated the club and captured the Cremation of Care ritual on video. (See Dark Secrets: Inside Bohemian Grove page 269)

Shearer was interviewed by Jon Ronson for a segment in his *Secret Rulers of the World* series for the Trio Network where he admitted he had been a visitor to the Grove on one occasion and that, "you don't have to be a conspiracy theorist to know that this is a get together of very powerful guys. Whatever it is they're doing there, whether they're running the world or just reliving their adolescence, they're a self selected group of powerful white Christian Americans. I love the theories, because I believe that these people are the only real good narrative writers left in the English language. They do write really good compelling narratives, but I just don't happen to think they're true. And they can keep you spellbound. And you can imagine, I'm in New York and they're keeping me spellbound. Imagine being isolated on a ranch in Montana with nobody except your son who you're teaching to shoot a rifle, this would be some amazing stuff coming through the night to you, you know. If you've ever been through a secret society in college, you know this stuff. Just add two zeros to the budget and you're doing what you did when you were eighteen years old."

[Ronson]: So it is a secret society, you think?

[Shearer]: Yeah but I mean it's a secret society the way the secret society that I was inducted into at UCLA in my senior year is a secret society. There is a lot of meaningless mumbo jumbo and the main conspiracy is to take it seriously.

In Shearer's film, the Bohemian Grove's Moloch statue is instead replaced with a large pelican. The human effigy, called "Care" by the club, is depicted as a neon clock in the film, and the members who dress up in red and black robes and participate in the ritual are depicted as men wearing Halloween-type witch costumes.

One of the plotlines in the film involves two employees of the club secretly videotaping the activities inside and exposing them, a plot clearly inspired by Alex Jones secretly videotaping the real Cremation of Care ritual in the year 2000.

Teddy Bears' Picnic was essentially a failure, and was released on DVD and not in theaters. Shearer's motivations for the film remain to be seen, but could have possibly been an attempt to discredit the claims of those who work to expose the Bohemian Grove and the powerful members who attend it.

The Brandon Corey Story

A fictional film produced to appear as a documentary called *The Brandon Corey Story* was actually believed to be a real documentary by some gullible viewers due to its extremely sophisticated production quality. The production company TruthseekerTV, marketed their film as a real documentary investigating the disappearance of a man who was investigating the Illuminati. They had hoped it would land them a pilot for a television show based on conspiracies.

The producers are fans of David Icke, who is known for his bizarre claim that the inner circle of the Illuminati are a hybrid race who are half human, half alien, and thought that their marketing plan would be successful in spreading David Icke's message. (See David Icke page 212) While some gullible viewers believed the film was real, there was also a tremendous backlash of people calling the producers frauds and the film a hoax.

This caused them to release a statement saying, "For the record, the movie *The Brandon Corey Story* is fiction based on fact. Our goal was to try and get this seen by the millions of folks who might not otherwise have heard of David or listened to him. We felt that the best way to do this was to market this as real. We realize now that we should have made it completely clear that it was a *movie*."[197]

The film's budget must have been substantial and the producers are extremely talented. It is sad that such talent has went to waste on the "reptilian bloodline" theories of David Icke, when it could have been put to good use making films about fully factual and documentable information instead of poisoning the well with such films as *The Brandon Corey Story*, by mixing legitimate issues such as the Bohemian Grove, with reptilian shape shifters.

The Long Kiss Goodnight

A 1996 action thriller starring Samuel L. Jackson and Geena Davis called *The Long Kiss Goodnight* includes a

---

[197] http://www.davidicke.com/content/view/4384/48/

chilling plotline involving false flag terrorism and mentions that the 1993 bombing of the World Trade Center was allowed to happen by the government, when, in fact, it was. *The Long Kiss Goodnight* was directed by Renny Harlin and written by Shane Black, who also wrote the screenplay for *Lethal Weapon*.

In the film, a CIA operative (played by Craig Bierko) explains, "1993, World Trade Center bombing, remember? During the trial one of the bombers claimed the CIA had advanced knowledge. (laughing) Well, the diplomat who issued the terrorist Visa was CIA. It's not unthinkable they paved the way for the bombing, purely to justify a budget increase."

[Samuel L. Jackson's character]
You're telling me you're going to fake some terrorist thing just to scare some money out of Congress?

[Craig Bierko's character]
Well, unfortunately Mr. Henesy, I have no idea how to fake killing 4,000 people, so we'll just have to do it for real. We'll blame it on the Muslims, naturally. Then I'll get my funding.

This element of *The Long Kiss Goodnight* is extremely significant because it not only includes corrupt elements in the CIA who orchestrated a terrorist attack to then blame it on Muslims, but it references an actual false flag attack, being the 1993 bombing of the World Trade Center. In the film, the CIA planned to detonate a chemical bomb in New York and blame Islamic terrorists.

Network

A popular 1976 film about the mainstream media that continues to reflect the reality of today is *Network*. The film is a drama about a struggling television network and a newscaster named Howard Beale whose ranting about society, the economy, and television itself causes the United Broadcasting System (UBC) to become a top rated network on TV.

The film contains several subplots including UBC producers becoming involved with a criminal Communist movement in order to get footage for a show about current events, but the main storyline revolves around Howard Beale becoming a television sensation for saying exactly what's on his mind as he becomes the "mad prophet" of the airwaves. The film was responsible for the phrase "I'm as made as Hell and I'm not going to take this anymore!" entering the pop culture lexicon. A transcript of Beale's most powerful rants follows, which he begins by telling the audience that the Chairman of the Board of UBC just died.

[Howard Beale]
So. A rich little man with white hair died. What has that got to do with the price of rice, right? And *why* is that woe to us? Because you people, and sixty-two million other Americans, are listening to me right now. Because less than three percent of you people read books! Because less than fifteen percent of you read newspapers! Because the only truth you know is what you get over this tube. Right now, there is a whole, an entire generation that never knew anything that didn't come out of this tube!

This tube is the Gospel, the ultimate revelation. This tube can make or break presidents, popes, prime ministers... This tube is the most awesome God-damned force in the whole godless world, and woe is us if it ever falls in to the hands of the wrong people, and that's why woe is us that Edward George Ruddy died. Because this company is now in the hands of CCA—the Communication Corporation of America. There's a new Chairman of the Board, a man called Frank Hackett, sitting in Mr. Ruddy's office on the twentieth floor. And when the twelfth largest company in the world controls the most awesome God-damned propaganda force in the whole godless world, who knows what shit will be peddled for truth on this network?

[Howard Beale]
[ascending the stage] So, you listen to me. Listen to me: Television is not the truth! Television is a God-damned amusement park! Television is a circus, a carnival, a traveling troupe of acrobats, storytellers, dancers, singers, jugglers, side-show freaks, lion tamers, and football players. We're in the boredom-killing business! So if you want the truth... Go to God! Go to your gurus! Go to yourselves! Because that's the only place you're ever going to find any real truth.

[Howard Beale]
[laughing to himself] But, man, you're never going to get any truth from us. We'll tell you anything you want to hear; we lie like hell. You're beginning to believe the illusions we're spinning here. You're beginning to think that the tube is reality, and that your own lives are unreal. You do whatever the tube tells you! You dress like the tube, you eat like the tube, you raise your children like the tube, you even *think* like the tube! This is mass madness, you maniacs! In God's name, you people are the real thing! *WE* are the illusion! So turn off your television sets. Turn them off now. Turn them off right now. Turn them off and leave them off! Turn them off right in the middle of the sentence I'm speaking to you now! TURN THEM OFF...

[collapses in a prophetic swoon as the audience erupts in thunderous applause]

END OF TRANSCRIPT EXCERPT

Beale's ranting eventually gets him in trouble with the network because he is giving the public too much information instead of keeping them entertained and out of the elite's way. This epic scene consists of the chairman of the company that owns UBC yelling at the top of his lungs that there are no more countries, there are only corporations and unleashed his anger saying, "You have mettled with the primal forces of Nature, Mr. Beale! And I won't have it! Is that clear?"

The film concludes with the UBC network executives planning Beale's murder to shut him up and he is later shot while doing a live broadcast by members of the Communist group that the network had been working with in the production of their show. It seems the rantings of the "mad prophet" fell on deaf ears, because since the film's release back in 1976, society has become completely mesmerized by television and it has increased its monopoly regarding the control of information. (See Mainstream Media page 33)

Star Wars

Nearly everyone in the world is familiar with the *Star Wars* films and the epic tales of good vs. evil that are woven into the storylines. In 2005 when *Episode III: Revenge of the Sith* was released in theaters, it contained a pivotal storyline which had such a resemblance to current affairs that large numbers of people saw the movie as a deliberate political statement regarding the Bush administration and the War on Terror.

In the film as the storyline unfolds it becomes clear that Chancellor Palpatine, who is the head of the Republic, is secretly working for the Dark Side and orchestrating events that will be used to justify eliminating laws which limit his power, allowing him to transform the Republic into an Empire, with him as the dictator. As he is announcing this transformation, Queen Padme (played by Natalie Portman) says, "So this is how liberty dies, with thunderous applause…"

The striking resemblance to the Bush administration using the threat of terrorism to pass the Patriot Act and eliminate valuable civil liberties that are outlined in the Constitution shows that George Lucas is very well aware of the tactics of dictators. There are also parallels between Chancellor Palpatine pretending to support the Jedi (the good guys) and democracy, just as George W. Bush pretended to be a Christian and support conservative ideologies. And, as it turns out in the film, Chancellor Palpatine actually is working with the evil Sith, just as George W. Bush is a member of Skull and Bones and one of the most willing servants of the Illuminati to ever hold the office of the president of the United States.

Lara Croft: Tomb Raider

In 2001 Angelina Jolie starred in the film adaptation of the video game *Tomb Raider*, which featured a plotline mentioning the Illuminati by name and depicted them as an evil power hungry organization that was after a special ancient artifact called the Triangle of Light that was believed to give whoever possessed it the power of God and the ability to manipulate time.

The Triangle of Light was broken into two halves and hidden on opposite sides of the earth in an attempt to prevent anyone from joining them together and harnessing its power. It was said that the power could be used for good or evil, and after it was abused in ancient times, the object was deemed too dangerous for anyone to use and it was hidden away. This Triangle of Light consisted of a metal pyramid with an all seeing eye in the center. Lara Croft's (Jolie's) father had told his daughter that it was her destiny to find the Triangle and destroy it before the Illuminati was able to find it. It turns out her father (played by Jon Voight, her father in real life ironically) was a member of the Illuminati and realized they were evil and had secretly planned to have his daughter find the object to prevent them from becoming all powerful.

Besides an abundance of Illuminati references and symbols, another interesting aspect to the film was that according the legend, the Triangle of Light could only be activated every 5,000 years when all nine planets in the solar system were aligned with each other. This is similar to the planetary alignment that will occur on December 21st 2012 which some mystics believe will mark the transformation of the earth into a New Age or possibly mark the birth or appearance of the New Age Christ. The screenplay for *Lara Croft: Tomb Raider* was written by Patrick Massett and John Zinman.

They Live

John Carpenter wrote a screenplay using the pseudonym "Frank Armitage" and then directed the 1988 science fiction film titled *They Live* which starred actor Rowdy Roddy Piper.

In the film, the economy is in shambles and tent cities are found throughout the country while the ruling class continues to maintain an abundant lifestyle. The plot follows Piper's character as he struggles to find work and discovers that a group of men at a tent city he is living at have discovered a secret as to the true identity of the ruling class, and their method of controlling the population.

In the beginning of the film as Piper wanders the streets looking for work he comes across a street preacher who gets hauled away by the police after delivering a message about the evils of society and how the people in power were feeding off of the less fortunate. One notable scene involves a group of hackers who illegally broadcast a brief message on the television in an attempt to inform people about why society is the way it is. A partial transcript of that pirate broadcast follows:

"Our impulses are being redirected. We are living in an artificially-induced state of consciousness that resembles sleep. The poor and the under-class is growing, racial justice and human rights are non-existent. They have created a repressive society and we are their unwitting accomplices. Their intention to rule rests with the annihilation of consciousness."

"We have been lulled into a trance. They have made us indifferent to ourselves, to others…we are focused only on our own gain. Please understand, they are safe as long as they are not discovered. That is their primary method of survival. Keep us asleep, keep us selfish, keep us sedated. We are their cattle. We are being bred for slavery."

Carpenter seemed to understand how the elite manage the population and there were numerous references to materialism and social ignorance in the film. While not exactly a blockbuster, *They Live* was well received among Rowdy Roddy Piper fans, who enjoyed the actor's rare appearance on the silver screen after building his career as a professional wrestler.

Hackers

A 1995 film that failed at the box office but developed a cult following in the underground community of hackers was the film titled *Hackers*. It starred Jonny Lee Miller and Angelina Jolie, and was written by Rafael Moreu.

The plotline involves a rivalry between groups of hackers, but there is a scene that stuck out to those aware of the New World Order when Eugene *"The Plague"* Belford (played by Fisher Stevens) sent a laptop containing a video message to a fellow hacker "Zero Cool" (played by Jonny Lee Miller). The message was, "You wanted to know who I am Zero Cool. Well let me explain the New World Order.

Governments and corporations need people like you and me. We are samurai. The keyboard cowboys, and all those other people out there who have no idea what's going on are the cattle. Moooo. I need your help. You need my help. let me help you earn your spurs. Think about it."

The Skulls

In the year 2000 a film called *The Skulls* was released in theaters which was clearly based on the Skull and Bones society at Yale. The plot in the film actually involves a fraternity at Yale University, called the Skulls, which is an elite invitation only secret society. The film stars Joshua Jackson, Paul Walker, and Leslie Bibb and was written by John Pogue. In 2002 *The Skulls 2* was released on video, and later in 2004, *The Skulls III* was produced as a direct to video release as well.

The Skulls plot focuses on the murder and ensuing cover-up of a student journalist who broke into the Skulls' clubhouse to take pictures and gather information for a story he was working on. In the film it is revealed that senators and judges are members of the Skulls and it is made clear that they have police and University officials under their control, primarily through blackmail. (See America's Secret Establishment page 85) (See Fleshing out Skull and Bones page 88)

The Good Shepherd

The Good Shepherd is a fictional film which claims to tell the story about the creation of the CIA. Since the Central Intelligence Agency was created by members of the Skull and Bones society at Yale University, the film includes several scenes showing Bonesmen involved in this process, but inaccurately portrays their motives for doing so. The film was released in 2006 and stars Matt Damon and

349

Angelina Jolie.

Damon portrays Edward Wilson who is based on James Jesus Angelton and Richard M. Bissell. Wilson (Damon) is asked to join Skull and Bones and the film shows an initiation ritual which is surprisingly accurate. A man wearing a black robe and dressed like the Grim Reaper tells the newly chosen members that they have been picked to become part of America's most powerful secret society, and brags that their membership has included a president, vice presidents, supreme court justices, congressmen and senators. The new recruits then lay nude in a coffin and tell the group all the secrets about their life that they've never told anyone before. (This is something that new members of Skull and Bones actually do.)

The film was written by Eric Roth, who also wrote the screenplay for *The Insider* (1999), the true story of the *60 Minutes* exposé of the tobacco companies, and *Munich* (2005) a historical film about Israel's secret retaliation of the murders of Israeli Olympic athletes in 1972.

The Good Shepherd depicts the men involved in creating the CIA as men concerned with and looking out for America during World War II and the Cold War, when in reality their sole purpose was to create a covert network that would aid in the construction of the New World Order, and provide those involved the cover and protection of "national security" for their operations. Throughout the film, the Skull and Bones society is painted as a group of patriotic Americans who sing choir songs and all say a prayer before dinner at their banquets on Deer Island.

It is advised that one watch a Dutch documentary titled *Skull & Bones* for an accurate history of the secret society. This film may be found on Google Video and starts out with a Dutch narrator for a minute or more, but then the rest of the film is in English. *The Good Shepherd* is a long and boring film, and can be added to the list of Illuminati whitewashing propaganda pieces which serve the purpose of tainting the

THE ILLUMINATI: FACTS & FICTION

facts to cover their dark past.

The Lord of the Rings

J.R.R. Tolkien's famous literary series, *The Lord of the Rings* was adapted to screenplays of which the first of the trilogy, *The Fellowship of the Ring* was released in 2001 starring Elija Wood and was directed by Peter Jackson.

The plot revolves around a hobbit (a fictional race of human-like beings) named Frodo Baggins (Elija Wood) who is trusted with the task of taking an ancient magical ring to a volcano called Mount Doom and throwing it in the lava to destroy it so it will not fall into the wrong hands. The films are amazing and visually stunning, but there are several aspects which stick out that ring of Illuminati overtones.

The first is the magical ring itself. According to the film (and the books) whoever wears the master ring will have supernatural powers beyond what anyone could imagine. Despite the good nature of anyone's heart, including Frodo Baggins, the power of the ring brings out the most selfish and corrupt nature of whoever has it. It seems that nobody is able to maintain their morality when given the power of the ring, which is why Baggins and his crew set out to destroy it. It is quite analogous to political power and Lord Acton's dictum "power tends to corrupt, and absolute power corrupts absolutely." One interpretation is that if the source of the Illuminati's power is benign, that simply having the power will lead them to use it in self serving and abusive ways.

Another, perhaps more interesting use of symbolism in the story is that of the Eye of Sauron. In the film, the evil ruler Sauron has sent his army out to find the ring so he may become invincible. But what is interesting is that a huge tower stands outside of his castle and contains one eye perched at the very top which can watch over the entire land and see everything, including sensing the location of the ring. This is quite a clear reference to the all seeing eye of the Illuminati that appears on top of the pyramid found on the back of the one dollar bill.

J.R.R. Tolkien's writings revolved around the forces of good and evil, and it is possible that he was aware of the Illuminati and their symbols, and incorporated them into his writings. Tolkien died on September 2nd 1973 at the age of 81.

Eyes Wide Shut

The bizarre 1999 film *Eyes Wide Shut* starring Tom Cruise and Nicole Kidman left the audience and critics alike confused, and some disappointed. The film was Stanly Kubrick's last production before he died and was inspired supposedly by a short book by Arthur Schnitlzer titled *Dream Story*.

In the film, Tom Cruise's charter (Dr. Bill Hartford) discovers that a secret group of wealthy men and women meet periodically in large mansions near New York City while wearing black robes and masks and participate in strange ceremonies and orgies.

Cruise obtains a black robe and a mask, and attends a party out of curiosity. He was only allowed in because a friend of his who played the piano at the parties had given him the secret password. At one point he is discovered while inside the mansion and it is clear that he is an uninvited guest. Before he is told of his punishment, a woman comes forward and asks that she be punished in his place. Days later he finds out the identity of the woman, and that she has turned up dead, leading him to believe that the group of masked partygoers killed her, as they were going to do with him before she volunteered to accept his punishment.

Some believe that the film was originally intended to depict the group of masked partygoers as a wealthy cult who sacrificed people and drank their blood while having an orgy, but that due to pressure, the screenplay was altered.

One also can't help but be reminded of the Bohemian Grove ceremonies when watching the film, and others see the storyline as a reference to actual Illuminati parties involving sexual orgies and human sacrifices and even necrophilia.

The Brotherhood of the Bell

A 1970 film titled *The Brotherhood of the Bell* depicts a college fraternity which acts as a recruiting ground for a criminal banking and business network involving the country's most successful men. The film was clearly a reference to the Skull and Bones society at Yale University. It was written by David Karp and directed by Paul Wendkos and nominated by the Directors Guild of America for outstanding directorial achievement in television.

After being sworn into the Brotherhood of the Bell, one of the initiates has a brief conversation with an elder of the organization who had attended the ceremony and joyfully says, "I'm a member of the establishment now," when the elder corrects him, "Not a part. *The* establishment."

The plotline involves an economics professor named Dr. Andrew Patterson (played by Glenn Ford) who receives a call from the group twenty years after joining, and is reminded of the oath he once took to follow any order regardless of what it was when given by the brotherhood, and his time to serve had come. He was told he needed to murder someone, and when he refuses, his entire life is turned upside down and the true power and reach of the brotherhood becomes apparent to him.

A Scanner Darkly

Keanu Reeves, Woody Harrelson, Robert Downey Jr., and Winona Ryder star in *A Scanner Darkly*, which was based on the 1977 science fiction novel by Philip K. Dick about a future dystopia in Orange County, California. The film was released in 2006 and is directed by Richard Linklater who also produced *Waking Life* and *Dazed and Confused.*

A Scanner Darkly was shot using real actors and then animated using a process called rotoscoping which gives it a very unique appearance of being a cartoon like animation. In the film, it is discovered that a drug rehabilitation center called New Way is funding the police department's investigations into the wide spread abuse of a drug called Substance D, but are secretly producing the drugs and forcing individuals enrolled in their rehabilitation program to cultivate the flowers used to create the drug. Anyone who is familiar with the real cause of the crack-cocaine boom in the 1980s can see that the film is making a statement about the CIA's major role in importing drugs into the United States.

The film included a brief cameo from Alex Jones and showed him standing on the street with a megaphone trying to inform people what was happening, and is quickly hauled away by police. One also can't help but notice the Illuminati's all seeing eye on the shirt worn by Robert Downy Jr.'s character. The fact that the director chose this as the character's wardrobe and included Alex Jones with his signature bullhorn, proves that this was no ordinary film. Clearly Richard Linklater was trying to make a statement with his film, as apposed to simply making an entertaining movie.

National Treasure

One of the films to bring Freemasonry and the topic of secret societies and their symbols into the public's awareness is *National Treasure* starring Nicolas Cage. The film was produce by Walt Disney Pictures and is about a lost treasure that the Freemasons and Knights Templar have hidden. While the film may be a family friendly adventure full of various twists and turns and clues and mysteries, it serves to whitewash the true history of the Knights Templars, the Freemasons, and the treasure from Solomon's Temple.

National Treasure basically paints the Freemasons as the good guys, who have had to protect their sacred treasure from pirates and criminals. In reality, the Knights Templar were the pirates and thieves who became the first international bankers, and later evolved into Freemasonry and the Illuminati. The story was written by a team of writers consisting of Jim Kouf, Oren Aviv, Charles Segars, Ted Elliott, and Terry Rossio. The screenplay was then written by a husband and wife team named Marianne and Cormac Wibberlev.

Shooter

Mark Wahlberg plays a Marine Corps Scout Sniper who is framed for an assassination by the CIA in *Shooter* which was released in 2007. In the beginning of the film, Wahlberg's character sits down at a computer to check the morning news and says to himself "let's see what lies they're feeding us today" as a copy of the *9/11 Commission Report* sits next to the keyboard.

There are several political statements woven into the storyline, including the lies promoted by the Bush administration that there were Weapons of Mass Destruction in Iraq. There was also a scene where a retired government agent says that the shooter on the grassy knoll was murdered and buried in the desert after he participated in the murder of John F. Kennedy.

While the majority of the population thinks that people who talk about actual conspiracies in the government get their ideas from watching films such as *Shooter*, the truth is that the writers of such films get their ideas from actual events. Subtle signs including the scene showing the *9/11 Commission Report* are often missed by the uninformed viewers, but serve to show those who have eyes to see that the writer or director is making a statement with their film. *Shooter* was based on the 1993 novel *Point of Impact* by Stephen Hunter, and was directed by Antoine Fuqua.

Air America

Mel Gibson and Robert Downy Jr. star in *Air America*, a 1990 film about the U.S. government shipping heroin into the country by using CIA agents in Laos, Vietnam. The screenplay was adapted from a non-fiction book by Christopher Robbins with the same name.

Air America is actually the name of a cargo airline that was owned and operated by the CIA from 1950 to 1976 which supplied covert operations in Southeast Asia during the Vietnam War. This airline was believed to be used to also transport heroine into the United States. This would ultimately be the inspiration for Christopher Robbins' book and *Air America* the film.

Wag the Dog

Robert De Niro and Dustin Hoffman star in the 1997 film *Wag the Dog* which eerily mirrored the events of the Monica Lewinsky scandal which was occurring at the same time the film was released. In the film, Dustin Hoffman plays a movie producer who helps the government concoct a war with Albania in order to distract the American people from a sex scandal involving the President and an intern.

As part of the plot, Willie Nelson was hired to write a theme song for the war in order to encourage patriotism and keep the public support as the government's corrupt propaganda campaign continued. In real life, Nelson would later become vocal about the 9/11 attacks and the World Trade Center being blown up by a controlled demolition, and has been an anti-war advocate for a long time. His decision to appear in *Wag the Dog* was most likely a result of his understanding how the film, while being fictional, showed how propaganda campaigns are waged to generate and keep public support for wars, and that the real reason for the war is rarely given to the public.

Wag the Dog was written by Hilary Henkin and David Mamet. It is believed that Henkin had an uncredited role in writing the screenplay for *V for Vendetta* (2006).

Oliver Stone's JFK

Perhaps the most popular "conspiracy" type of film is Oliver Stone's *JFK* which was released in 1991 and starred Kevin Costner. The film was both attacked and praised, depending on how critics felt about the idea of who killed President Kennedy. The film is a dramatized version of events surrounding the assassination of John F. Kennedy in 1963 and depicts the idea that Oswald was not the only shooter and that Kennedy was killed as a larger plot by the CIA. Aside from being attacked by critics, Stone actually received death threats over the film's production.

In 1991 when it was released, a writer for the *Chicago Tribune* wrote that it was "an insult to the intelligence" and George Larnder, who worked as the national security correspondent for the *Washington Post* attacked "the absurdities and palpable untruths in Garrison's book and Stone's rendition of it."[198]

Bernard Weinraub wrote an article in *The New York Times* titled "Hollywood Wonders If Warner Brothers let *JFK* Go Too Far" and suggested that the studio should have killed the film before it went into production, saying, "At what point does a studio exercise its leverage and blunt the highly charged message of a film maker like Oliver

---

[198] Lardner, George – *On the Set: Dallas in Wonderland*, The Washington Post 5-19-1991

Stone?"[199]

Conversely, the *Miami Herald* said, "the focus on the trivialities of personality conveniently prevents us from having to confront the tough questions his film raises." And film critic Roger Ebert wrote, "The achievement of the film is not that it answers the mystery of the Kennedy assassination, because it does not, or even that it vindicates Garrison, who is seen here as a man often whistling in the dark. Its achievement is that it tries to marshal the anger which ever since 1963 has been gnawing away on some dark shelf of the national psyche."[200]

The president of the Motion Picture Association of America, Jack Valenti, released a seven page statement about the film saying, "In much the same way, young German boys and girls in 1941 were mesmerized by Leni Reifenstahl's *Triumph of the Will*, in which Adolf Hitler was depicted as a newborn God. Both *J. F. K.* and *Triumph of the Will* are equally a propaganda masterpiece and equally a hoax. Mr. Stone and Leni Reifenstahl have another genetic linkage: neither of them carried a disclaimer on their film that its contents were mostly pure fiction."[201]

Despite being barraged with attacks, the film was ranked the fourth best of the year by *Time Magazine* and Robert Ebert called it the best film of the year and one of the top ten films of the decade.[202] It was nominated for eight Academy Awards including Best Picture, and Stone was nominated for Best Director by the Directors Guild of America, and won a Golden Globe for Best Director. During his acceptance

---

[199] Petras, James (May 1992). "The Discrediting of the Fifth Estate: The Press Attacks on *JFK*," *Cineaste*, pp. 15

[200] Ebert, Roger (1991-12-20). "JFK", *Chicago Sun-Times.*

[201] Weinraub, Bernard (1992-04-02). "Valenti Calls *J.F.K.* 'Hoax' and 'Smear'", *The New York Times*

[202] Ebert, Roger (2004-12-15). "Ebert's 10 Best Lists: 1967-present," *Chicago Sun-Times*

speech he said, "A terrible lie was told to us 28 years ago. I hope that this film can be the first step in righting that wrong."[203]

In 2006 when word started to circulate that Oliver Stone was working on a film about the 9/11 attacks, many had hoped, (and others feared) that he was going to produce a similar "conspiracy" type of film showing a dramatized version of how elements within intelligence agencies pulled strings to aid and allow the 9/11 attacks to happen. It turned out that the film, which was titled *World Trade Center*, focused on the rescue of two New York City Port Authority workers.

Then several years later it was discovered that Stone was working on a film about George W. Bush, and hopes were revived that he would finally take up the task of exposing the 9/11 inside job to a world wide audience. Sadly Stone failed to deliver and instead produced *W.* which was a biopic attack on George W. Bush and the war on terror, but did not include anything about Bush and his Illuminati cohorts aiding in the 9/11 attacks.

As a result of Stone's avoidance of these issues, despite them growing from a small underground movement to boiling over into the mainstream, many suspect that Stone has sold out and some even consider him an accomplice in the 9/11 cover-up for not addressing the topic after producing two films about 9/11 and George W. Bush.

Bulworth

Warren Beatty starred in *Bulworth*, a film about a California Senator named Jay Billington Bulworth (Beatty) who decides to speak his mind and tell the public exactly

---

[203] Reeves, Phil (1992-01-20). "Top award for Kennedy film", *The Independent*, p. 12.

how things work in politics as he runs for re-election. Bulworth is ultimately murdered by a medical insurance representative because of his push for socialized medicine which would put the insurance companies out of business. The film was release in 1998 and was co-written and co-produced by Beatty himself.

The final scene shows a homeless man as he says, "Bulworth, you've got to be a spirit. You can't be no ghost," meaning he was a spirit of truth and died a martyrs death.

Conspiracy Theory

Mel Gibson and Julia Roberts star in the 1997 film *Conspiracy Theory* about a taxi driver who everyone thinks is a lunatic and a conspiracy theorist because he thinks the government is involved in all kinds of conspiracies.

The film starts off with Jerry Fletcher (Gibson) driving a cab and talking to his passengers about how the government adds fluoride to the drinking water to dumb the population down and make everyone a slave to the state and that pets are getting implanted with computer identification chips and soon they'll be implanting them in humans.[204] He continues to say that George Bush (senior) is a 33rd degree Mason and the former director of the CIA and that "he knew what he was saying when he said 'New World Order' during his State of the Union speech in 1991."

Fletcher (Gibson) had become friends with Julia Robert's character (Alice) after he saved her from being mugged in the past, and she basically feels like she has to be nice to him and listen to his seemingly paranoid conspiracy theories every time she sees him. Alice is an attorney for the Justice Department and is haunted by her father's mysterious

---

[204] This was a reference to the VeriChip implantable RFID tag which is designed to do just that.

murder.

As it turns out, a man named Dr. Jonas (played by Patrick Stewart), worked for the CIA on MK-ULTRA mind control experiments and was involved in brainwashing Gibson's character into becoming a mind controlled assassin in the past. The film mentions MK-ULTRA by name and makes several references to Manchurian Candidate mind control. For example, Fletcher is shown to have an obsession with *The Catcher in the Rye*. When the book is discovered in his belongings, a police officer observes out loud that Mark David Chapman had that book on him when he shot John Lenin, and another officer remarks that the same book had been found in John Hinckley's possessions after he had shot Ronald Reagan in an assassination attempt. Both Chapman and Hinckley are suspected to be victims of mind control who were programmed to be assassins. There are also casual references to the Kennedy assassination and Oswald, as well as secret handshakes and the Military Industrial Complex.

It is obvious that the script was inspired by actual events such as the MK-ULTRA program, and the writer was very familiar with "conspiracy theory" culture. The only disappointing aspect of the film is that Fletcher (Gibson) was portrayed as a lunatic who happened to be right. Mixed with historical conspiracies and sinister government projects are paranoid delusions and gibberish which erodes from the credibility of Fletcher's claims. *Conspiracy Theory* was written by Brian Helgeland, who is credited with writing or producing a variety of films, including *Assassins* (1995), *A Knight's Tale* (2001), and *The Order* (2003).

The Manchurian Candidate

In 2004 a remake of the 1964 film, *The Manchurian Candidate* was released starring Denzel Washington which depicted a Gulf War veteran named Major Ben Marco

(Washington) who comes to discover that he and his military unit were the victims of a top secret government program involving brainwashing.

Those who orchestrated his brainwashing operation planned to have him assassinate the president of the United States so that the vice president (played by Liev Schreiber) would take control of the White House and thus aid the profits and actions of the Manchurian Global Corporation, the very corporation that was behind the brainwashing experiments.

The film is based on actual experiments in the MK-ULTRA program, where drugs, hypnotism, and trauma-based mind control experiments were conducted in attempts to actually create a mind controlled assassin who would carry out orders without question, just like the one in the film.

Some believe that Sirhan Sirhan, the man who killed Robert Kennedy, was a victim of MK-ULTRA mind control programs. Others suspected of being programmed assassins by the CIA include John Hinckley Jr., who shot President Ronald Reagan in 1981 in an assassination attempt. The Hinckley family maintained a close relationship with the Bush family, and some suspect that John Hinckley's attempted murder of President Reagan was orchestrated using mind control techniques so that George H.W. Bush, who was then the vice president under Reagan, could become the president. For three generations, the Bush family have been members of Skull and Bones and knowingly and willingly serve the Illuminati. (See America's Secret Establishment page 85) (See The Search for the Manchurian Candidate page 115)

Enemy of the State

Will Smith stars in *Enemy of the State* which was released in 1998 and showed the technological capability of the National Security Agency, and what could happen if the systems were abused. While the capabilities of the technology shown in the film were considered the design of science fiction, systems such as Echelon and spy satellites are very much a reality. The American people came to know after 9/11 that such systems were being used to illegally listen to people's phone calls and have the ability to activate the microphone in a cell phone and use it as a listening device to pick up conversations in the surrounding areas, even when the phone is turned off.[205] *Enemy of the State* was written by David Marconi who was also one of the writers for the story of *Live Free or Die Hard* (2007) which was part four of the *Die Hard* series starring Bruce Willis.

Batman Returns

Michael Keaton, Christopher Walken, and Danny DeVito star in *Batman Returns* (1991) which includes multiple Illuminati symbols and references to actual false flag terror attacks. For example, at a costume party one of the bad guys, Max Shreck (Walken), is dressed as a genie with an all seeing eye inside of a pyramid placed on his forehead. At another point in the film he is shown displaying a model of a power plant he would like to build which is in the shape of a pyramid with the capstone missing. Another antagonist, the Penguin, has an umbrella which contains the pattern of the Knights Templars' red cross. While some may see these symbols as nothing more than random costume and set designs, one scene contains a blatant reference to actual historic false flag terror attacks.

At one point Shreck (Walken) and the Penguin (DeVito) are plotting to install Penguin as the mayor and use their

---

[205] CNET News *FBI taps cell phone mic as eavesdropping tool* By Delcan McCullagh and Anne Broache December 1, 2006

power to take over the city of Gotham. As the two are discussing their plans, Shreck proposes "an incident like the Gulf of Tonkin or the Reichstag fire" and the two laugh with delight. Both events were, in reality, false flag events. (See Terrorstorm page 274) *Batman Returns* was written by San Hamm and Daniel Watters.

Dragnet

The 1987 comedy *Dragnet* starring Dan Aykroyd and Tom Hanks is about two police detectives who are given an assignment to investigate a religious cult in Los Angeles.

The two men eventually follow a popular televangelist to a ceremony put on by a group called P.A.G.A.N. (People Against Goodness And Normalcy). The ceremony the group is about to participate in is a human sacrifice. The parallels are subtle yet similar to the activities in the Bohemian Grove, and it is not far fetched to think that the writer and producers either knew of, or had heard rumors of the activities within the club, which then served as the inspiration for the plot of *Dragnet*.

The word bohemian actually means, "one who lives and acts free of regard for conventional rules and practices," and was likely the inspiration for the group P.A.G.A.N. (People Against Goodness And Normalcy), found in the film. The screenplay was written by a collaboration of Jack Webb, Dan Aykroyd, Alan Zweibel, and Tom Mankiewicz.

Television Show References

Aside from the Illuminati being worked into the plotline of various Hollywood movies, the subject matter is also occasionally referenced in television shows as well. Popular shows from *The Simpsons* and *South Park*, to lesser known TV series such as *Wild Palms* and *The Lone Gunmen* have all included plotlines stemming from actual events that the Illuminati have organized or participated in. To an uninformed audience, these aspects are merely seen as another fictional storyline, but the more informed viewer sees these issues as deliberate insertions by the shows' writers or producers to make a larger statement as their art imitates life.

South Park

A trashy, foul mouthed cartoon for adults, *Southpark*, has lampooned various people and institutions by simply presenting various bizarre facts in a humorous way. For example, an episode about Mormonism presented the actual beliefs about the Mormon Church and put a banner on the bottom of the screen saying, "This is actually what Mormons believe," and it was what they believe. An episode about Scientology used the same method when presenting information about the organization. It was funny for most of the audience, although insulting for members of such organizations.

A more disturbing episode also used the tactic. An episode about a group the show called the "Super Adventure Club" was about an international organization of pedophiles who travel around the world to have sex with young boys because they believe that it gives them magical power.

In the cartoon, the current leader of the group explains, "Our club offers hope. Do you think we go around the world molesting children because it feels really good? No. Our club has a message and a secret that explains the mysteries of life."

The man goes on to explain the history of the club and how a man named William P. Finius was a great traveler and explorer who also was a pedophile. After talking about all countries the man traveled to, he continued to say, "But now the most wonderful part. You see, after having sex with all those children, Finius realized that molesting all those kids had made him immortal. He discovered that children have things called marlocks in their bodies and when an adult has sex with a child, the marlocks implode feeding the adult's receptor cavity with energy that causes immortality."

While this is completely disgusting, and not funny at all, what many of the viewers didn't know is that one of the most hidden secrets in the occult is the belief that by having sex with a male child, an individual can experience altered states of consciousness and achieve a level of super enlightenment or immortality. Trey Parker and Matt Stone must have been aware of this esoteric occult practice and wrote it into their show. I'm not saying they have participated in such activities, but they must be familiar with the Illuminati and such material. (See Sex Magic page 305)

Again, just like the episodes making fun of Scientology and the Mormons, they inserted a banner on the bottom of the screen saying "This is what the Super Adventure Club actually believes." How else could they have come up with such an idea, and why would they put the banner on the screen explaining it's what these people actually believe, in the same way they did in other episodes about strange religious beliefs?

Rescue Me

The television series *Rescue Me* which airs on the FX network is a show about New York City firefighters starring

Dennis Leary. In 2007, the show's costar Daniel Sunjata created a stir on the Internet when he came on several patriot radio shows to discuss his stance that the 9/11 attacks were an inside job. Sunjata is extremely knowledgeable and articulate and while other actors who voiced similar beliefs seemed afraid to blatantly state that the 9/11 attacks were an inside job, Sunjata makes no bones about it. The mainstream media did not attack Sunjata for his comments, possibly because he is not a household name like Charlie Sheen or Rosie O'Donnell, who made headlines for speaking about such issues.

Several years after Sunjata's radio interviews about 9/11, writers for *Rescue Me* had incorporated some of his personal views into his character. In one scene, Franco (Sunjata) was being interviewed by a reporter when he states, "What you're going to hear from me, you're not going to hear from anybody else. Because, my opinions, let's just say they're not popular. 9/11? Inside job. Plain and simple. And all you gotta do is connect the dots. And I'm not talking bout the dots everyone has heard about... I am talking about a massive neoconservative government effort that's been in the works twenty years. Ever heard of PNAC? Project for a New American Century? According to them, the end goal of their effort is American global domination. Full spectrum dominance, they call it. Now, first question that pops into my mind is: How do you pull that off in this day and age?"

The reporter, played by Catherine Zeta Jones, sits quietly and continues to listen. Franco (Sunjata) goes on, "Well, according to them you do it in four steps. First, we must control the world's oil. Now I don't have to remind you that Bush and Cheney came into power with plans all ready to attack Afghanistan and Iraq. Number two, we have to make huge technological advances with our armed forces. Number three...surprise, surprise, huge increases in military spending to pay for the above. Number four, and this is key. We change the definition of preemptive attack so we can unilaterally bomb the shit out of, invade, and occupy countries even if they pose no credible threat or had nothing to do with 9/11. One problem. How are you going to put that into action? I mean, the American people are never going to go for no shit like that, right? Damn straight. Now what you need is an event. An event that gets everyone's heads turned around the right way. What you need is a new Pearl Harbor. That's what they said they needed. You're looking at a guy who went to fifty-eight funerals in twenty six days, I can tell you that is sure as shit what they got."

Many of the viewers might not know the story behind how this idea was worked into the script. In an interview Sunjata explained, "I'm really gratified that they allowed that to be focused through my character, because I happen to subscribe to a lot of those theories and beliefs that 9/11 was an inside job."[206]

This surprised the interviewer, and when asked to clarify this, Peter Tolan, the show's co-creator explained, "That's part of the reason why we wrote it, is because Danny actually has—is actually well-read on—he's done a lot of research on this and has told us about it. And, you know, look, obviously not all of us buy in. But we went, wow, that's interesting, and he's passionate about it. Let's use that."[207]

Sunjata went on to say, "there are some very, very well-thought-out ideas and theories that seem to me to make a lot more sense than the ones that are popularly espoused. And anyway, the fact that they've allowed that conversation to be had within the world of *Rescue Me*, I think, is admirable and should be applauded."[208]

---

[206] Kansas City Star *"Rescue Me" character believes 9/11 was an inside job ... and so does the actor playing him* January 19, 2009
[207] Ibid
[208] Ibid

The Lone Gunmen

A television series that ran on Fox in 2001 called *The Lone Gunmen* aired an episode March 4, 2001 with a plot of a corrupt faction within the government hijacking a jet and trying to crash it into the World Trade Center to further the objectives of the Military Industrial Complex. Watching the episode is like watching a made for TV movie about the September 11th attacks only it was produced months prior to the event.

One of the stars of the show, Dean Haglund, later came forward and said the FBI and NASA would approach Chris Carter, the show's creator, with story ideas for various shows. Haglund also said that since the 1980s the CIA had hired informants who attend Hollywood parties and report back to the CIA on general trends and issues that writers and producers were focusing on. Haglund believed this was to tip-off the CIA if any famous writers or film makers were developing a project that would be potentially damaging to the government's image or incite people to react in an unfavorable fashion.

It is certainly possible that the plot for *The Lone Gunmen* involving the government attempting to crash a jet into the World Trade Center in order to use the incident to justify military expansion was an idea that was given to the show's writers by the FBI consultants who worked with the producers. The purpose for this would be to point to the show as the source of such "conspiracy theories" when people started to figure out that elements within the government aided in the 9/11 attacks.

Another explanation, of course, is that the writers were aware of how governments use false flag terrorism, and had read reports about terrorist groups planning to hijack planes and crash them into prominent buildings in America prior to September 11th 2001. While many American's still believe that the 9/11 attacks were a complete surprise and that intelligence agencies had never heard of such plans, the truth is that as far back as 1995 the CIA was aware of plans to hijack planes and crash them into the World Trade Center.[209] The Islamic terrorists who had planned this plot called it Project Bojinka.

24

The show *24* is a popular television action drama broadcast by Fox which has aired since November 2001. The show stars Keifer Sutherland, who plays Jack Bauer, an agent for the fictional Counter Terrorism Unit (CTU). The show is a high budget action packed hour which features Bauer (Sutherland) and his fellow CTU officers tracking down domestic terrorists and saving America from various terrorist attacks including nuclear and biological.

In the show, Bauer frequently violates the law and the Constitution in order to save the country from the terrorists. He doesn't follow legal statutes, and tortures suspects in an attempt to extract information from them. Instead of being seen as a corrupt agent who is a danger to the integrity of the United States, Jack Bauer is seen as a hero defending America. Numerous episodes depict the people who are against Bauer torturing people as the reason that the terrorists get away. Such plots are created to serve as government propaganda and teaches the audience that it's ok for government officials to break the law and torture people, because it is believed such actions are necessary to keep us safe from terrorists. Sutherland's character is presented as a hero who is only hindered by the law, and must continuously take matters into his own hands in order to do what is right for the country.

---

[209] New York Times *Plot Echoes One Planned by 9/11 Mastermind in '94* by Ramond Bonner August 10, 2006

All experts who are not on the Illuminati's payroll agree that using torture as a method to extract information from suspects is not a reliable method because if the suspect doesn't know the information his captors desire, he will simply start agreeing with whatever they ask, with hopes that it will satisfy them so they will end the torture. Such practices are a violation of international law, but that didn't stop the Bush administration from approving waterboarding suspects in the War on Terror. Waterboarding basically consists of strapping a suspect down on a table and pouring water down their throat until they nearly drown. Such a practice had previously been classified as torture by the Department of Defense, but officials simply use the term "enhanced interrogation techniques" and used the practice in secret until such methods were exposed to the public. Other suspects are transferred to foreign countries which then torture them on behalf of the U.S. so America can claim their hands are clean. Such a practice is labeled "rendition" and is used to torture suspects by proxy.

Shows like *24* serve only as Illuminati propaganda to desensitize people to the inhumane practices of the government and lead everyone to believe that all suspects are guilty and can be treated worse than animals. Anytime any illegal or inhumane strategies are faced with opposition, the government accuses those who oppose it as being un-American, or aiding the terrorists.

Gargoyles

A cartoon airing on the Disney Channel from 1994 to 1997 called *Gargoyles* included several episodes which mentioned the Illuminati and one of the main characters was shown to be a member.

The cartoon featured several creatures, called Gargoyles, which turned to stone during the daytime and were animated during the night. The series was produced by

Greg Weisman and Frank Paur. Weisman also was a writer for the *Men in Black* animated series which aired on the Kid's WB for several seasons.

Wild Palms

A 1993 mini-series airing on ABC titled *Wild Palms* is about a power-mad corporation which hopes to brainwash society by using its advanced virtual reality technology. Oliver Stone and Bruce Wagner were the executive producers of the series. It starred James Belushi, Dana Delany, Angie Dickinson, and Kim Cattrall.

While the series is extremely dull and drawn out with bad acting, it contains some interesting aspects which were undoubtedly inspired from actual events. Basically, the series is about a California senator named Tony Kreutzer (played by Robert Loggia) who is also the head of the Channel 3 television station and the founder of a popular religion called Synthiotics. This new "religion" was obviously a reference to Scientology. As the series continues, the viewer discovers that there are two political groups that oppose each other, the Friends, and the Fathers. The Friends are libertarians and support the Bill of Rights, where the Fathers are ruthless and fascistic.

The Fathers are planning for the senator to run for president and then become all powerful using the hologram technology. Members of this group have small tattoos on their hand which awards them special privileges in society. At one point, the libertarian Friends try to warn James Belushi's character about the fascistic Fathers and explain that they had planned the Great Depression and major terrorist attacks and wars.

There is a brief scene where a television is on in the background which shows Oliver Stone being interviewed on a talk show and the interviewer says to Stone, "15 years after the release of your film *JFK* the documents are released, and you were right. The conspiracy turned out to be so much larger than you presented in the film. Can you comment on that?"

Recall that *Wild Palms* aired in 1993 and takes place in the future. The producers were trying to show that the JFK assassination had been proven to be a conspiracy, and was now public knowledge.

At the end of the series as the senator's plans are foiled, he freaks out and yells, "I am a soldier. I am mustering my troops! And we are storming Heaven!"

The Simpsons

In a 1995 episode of the popular animated cartoon, *The Simpsons*, Homer joins an all male fraternity in Springfield called the Stonecutters, an obvious reference to the Freemasons. The Freemason fraternity evolved out of ancient stone masons and trade guilds who kept knowledge secret about how to work with stone and build cathedrals and castles. The episode is titled "Homer the Great" and starts of with Homer noticing that two of his friends, Lenny and Carl, are enjoying special privileges around town and at work such as comfortable chairs and premium parking spots. After Homer becomes suspicious, he finds out that they are members of the Stonecutters secret society, and is allowed to become a member himself.

The episode contains numerous humorous incidents, and references to Freemasonry. Homer ultimately ends up accidentally destroying the society's sacred parchment, which is an ancient document containing secrets of the group that had been handed down for generations. The Stonecutters were also waiting for "the Chosen One" who would one day lead the organization to glory. The episode was written by John Swartzwelder.

In one entertaining scene, all of the members sing a quick song while inside their lodge and drinking beer. The song is titled *We Do* and was nominated for an Emmy Award for "Outstanding Music And Lyrics." The lyrics are about how the Stonecutters secretly rule the world, held back the production of the electric car to benefit the oil companies, and keep information about aliens from becoming public.

Another funny storyline that the show's creators worked into a plot for a different episode was also clearly inspired from actual events. In the show immediately preceding the 2008 presidential election, the cartoon included a scene showing Homer entering a voting booth which contained an electronic voting machine. When Homer used the touchscreen to press the "Obama" button, the electronic voice announced, "One vote for McCain." Homer seemed puzzled and pressed the "Obama" button again, only to have the machine say "Two votes for McCain." "Wait a minute! This machine is rigged!" Homer yells. Then a trap door in the machine opens and starts sucking him down a tube. As he's being pulled in he says, "This doesn't happen in America. Maybe in Ohio, but not America!"

It is interesting that the writers included this short little segment into the show, but it is even more interesting that they included the comment about Ohio. In case you don't see the significance of this statement, the Illuminati used electronic voting machines in Ohio (as well as other states) to steal the election for George W. Bush in 2004. This is why all the exit polls in Ohio showed John Kerry would win the state on election night, but it ultimately went to Bush. (See Hacking Democracy page 295)

The YouTube clip titled *Homer Simpson tries to vote for Obama,* which depicts this scene had received 6.4 million views at the time of this writing, and may or may not still be available online.

One other brief reference to Freemasons in the cartoon which was likely missed by most of the audience is a scene when Mr. Burns has become a germaphobe and as he is looking at his assistant's face he hallucinates that it is covered with bacteria and in a high pitched tone they say "Freemasons run the country."

The Cartoon Network

Lucy, Daughter of the Devil is an adult cartoon shown on Turner Broadcasting's Cartoon Network late at night as part of the network's "Adult Swim." It is a ten minute CGI comedy with a plot involving Satan who lives in San Francisco and is trying to convince his 21-year-old daughter, Lucy, to fulfill her role as the Antichrist. Lucy's boyfriend is DJ Jesús, a techno DJ who is actually Jesus Christ.

On October 7th, 2007 an episode aired titled *Human Sacrifice* in which the Devil is invited to attend a human sacrifice ritual at the Bohemian Grove which will honor a senator who has been chosen to be elected as the next president.

DJ Jesús is chosen as the human sacrifice and is lured to the Bohemian Grove under the pretense that he will be DJing a party. He is actually told the party will be like the film *Eyes Wide Shut* and that Alan Greenspan (former chairman of the Federal Reserve Bank) will be there.

The Bohemian Grove in the cartoon is clearly modeled after the actual Grove or from the footage of Alex Jones' film *Dark Secrets Inside Bohemian Grove*. The ritual begins with people lighting torches, which is also identical to the real Bohemian Grove, and then shows the audience which is said to contain half of Washington, chanting "hail Satan." Before the sacrifice, Satan tells the audience that ten presidents have announced their candidacy in the Bohemian Grove.

In the end, DJ Jesús escapes without being killed, and the show concludes by zooming out to an aerial view showing the location of the incident being in Northern California, where the actual club is located.

Corporate Logos

Since the teachings and secret knowledge that is given to Illuminati members as they climb the ranks within the hierarchy gives them a tremendous advantage in business and politics, it is no surprise that most major multinational corporations were started by Illuminati families and members. By using their advanced knowledge, backroom deals, and unconscionable practices, they have created and maintained the corner of the market in multiple industries such as oil, banking, entertainment, and news media. What is even more interesting is that an extremely large number of these companies have incorporated Illuminati symbolism into their logos. All seeing eyes, pyramids, the sun, and mythical figures are found in numerous logos from CBS to America Online.

CBS's logo is actually an all seeing eye. Mobile Oil prints their logo in blue with exception of the letter o in Mobile, which is printed in red to signify the sun. The symbol for Infinity automobiles is a pyramid with a sun behind it. Fidelity Investments' logo is a pyramid with an all seeing eye on the top. The o in Morning Star investments represents the sun and is a different shape than the rest of the letters. Lucifer is often called the Morning Star. The list goes on and on.

Many logos for Hollywood production studios also include Illuminati symbolism. Paramount Pictures' logo is a huge mountain shaped like a pyramid surrounded by a ring of stars; Tri-Star's logo is a winged Pegasus; Columbia Pictures' logo features the goddess Semiramis holding a torch; Prometheus Entertainment, Orion, Icon, Lion's Gate Films, DreamWorks, and many other companies have Masonic/occult symbolism in their logos.

Music References

A small number of musicians have occasionally referenced the Illuminati in their songs, although most of these artists are underground and are rarely, if ever, played on the corporate owned airwaves on stations like Clear Channel or similar monopolized markets. Some of these artists, such as Paris and Prodigy, mention the Illuminati by name, while others from rappers to rockers seem to be very well aware of the evil deeds of the brotherhood, a fact that becomes clear by simply listening to the lyrics of their songs or watching the music videos that accompany them. Below is just a sample of musicians, some of which are extremely well known, who have made such references in their songs.

It's important to note that the Illuminati financially supports musicians whose music preaches socially destructive messages, and builds them up as role models which the brain-dead masses worship as idols. The fact that many musicians achieve massive success isn't necessarily that they are extremely talented, it's that they have been chosen to be promoted because their music encourages violent, immoral, and social destructive behavior. Their music is literally used to brainwash the listeners. Occasionally an artist who is an unknowing Illuminati pawn will actually write a song which counters their very purpose for being promoted, as in the case of Eminem.

Eminem

Marshall Mathers, aka Slim Shady, aka Eminem released a music video just before the 2004 presidential election for his song titled *Mosh* which is a scathing attack against George W. Bush and his fear mongering surrounding the War on Terror.

The video starts with a parody of George W. Bush

reading *My Pet Goat* to a classroom of school children as a jet flies over the school and crashes into the World Trade Center. It then cuts to Eminem standing in front of a wall covered with newspaper clippings and headlines about Bush's foreknowledge of the 9/11 attacks, including the *New York Post's* front page headline "Bush Knew."

Eminem roars "look in his eyes it's all lies" as the music video cuts from President Bush to a cardboard cutout of Osama Bin Laden on a soundstage controlled by Donald Rumsfeld and Dick Cheney. Eminem rallies dozens of people and they surround the Capitol building and head up the stairs and start pouring inside in what appears to be the beginning of a riot, when it is revealed that they are all lining up to vote. The song itself is extremely powerful, but the music video, which was produced by the *Guerilla New Network* is historic and presents a powerfully positive message about activism and power in numbers.

Despite this powerful song, Eminem is actually an unknowing pawn of the Illuminati and was promoted by them as a role model for the youth because the vast majority of his music preaches violence, immorality, and irresponsibility. His song *Mosh* is mentioned in this book because despite his dark and troubled soul, it appears that even Eminem could see through the lies of the Bush administration.

Dr. Dre

Rapper Dr. Dre included a line about buying his own island before the year 2000 and that he "ain't trying to stick around for Illuminati" in his song *Been There, Done That*.

Neil Young

In 2006 Neil Young released an entire album of war protest songs titled *Living with War*. One of those songs,

Let's Impeach the President, was nominated for a Grammy Award and contained lyrics referring to the shadow government, spying on American citizens, and George W. Bush hijacking Christianity to get elected.

Don Henley

In 2000, Don Henley, the singer from *The Eagles*, released a solo album titled *Inside Job* which contained a song with the same title which speaks universal truths regarding government corruption and inside jobs in general. While the song was recorded and released before the September 11th attacks, it has become a theme song for what really happened that fateful day and a warning for what lies ahead.

"It was an inside job by the well connected" Henley sings. Other lyrics include that they know what you've had for breakfast and what you've hid beneath the mattress. "Chalk it up to business as usual," Henley concludes.

Megadeth

The heavy metal band Megadeth has a song titled *New World Order* with lyrics that talk about how all currency has become obsolete and that "Revelation has come to pass" and "all rights will be denied…without the mark you shall die," referring to the mark of the Beast.

Ministry

In 2006 the industrial metal band, Ministry, released an album titled *Rio Grande Blood* which contained several songs about the War on Terrorism and 9/11. The song *Lies Lies Lies*, actually sampled sound bites from the film *Loose Change* saying, "Do you still think that jet fuel brought down the World Trade Center?"

THE ILLUMINATI: FACTS & FICTION

Jadakiss

In 2004, rapper Jadakiss released his second album titled *Kiss of Death* which included a track titled *Why?* which contained one line that set off a media firestorm and would cause his song to either be pulled from the radio, or the one line censored when it was played.

The line which resulted in so much controversy was, "Why did Bush knock down the towers?" referring to the World Trade Center. Fox News' Bill O'Reilly publicly stated that President Bush should sue Jadakiss for slander.

Flowbots

Flobots are an American alternative hip hop band from Denver, Colorado who got mainstream exposure in 2008 with their song *Handlebars* which was released in 2007 on their album *Fight with Tools*. The song and the accompanying video ring of overtones attacking the War on Terror and the rise of dictatorial powers. The video also depicts mob mentality and shows how easily the population can be "led by a microphone."

Conspirituality

The Vancouver rap duo Conspirituality released a song titled *AmBUSHED* in 2009 on their debut album which contains lyrics about 9/11, Bohemian Grove, the Illuminati, and the Bush administration's torture of prisoners and other war crimes. The video was produced by DJ Ball and depicts men in orange prison jumpsuits chasing down President Bush, Dick Cheney, Condoleezza Rice and others as they run for their lives to avoid paying the penalty for their crimes.

Paris

A rapper named Paris on the Guerilla Funk record label has produced numerous songs about the New World Order and the Illuminati. One of his most popular tracks is *What Would You Do?* In the song, Paris exposes the Illuminati's agenda in a venomous poem which is delivered with the precision and quality of any chart-topping single. Paris raps, "The Illuminati triple six all connected. Stolen votes they control the race and take elections."

Immortal Technique

Another popular underground artist is Immortal Technique, a rapper whose every word is a blistering attack on 9/11 in songs like *Bin Laden* and *Cause of Death* which inundate the listener with hard facts and evidence delivered with the power and poise of Martin Luther King.

Sean "P. Diddy" Colmes

In 1997, Sean "P. Diddy" Colmes released a music video for a song titled *Victory* featuring the Notorious B.I.G. and Busta Rhymes. The video takes place in the "New World Order" in the year 3002 AD which is a Big Brother police state and depicts Sean Colmes as being pursued by the police as part of a televised game show which was most likely inspired by the film *The Running Man* (1987).

Prodigy

Albert Johnson, known by his stage name Prodigy is a rapper and member of the duo Mobb Deep. Prodigy's third solo album titled H.N.I.C.2 was released in April of 2008 and included a song titled "Illuminati." The song is entirely about the Illuminati secret society and includes a chorus saying, "Illuminati want my mind, soul and my body. Secret society trying to keep their eye on me."

During the 2008 presidential campaign when practically every African American entertainer or celebrity was thrilled that Barack Obama was running for president, Prodigy called him a phony and a plastic president. He said, "I wish nothing but love and happiness for him, but he's either gonna be assassinated to create chaos and bring about martial law or he'll live and then years down the line, at the end of his term everybody will see that he's just like the rest of these plastic presidents, who does absolutely nothing good. Just another puppet for the Royal family."[210]

Prodigy also publicly voiced support for Congressman Ron Paul (R-Texas) who ran for president in 2008.

Jay-Z

Rapper Jay-Z (real name Sean Carter) has included some occult and Illuminati references in his music, but not as a way to expose the activities of the organization, but rather as a tribute to them. It seems that Jay-Z is familiar with the Illuminati and chose to aid them instead of fight them. Jay-Z is the founder of Roc-A-Fella Records, a name that refers to the Rockefeller Illuminati family.

A song titled *Lucifer* which was released on *The Grey Album* in 2004 which was produced by Danger Mouse, contains some disturbing messages. When listening to the song it is clear that a small part is playing backwards and is uninteligable. When the song is played in reverse, you can clearly hear Jay-Z saying, "Six six six, murder, murder Jesus" and "Catholics, I gotta murder them, I can introduce you to demons, leave niggas on death's door, and I can

[210] http://www.ballerstatus.com/article/news/2008/06/4838/

introduce you to evil."

It's important to stress that this is not a "subliminal message" meant to be picked up subconsciously by the listeners. It is more of a marketing ploy and a way to get Jay-Z fans talking about this unique aspect of one of his songs. It's also important to understand that the message is clearly understandable and is not the result of someone interpreting a series of sounds as saying such things.

When people hear the allegations of the reverse messages in the song *Lucifer*, most Jay-Z fans refer to the original song *Lucifer* which is found on Jay-Z's Black Album. Danger Mouse remixed the song for The Grey Album and edited Jay-Z's voice to say the disturbing things found in the song. Jay-Z never denounced Danger Mouse for doing such a thing and appears to be acceptant of if.

A popular photo of Jay-Z shows him making a pyramid with his index fingers and thumbs with his left eye in the middle, which is a popular Illuminati symbol. A letter that Prodigy wrote to his record label while in jail reveals that he believes Jay-Z is knowingly cooperating with the Illuminati and cites that as the reason he became so wealthy.

In a video posted to YouTube that was shot inside the studio when Jay-Z was recording the original song *Lucifer* for his Black Album you can hear him make a comment where he brags, "I swear I never read the Bible in my life, I don't even know…(uninteligable)." In his song *D'Evils* he raps a verse where he says he never prays to God, he prays to Gotti (John Gotti the gangster).

Nas

Rapper Nas (real name Nasir Jones) is another rapper some believe is aware of the Illuminati, and is secretly a supporter and servant for them. In the song *Be a Nigger Too*, Nas raps, "My click's still real QB gangsters. Click still moving like Freemasons so if I'm on the flow from the law there's lodges all across the nation. Nas is bred for the plan. To hold a grand dragon's head in my hand. Come and get me, here I am."

There is also a picture on the Internet of Nas and Jay-Z using what looks to be a Masonic handshake. Nas has frequently referred to himself as "God's son" which was also the title of one of his albums.

Tupac Shakur

Rapper Tupac Shakur, who was shot and killed in Las Vegas in 1996, released an album shortly before his death titled *The Don Killuminati: The 7 Day Theory* which remains the topic of speculation among his fans who think the title was a reference to killing the Illuminati. "The Don" is a mafia term for a mafia boss or leader, which leads some of Tupac's fans to think that he had learned about the Illuminati and the album title was a coded name meaning he was the leader of the killers of the Illuminati.

Black Eyed Peas

The Los Angels hip hop group Black Eyed Peas told people to "be prepared for the New World Order" in their song *Say Goodbye* which talks about what a mess the world is in and how society is falling apart.

Fat Boy Slim

The British DJ, Fat Boy Slim (Norman Quentin Cook) produced a song for the film *Lara Croft: Tomb Raider* which was titled *Illuminati*. In the film, Lara Croft is opposed by the Illuminati as they search for a mystical artifact. Fat Boy Slim's song is basically an instrumental song but it starts by saying, "Illuminati. A secret society do exists." Note: The lyrics actually read, "a secret society *do* exist" and is not a typo.

Skinny Puppy

The Canadian electronica band Skinny Puppy produced a song titled *NeuWerld* which says, "I trust we must distrust the owners of the New World Order."

Poker Face

The American rock band Poker Face is known as a protest rock band and includes many themes about the New World Order and out of control governments in their music. The insert for their CD *Made In America* includes a montage of Illuminati symbols including the Skull and Bones logo, Masonic symbols, and the street layout of Washington D.C. Tracks such as *Kontrol* and *Revolution* are powerful songs promoting gun rights, the Constitution and exposing mainstream media propaganda.

Killarmy

In 1997 an affiliate of the rap group Wu-Tang Clan called Killarmy released their debut album titled *Silent Weapons for Quiet Wars* which was a reference to a document that author William Cooper published in his 1991 book, *Behold a Pale Horse*. (See William Cooper page 215) Wu-Tang Clan member Killah Priest is aware of the Illuminati and had contacted Antony J. Hilder in 2006 and invited him to the studio to record some sound bites for an album he was working on.

Meat Beat Manifesto

A UK electronic music group called Meat Beat Manifesto (MBF) produced a song called *No Purpose No Design* which includes several references to the Bavarian Illuminati.

The Jurassic 5

An American alternative hip hop group, *The Jurassic 5*, produced a song titled *Concrete Schoolyard* which contained one line saying the artist was anti-Illuminati.

Gamma Ray

A German metal band released an album in 2001 titled *No World Order* and has several references to the New World Order and the Illuminati. The songs were written by Kai Hansen.

The KLF

The KLF (also known as The Justified Ancients of Mu Mu—or the JAMMs were a British band from the 1980s which frequently used themes from Robert Anton Wilson's *Illuminatus! Trilogy* novels. (See The Illuminatus! Trilogy page 309)

Agent Steel

A speed metal band named Agent Steel released an album in 2003 called *Order of the Illuminati*. The band is well known for basing its lyrical concepts on conspiracy theories.

Killer Squirrel

An underground punk band named Killer Squirrel recorded a song in 2005 called *The Cowboy Illuminati Get Their Revenge* which mentions the Skull and Bones society at Yale University. The group's previous album *Self Released (And Loving It)* had a cover which featured artwork showing an eye on top of a pyramid.

Hed PE

A rock band from Huntington Beach, California named Hed PE (also known as (hed) planet earth) released an album in 2006 titled *Back 2 Base X* which contains several Illuminati and New World Order references in the lyrics and on the album artwork.

Bobby Conn

Bobby Conn is a pop-rock musician from Chicago who references the Illuminati and global domination in sarcastic and satirical ways. He once said he invented "The Continuous Cash Flow System" in order to bankrupt America by dramatically increasing the national debt. He also once claimed to be the Antichrist.

Malice Mizer

The Japanese rock band Malice Mizer produced a song titled *Illuminati*, which includes references to Biblical and sexual themes. The band officially went on an indefinite hiatus starting in December 2001.

Infected Mushrooms

In 2003 an Israeli psychedelic trance band called Infected Mushrooms released an album titled *Converting Vegetarians* which contains a song called *Illuminaughty* which contained lyrics talking about eating forbidden fruit and having one's eyes opened.

The Matthew Good Band

Singer Matthew Good has a song titled *Lullaby for the New World Order* which is a vague song with lyrics about how God gave us a voice and we should use it, and asks how can we get ourselves out of this trouble.

The Alan Parsons Project

The British progressive rock band The Alan Parsons Project has a song titled *Eye in the Sky* which has strange lyrics saying that the eye in the sky can read your mind and "I am the maker of rules...dealing with fools...I can cheat you blind." The album cover contains the Egyptian eye of Horus.

Solutions

When one comes to grips with the reality of a secret occult society which, for hundreds, perhaps thousands of years has pulled the strings from behind the scenes and has been operating an underground network to advance their own personal and political agendas and accumulate unimaginable wealth as a parasitic vampire feeding off the uninformed and uninitiated, one can be overcome with fear and anxiety. A dramatically large amount of information concerning such things is fully verifiable and accurate. And if even only ten percent of the more outrageous and disturbing claims are true, then certainly a monstrous and immeasurable evil is functioning in our world.

With such revelations, one must not retreat from society or become paralyzed from fears or paranoia. These things were happening long before you became aware of them, and they may continue to happen until the end of time. Nothing has changed in your life except your awareness of the hidden reality beneath the facade of lies that most people accept as the truth. But now that you see beyond this false reality that is presented to the world, there are several things you can do to either minimize, or in many cases, completely avoid the effects of such things on your life and on your family.

You have already used the first key to unlock your prison cell, and that is awareness. One cannot make the proper decisions if the information one has is inaccurate. Now you have accurate information, and the means by which you can obtain it to see through propaganda, lies, half-truths, and distortions. Now you see the bigger picture of why things are happening the way they are. By simply knowing how the system works, you can effectively maneuver through the world and avoid many of the traps and snares that have been set for you.

It is strongly advised that you take several precautions

as insurance to protect yourself and your family from the dangers we face. You should purchase several firearms, including a hand gun, shot gun, and riffle, and learn how to responsibly handle and store them. Other simple self defense devices such as clubs and knives should also be possessed. Hand to hand combat and self defense training is also advised. You should keep your home fully stocked with food and water incase of an emergency such as a natural disaster, terrorist attack, or civil unrest.

You should invest in physical gold and silver coins and hold them in your possession or in a safety deposit box. You should also keep several thousand dollars in cash on hand as well. If there is an economic collapse (or computer failure) and credit and debit cards are no longer functioning or accepted, you will need to have cash to buy food, gas, and other necessities. Such a disaster will cause a run on the bank and ATM machines, and cash may be impossible to get for a considerable amount of time. Therefore a stash should be well hidden in your home or safety deposit box so you will not be like the countless herds who rush to the bank, and are likely turned away and return home penniless. Do not stash all your money in one hundred dollar bills, but instead keep a variety of denominations since it may be difficult to spend $100s and get back change during this time of crisis.

One of the most important things is to cultivate a healthy social circle of friends, family, and neighbors. The New World Order has isolated people from each other, and many live in their own world not even knowing the names of the very neighbors who they live next to. A close knit, safe and trustworthy community will prove to be a priceless asset as the New World Order solidifies.

You should also reach out and educate others. For those who want to know the truth and are seeking answers, the insights you share with them will help put them at ease by showing them the big picture. Giving them a copy of *The Illuminati: Facts & Fiction* or *The Resistance Manifesto* is also a great way to educate people since these books will present the most important information regarding the Illuminati and the New World Order. It is also pivotal that we befriend and educate the police and military. The more law enforcement officers and military personnel we have on our side, the safer we will be. When things get out of control and orders are given to blatantly violate the Constitution, many informed troops will simply refuse to participate and hopefully stand up to their superiors with their fellow troops who are informed as well. We also need assets of our own to covertly work within the system, who report back to us about the orders being given and secretly sabotage the New World Order's plans.

Financial responsibility is also another key ingredient to avoid entrapment by the New World Order. By not mindlessly participating in the materialistic shallow culture that is being perpetuated, you can minimize or even avoid the financial hardships that such behaviors ultimately lead to. Expensive status symbols that have no practical value suck money out of peoples' pockets as they joyfully indulge themselves with their material idols. Manufactured social pressures and the status quo uphold an illusion that one has substandard value if they do not participate in the rat race. By freeing yourself from the worry of judgment from others, you free yourself from the unnecessary burdens that such fears bring. Many fear the judgment from friends, and often from total strangers if they don't have the right brand of clothes, watch, or car. And it is this very fear that keeps them enslaved.

Running for public office yourself can lead to real and measurable changes in your community. While you will not, nor would you want to become the president of the United States, you can certainly run for any number of local and even state offices. The Illuminati does not have complete control of the political system on a small local level, and by becoming involved instead of throwing your hands up in submission, you can realistically bring tremendous benefits to your town, or even your state.

Finally you must live in a state of love and not fear. Learning about the Illuminati can be extremely terrifying, but you must not let the fear overshadow your love. By living by the golden rule of life and treating others the way you want to be treated, you will set in motion a chain of events that will spread in ways you cannot even begin to fathom. One small selfless act will encourage another, and another, in a never-ending chain of events.

If you treat someone with undeserving hostility, they will return that hostility directly back at you or to others, which in turn will have the same chain reaction and may echo around the world in ways you do not understand. If you are faced with such a negative energy, you may neutralize it with love instead of amplifying it with more negativity. You must be an example for others since you are enlightened with the truth. You must resist at all costs any temptation to sink to the immoral level of the Illuminati which we fight. This is not only a political battle which we are fighting, but a spiritual one as well. As you close this book after having absorbed the insights found within, I wish you the best on this journey of life. You are now armed with some of the forbidden knowledge that the Illuminati has done their best to keep hidden from you. As Jesus said, you now know the truth, and the truth shall set you free.

Illuminati Controlled Organizations

The Bilderberg Group

A yearly secret meeting of the world's leading politicians, media moguls, business titans, bankers, and royalty, who discuss and dispense their agenda for the coming months and years.

Council on Foreign Relations

A private organization that masquerades as a government committee which has tremendous influence over foreign policy and is used to construct the New World Order.

The Trilateral Commission

A private organization set up by David Rockefeller for the purpose of organizing America, Europe, and Japan into the New World Order.

The Bohemian Grove

A secluded 2700 acre redwood forest in Northern California where members meet every July to have private discussions of the next years events, and participate in a human sacrifice ritual to Moloch using a life-size paper mache effigy.

The Federal Reserve

A private bank that most Americans think is a government agency simply because of its name. The bank controls the money supply, interest rates, and loans money to the federal government for interest.

Freemasonry

A fairly well known global secret society in the form of a men's fraternity which is harmless on the lower levels, but within the cloak of secrecy at the top, members are intimately involved with nefarious occult activities and worship Lucifer.

Skull and Bones
An elite fraternity at Yale University in Connecticut which chooses fifteen new members each year and inducts them into the Illuminati with satanic rituals and pretend human sacrifices.

The Military
The Joint Chiefs of Staff, who are the head officials of each military branch, are carefully promoted and chosen for their willingness to serve the Illuminati. Secret cells committed to black ops are also under their control.

The Vatican
Once seen as the enemy of the Illuminati, the leadership within the Catholic Church and the secretive Jesuits have been working hand in hand with them for many years. The pope could one day be the false prophet talked about in the Bible who will tell the world that the antichrist is the return of Jesus.

Knights of Malta
An organization within the Catholic Church that is believed to contain an inner circle of individuals who work in tandem with the Jesuits (the Society of Jesus) to secretly maintain and expand the wealth and influence of the Catholic Church.

Radical Islam
Radical Muslims who kill innocent civilians and carry out deadly terrorist attacks around the world are funded and encouraged by the Illuminati to create an enemy and instill fear in populations so that freedoms and civil rights may be removed as part of the so-called solution to the problem.

Communism
While seen as the enemy of America and Capitalism, Communism is actually a creation of the Illuminati and is used as a controlled opposition to continue the construction of the New World Order.

World Council of Churches
A Christian unity organization containing over 300 churches in more than 120 countries. The combined membership of church bodies in the organization exceeds 550 million Christians. Its purpose is to merge Christianity into a one world religion.

Election Fraud
Besides using their control of the media and their unlimited supply of money to finance candidates who will serve their secret agendas, the Illuminati also have a strangle hold on elections through electronic voting machines and other fraudulent tactics to ensure the outcomes they desire.

The British Monarch
The British royal family secretly believes they are descendents of the lost tribe of Dan, and that they have the Divine right to rule as kings.

Royal Order of the Garter
An order of Knighthood in Europe involving the Prince of Wales and twenty-four other members of the British royal family or foreign monarchs.

MI-5 and MI-6
Just like all law enforcement branches and intelligence agencies in America have Illuminati handlers at the highest levels, the same is true for British MI-5, which is equivalent to the FBI, and MI-6 which is equivalent to the CIA.

Council of Chatham House

Formerly called the Royal Institute of International Affairs, the Council of Chatham House is the British version of America's Council on Foreign Relations. They gather prominent politicians, policy makers, members of business, academia, diplomats, the media, and researchers to formulate and dispense propaganda and agendas to the British government.

The Group

A secret society at Oxford University in England and is Europe's version of the Skull and Bones society found in America at Yale University.

The Triads

The Asian branch of the Illuminati mainly in China which is involved in organized crime of every kind from drug trafficking and money laundering to contract killings. Its membership ranges from low level street thugs to billionaire businessmen.

The CIA

The Central Intelligence Agency is responsible for overthrowing or implementing governments or dictators around the world so that the global goals and interests of the Illuminati may be carried out. It is not only an intelligence agency, but a covert terrorist organization and drug running agency.

The NSA

The National Security Agency built and maintains Echelon, the most sophisticated spy system ever created. Every form of electronic communication is monitored or recorded. Keywords, voiceprints, and specific phone numbers are tagged and intercepted among the billions of communications around the globe.

The FBI

FBI infrastructure and manpower is used to obtain wiretaps on politicians, activists, and whistle blowers, which are then used for blackmail purposes so these individuals can be controlled, contained, or eliminated.

The DEA

While most people who work in the Drug Enforcement Agency are trying to reduce illegal drugs on the streets, there is an inner circle who work hand in hand with drug cartels to import drugs and launder money.

Pharmaceuticals

Prescription drugs are designed and advertised as magic pills for every ailment from depression to anxiety, and mask the symptoms while ignoring the root cause behind these ailments to help keep the population legally sedated, and out of the way.

Entertainment

Money is funneled to promote musicians, TV shows, and films which teach and encourage immorality and violence, and help to keep the masses mesmerized and out of the way of political and social agendas that are being implemented.

The Mormon Church

This pseudo Christian cult was founded by Joseph Smith in 1830 based on his fraudulent *Book of Mormon*, and has steadily grown in wealth and size ever since. They teach and believe that Mormons are the only "true" Christians.

Jehovah's Witnesses

Founded in the late 19th century by Charles Taze Russell, this Christian cult teaches a dramatically different doctrine than traditional Christianity, and serves as a poison to Christian theology.

Rhodes Trust

Named after Cecil Rhodes, as it was written in his will, the Rhodes Scholarship is an award given by the Rhodes Trust for a student to study at the University of Oxford in England. Students who are seen as potential assets for the Illuminati and their plans are given this scholarship.

The Cosmos Club

A social club founded in 1878 in Washington D.C. whose goal is "the advancement of its members in science, literature, and art." Its members have included many recipients of the Nobel Prize, Pulitzer Prize, and Presidential Medal of Freedom.

Club of Rome

A global think tank founded in 1972 with the purpose of creating scientific reports which support the idea of population reduction in the world. Their report *Limits to Growth*, which was first published in 1972, began spreading information about the Illuminati's plan to reduce the world's population.

DARPA

The Defense Advanced Research Projects Agency (DARPA) is an agency of the Department of Defense which develops new technology for the United States military. Some completed projects include the directed energy weapons such as the Active Denial System (ADS), the High Energy Liquid Laser Area Defense System (HELLADS), and the Predator drones.

Supreme Council of Wise Men

The top 10 most powerful men in the Illuminati form this inner circle of so-called wise men who are the puppet masters whose directives and orders flow down the pyramid to be spread and carried out by the proper organizations or delegated to others to follow.

The Council of 13
The executive branch of the Illuminati consisting of the heads of the top 13 Illuminati bloodlines known as kings. These kings, along with their queens, princes and princesses direct those below them in the Committee of 300 or directly run organizations themselves.

The Committee of 300
Directly under the Council of 13, the Committee of 300 are representatives of the top bloodlines and in key positions of power who have entire organizations that they are personally the heads of.

The Jasons
A scientific organization whose members are used as researchers and consultants for the Department of Defense. Jason members are made up of the brightest scientific minds in the country in an array of fields including theoretical physics, engineering, chemistry, and biology.

MJ-12
Also known as Majestic 12 or the Majestic Trust, this is believed by some to be a secret organization of scientists involved with research surrounding UFOs and aliens.

The Mothers of Darkness Castle
The Château des Amerois, also known as the Mothers of Darkness Castle, is an enormous castle located in Belgium near the village of Muno. Some believe that satanic ritual parties and child sacrifices take place in the castle annually by Illuminati members.

The Pilgrims Society
A private organization of elite U.S. and British politicians, diplomats, and business men who host dinners for members each time a new U.S. Ambassador to the United Kingdom or British Ambassador to the United States is chosen in order to indoctrinate them with Illuminati goals.

The Priory of Sion
This alleged organization supposedly hides and protects a secret bloodline of Jesus and Mary Magdalene. The bloodline myth is, in reality, a cover story for the bloodline of what will one day give birth to the antichrist so he can claim the Divine right to rule according to the prophecy of the Old Testament with regards to the bloodline of the messiah.

Satanic Cults and Churches
Organizations like the Church of Satan, the Temple of Set, the Brotherhood of Saturn, the Order of the Golden Dawn, and the Ordo Templi Orientis (OTO), act as recruiting grounds for entry level occultism.

United Nations
Founded in 1945 after World War II under the premise to prevent war between nations, the UN's formation began the framework for the New World Order super state.

International Monetary Fund
Based in Washington D.C., the IMF is an international organization that oversees the global financial system and exchange rates and is following the plan to create a single global currency.

The World Bank

A private bank which loans money to developing countries for the purpose of building infrastructure such as roads, schools, water treatment facilities, etc. Often these projects are then taken over by private foreign corporations instead of the host country's government, and run for profit by taking advantage of the population's reliance on such projects.

Foundations

Numerous supposedly non-profit organizations are created and maintained which carry out tasks including research aimed at furthering Illuminati goals and presenting positive public relations to reduce resistance to their implementation. While categorized as non-profit, the directors and leadership of these foundations often earn hefty six figure salaries. The Rockefeller Foundation, for example had $3.7 billion in assets in 2006.

Bank for International Settlements

An international organization of banking institutions that operates as a bank for central banks. As of 2007 the BIS held over $400 billion in assets, including 150 tonnes of gold.

Central Banks

The large banks responsible for the monetary policies of countries and member states. They control the stability of the national currency and money supply, as well as interest rates. They lend money to smaller banks such as your local small town branch.

Global Environmental Facility

An organization consisting of nearly two hundred countries, international institutions, and non-governmental organizations (NGOs), which provides grants related to global warming, land degradation and biodiversity.

Monopoly Corporations
For generations the Illuminati has created and maintained businesses which form monopolies that are relied upon by populations. Oil companies such as Shell Oil, British Petroleum, Exxon Mobile, and others have been their primary cash cows aside from banking. De Beers diamonds and Monsanto are examples from other industries.

Regional Federations
The North Atlantic Treaty Organization (NATO), the European Union (EU), the North American Union (NAU), and others are incremental steps to streamlining laws, trade, and ultimately currency for the New World Order.

The United Grand Lodge of England
Founded in 1717, this is the oldest Masonic Grand Lodge in the world and is the main governing body of Freemasonry in England and Wales. A Grand Lodge, or "Grand Orient," is the governing body of Freemasonry in a particular jurisdiction.

Unity Church
Formally known as the *Unity School of Christianity*, this is another New Age Christian Church based on a variety of spiritual, metaphysical, and philosophical ideas. It was founded in 1889 by Charles Fillmore.

Unitarian Universalist Association
A liberal religious association of Unitarian Universalist congregations formed by the consolidation of the American Unitarian Association and the Universalist Church of America in 1961.

Unification Church
Founded and lead by Sun Myung Moon, a Korean billionaire

who claims to be the second coming of Christ. He is the founder and owner of the *Washington Times* and gives millions of dollars to U.S. politicians.

Temple of Understanding
A 501 (c) (3) tax exempt non-profit organization founded in 1960 by Juliet Hollister and has representatives with the United Nations who are implementing their eight Millennium Development Goals, they hope, by 2015. They focus on "furthering education for global citizenship."

Bahai
The Bahai faith is a religious movement started in 19th century Persia with an estimated five to six million followers in more than 200 countries and territories. The teachings emphasize unifying the major world religions.

Rosicrucians
An enlightenment group dating back to the 1400s. While currently not a very powerful organization, the teachings within Rosicrucianism and the activities of its members were important aids in the enlightenment era and the overthrow of the Catholic Church's rule.

The Aspen Institute
An international non-profit organization founded in 1950 which is dedicated to "fostering enlightened leadership, the appreciation of timeless ideas and values, and open-minded dialogue on contemporary issues." It is largely financed by the Rockefellers Brothers Fund, (Not to be confused with the Rockefeller Foundation), which was set up in 1940 by the five famous Rockefeller brothers: John D., Nelson, Laurance, Winthrop, and David.

World Trade Organization

The World Trade Organization negotiates, implements, and oversees the rules of trade between nations around the world. 95% of all world trade is policed and governed by the WTO. Labor laws and environmental regulations are circumvented or ignored in poor and undeveloped countries, whose people are taken advantage of by rich countries and multinational corporations through the WTO.

KGB

The Russian Secret Service which operates as an organized crime network and controls Russian leadership, illegal weapons sales, drug running, money laundering, assassinations, and political kingpins.

La Cosa Nostra

The Italian mafia has become somewhat mythical as a result of Hollywood movies, but the mob has worked hand in hand with corrupt politicians, the CIA, Freemasonry, and other elements of the Illuminati in order to make money, eliminate obstacles (assassinations), and to break businesses and worker unions.

FEMA

The Federal Emergency Management Agency gives the president of the United States sweeping powers that in a declared emergency can be used to place citizens in detention centers or prison camps. Police and Military are also given authority to walk door to door in communities and confiscate guns from registered gun owners who are law abiding citizens.

Mossad

Israel's intelligence agency works hand in hand with the CIA, KGB, and other agencies around the world to coordinate and share information, carry out intimidation and assassinations, and to secretly pull the strings in Israel's government and with regards to their foreign policies.

UNESCO
United Nations Educational, Scientific and Cultural Organization (UNESCO) is an agency of the United Nations established in 1945. Its purpose is to create propaganda and push agendas favorable to the UN and the New World Order. It was responsible for the creation of an agenda supporting a "New World Information and Communication Order" which attempted to curb freedom of the press.

Planetary Congress
The Association of Space Explorers holds a Planetary Congress which is a forum for international astronauts and cosmonauts to exchange technical information concerning space operations, scientific research, mission development and astronaut training.

Environmental Groups
Various environmental groups have been created to push global warming and climate change propaganda which is being used to implement carbon taxes and increased regulations.

Lucis Trust
Originally created as Lucifer's Trust and renamed years later, the Lucis Trust is one of the premier publishers of New Age books and material. Its headquarters is located on Wall street in New York City, just blocks away from the New York Stock Exchange. One of the most famous books from the company is Alice Bailey's *Externalization of the Hierarchy* which is mandatory reading for all Illuminati members.

World Union

Another "non-profit" organization dedicated to paving the path for a New Age unified religion is the World Union, which was founded in 1958. The inspiration of its founders came from Indian mystic Sri Aurobindo.

Esalen Institute

Located in Big Sur, California, this nonprofit organization is dedicated to science that will help humanity realize what Aldous Huxley called the "human potential."

Commission on Global Governance

Founded in 1992 with the support of the United Nations Secretary General Boutros Boutros-Ghali, this commission produced the controversial report titled *Our Global Neighborhood* which called for countries to give up their national sovereignty in order to strengthen the United Nations.

Interpol

The International Criminal Police Organization, better known as Interpol is an organization facilitating international police cooperation. It will ultimately be used to create the New World Order's global soldiers with no allegiance to the country they are working in.

Information Awareness Office

The Information Awareness Office (IAO) was established by the DARPA for the purpose of creating information technology able to monitor and track all electronic communications and transactions under the guise of national security in order to achieve what the office called "total information awareness." The official seal for the office is a pyramid with an all seeing eye as the capstone with a light shining out of it over the entire earth.

Tavistock Institute
A "charity" organization which engages in research and experiments in social science and applied psychology. The institute's primary clients are the British government, the European Union, and private clients interested in manipulating populations and groups of people.

Underground Bases and Tunnels
A series of tunnels and secret bases span the country, possibly the globe, which were created largely by the Army Corps of Engineers. The tunnels are likely equipped with subway type systems which allow individuals to pass underground to different parts of the country in the case of an emergency such as a nuclear attack.

The Project for a New American Century
Founded in 1997 by prominent neocons including Dick Cheney, Paul Wolfowitz, William Kristol, Richard Pearlman and others, this organization produced the infamous *Rebuilding America's Defenses* documents which recommended a terrorist attack like a new Pearl Harbor would be needed to implement their plans in the Middle East.

Others
Various other private organizations or secret societies masquerading as college fraternities exist as both recruiting grounds for Illuminati supporters, and as a private environment where networking may take place between elite businessmen, politicians, and royalty.

Bibliography
Books

Allen, Gary *None Dare Call It Conspiracy* 1971 Concord Press

Baddeley, Gavin *Lucifer Rising: Sin, Devil Worship, and Rock and Roll* 1999 Plexus Publishing   ISBN: 0-85965-378-1

Barruel, Abbe *Memoirs Illustrating the History of Jacobinism* Vol 3 (1799) Printed by Isaac Collins, for Cornelius Davis, No 94 Water-street

Barruel, Abbe *Memoirs Illustrating the History of Jacobinism* Vol 4 (1798) Translated to English by Robert Clifford. Printed by the Translator by T. Burton, No 11, Gate Street, Lincoln's-Inn Field. Sold by E. Booker No. 56, New Bond Street.

Bailey, Alice *The Externalization of the Hierarchy* Lucis Publishing Company 1957 ISBN: 0-85330-106-9
Bailey, Alice *A Treatise on White Magic* Lucis Publishing Company (June 1998) ISBN-10: 0853301239

Barton, Blanche - *The Secret Life of a Satanist: the Authorized Biography of Anton LaVey*) (1990, 1992,) Funeral House ISBN: 0-922915-12-1

Blavatsky, Helena .P. - *The Secret Doctrine v. I & II*   The Theosophical Publishing Company 1888 ISBN: 1-55700-002-06

Brown, Dan *Angels and Demons 2000* Pocket Star Books ISBN-10: 0671027360

Burkett, Larry *The Illuminati* Thomas Nelson; New edition (October 6, 2004) ISBN-10: 1595540016

Christian, Robert *Common Sense Renewed* 1986 Stoyles Graphic Serves Lake Mills Iowa ISBN: 0-89279-078-4

Crème, Benjamin. *The Reappearance of the Christ and the Masters of Wisdom.* 2007 Share International Foundation ISBN: 90-71484-32-7

Crowley, Aleister. *Magick: In Theory and Practice* 1979 Smith Peter ISBN: 0844654760

Crowley, Aleister. *Book of the Law* 1938 Ordo Templi Orientis ISBN: 087728-334-6

DeCamp, John W. *The Franklin Cover-up: Child Abuse, Satanism, and Murder in Nebraska* ISBN: 0963215809 A W T, Incorporated 1992

Elberton Granite Museum. *The Georgia Guidestones "Elberton's Most Unusual Granite Monument"* 1980 Elberton Granite Museum and Exhibit Pamphlet. Elberton, GA 30635

Estulin, Daniel *The True Story of the Bilderberg Group* 2007 TrineDay ISBN: 0-9777953-4-9

Finkbeiner, Ann The Jasons: The Secret History of Science's Postwar Elite (2006) The Penguin Group ISBN: 0-670-03489-4

Gardner, Gerald B. *The Book of Shadows*

Griffin, G. Edward *The Creature from Jekyll Island* American Media; 4th edition (2002)

Hall, Manly P. *The Lost Keys of Freemasonry: Or, the Secret of Hiram Abiff* 1994 ISBN: 0880530448 Macoy Publishing & Masonic Supply Company

Hall, Manly P. *The Secret Teachings of All Ages* the Philosophical Research Society Press Philosophical Research Society 1999. ISBN: 0893145483

Hanson, Mike. *Bohemian Grove: Cult of Conspiracy* ISBN: 0595326749 iUniverse 2004

Knight, Christopher & Lomas, Robert - *The Book of Hiram* Barnes & Noble (2005) ISBN-10: 0760776334

LaVey, Anton *The Satanic Bible* Avon (December 1, 1976) ISBN-10: 0380015390

Leverett, Mara. *The Boys on the Tracks: Death, Denial, and a Mother's Crusade to Bring her Son's Killers to Justice* 1999 St. Martin's Press ISBN: 0312198418

Levi, Eliphas. *Transcendental Magic: Its Doctrine and Ritual* (1910)
1998 Kessinger ISBN: 0766102971

Levi, Eliphas – *History of Magic* (1913) Red Wheel / Weiser (1999)
ISBN-10: 0877289298

Lewin, Leonard C. *The Report From Iron Mountain* The Dial Press, Inc.;
First edition (1967)

Mackey, Albert G *The Lexicon of Freemasonry* Barnes and Noble Books
(2004)

Marks, John. *The Search for the "Manchurian Candidate": The CIA
and Mind Control, the Secret History of the Behavior Sciences* 1979
Norton and Company, New York ISBN: 0393307948

Marrs, Texe. *Codex Magica* RiverCrest Publishing (November 1, 2005)
ISBN-10: 1930004044

Marx, Karl and Fridrich Engels. *The Communist Manifesto* 1998
Reprinted Oxford University Press Inc. New York Firs published as a
World's Classics paperback in 1992 ISBN: 0-19-283437-1

Millegan, Kris. *Fleshing our Skull and Bones: Investigations into
Americas Most Powerful Secret Society.* TrineDay, LLC Walterville, OR
2003 ISBN: 0-9752906-0-6

Miller, Judith *Occult Theocrasy* (1933) Christian Bookclub of America
(Reprinted in 2007)

O'Brien, Cathy *Trance Formation of America* Fourteenth Edition 1995
Reality Marketing ISBN: 0-9660165-4-8

Orwell, George *Nineteen Eighty Four* (Centennial Edition) Plume
Printing (1983) ISBN: 0-452-28423-6

Ovason, David. *The Secret Architecture of our Nation's Capitol:The
Masons and the Building of Washington, D.C.* 2002 Perennial Currents
ISBN: 0060953683

Payson, Seth *Proof of the Illuminati* Invisible College Press, LLC
(January 1, 2003) ISBN-10: 1931468141

Pike, Albert. *Morals and Dogma of the Ancient and Accepted Scottish Rite Freemasonry* Reprinted by Kesslinger Publishing ISBN: 0-7661-2615-3

Quigley, Caroll *Tragedy and Hope A History of the World in Our Time* G. S. G. & Associates, Incorporated (June 1975) ISBN-10: 094500110X

Quigley, Caroll *Anglo American Establishment* 1981 C P A Book Pub ISBN: 0913022454

Rockefeller, David - *David Rockefeller: Memoirs* 2002 Random House ISBN-10: 0679405887

Robbins, Alexandra *Secrets of the Tomb: Skull and Bones, the Ivy League, and the Hidden Paths of Power* Back Bay Books (September 4, 2002) ISBN-10: 0316735612

Robison, John. *Proofs of a Conspiracy* 1798 Boston: Westerland Islands, 1967.

Robertson, Pat. *The New World Order* Word Publishing USA 1991 ISBN: 0-8499-0915-5

Sauder, Richard Ph. D. *Underground Bases and Tunnels: What is the government trying to hide?* Adventures Unlimited Press. 1995 ISBN: 0-932813-37-2

Scnoebelen, William. *Masonry: Beyond the Light* Chick Publications 1991 ISBN 0-937958-38-7

Simon *The Necronomicon* Avon (March 1, 1980) ISBN-10: 0380751925

Springmeir, Fritz *Bloodlines of the Illuminati* 2002 Ambassador House ISBN: 0-9663533-2-3

Sutton, Antony C. *America's Secret Establishment: An Introduction to the Order of Skull and Bones* Trine Day. 2003 ISBN: 0972020705

Thompson, Hunter S. *Fear and Loathing in Las Vegas: A Savage Journey to the Heart of the American Dream* Vintage; 2nd edition (May 12, 1998) ISBN-10: 0679785892

Tucker, Jim *Jim Tucker's Bilderberg Diary* American Free Press (2005) ISBN-10: 0974548421

Tulbure, Solomon *The Illuminati Manifesto* Writers Club Press (December 1, 2001) ISBN-10: 0595210554

Webster, Nesta Secret Societies and Subversive Movements (1924) A&B Publishing Group ISBN 1-881316-88-2

Wilson, Robert Anton *The Illuminatus Trilogy: The Eye in the Pyramid, The Golden Apple, Leviathan* Dell (December 1, 1983) ISBN-10: 0440539811

Other Documents

Operation Northwoods File can found at the National Security Archives online and is named: Chairman, Join Chiefs of Staff, Justification for US Military Intervention in Cuba [includes cover memoranda], March 13, 1962, TOP SECRET, 15 pp.
http://www.gwu.edu/~nsarchiv/news/20010430/

Presidential Daily Briefing August 6, 2001 *bin Ladin Determined to Strike in US* Declassified on April 10, 2004 after pressure from the September 11th Commission

MKUltra Documents CIA, Memorandum for the Record, Subject: *Project ARTICHOKE*, January 31, 1975, 5 pp.

Rebuilding Americas Defenses: Strategy, forces resources and for a new century. A report from the Project for the New American Century 2000

From PSYOP to Mindwar: The Psychology of Victory by Colonel Paul E. Valley with Michael A. Aquino Headquarters, 7th Psychological Operations Group United States Army Reserve Presidio of San Francisco, California 1980

The Protocols of the Elders of Zion

Printed in Great Britain
by Amazon.co.uk, Ltd.,
Marston Gate.